States, War and Capitalism

States, War and Capitalism

Studies in Political Sociology

Michael Mann

Basil Blackwell

Copyright © Michael Mann 1988

First published 1988

Basil Blackwell Ltd
108 Cowley Road, Oxford, OX4 1JF, UK

Basil Blackwell Inc.
432 Park Avenue South, Suite 1503
New York, NY 10016, USA

All rights reserved. Except for the quotation of short passages for the purposes of criticism and review, no part of this publication may be reproduced, stored in a retrieval system, or transmitted, in any form or by any means, electronic, mechanical, photocopying, recording or otherwise, without the prior permission of the publisher.

Except in the United States of America, this book is sold subject to the condition that it shall not, by way of trade or otherwise, be lent, re-sold, hired out, or otherwise circulated without the publisher's prior consent in any form of binding or cover other than that in which it is published and without a similar condition including this condition being imposed on the subsequent purchaser.

British Library Cataloguing in Publication Data

Mann, Michael, 1942–
  States, war and capitalism: studies in political sociology.
  1. Capitalism   2. War–Economic aspects.
  I. Title   HB501
  303.6'6
  ISBN 0–631–15973–8

Library of Congress Cataloging in Publication Data

Mann, Michael, 1942–
  States, war, and capitalism: studies in political sociology/ Michael Mann.
    p. cm.
  ISBN 0–631–15973–8
  1. War-Economic aspects. 2. Militarism-Economic aspects.
  3. Capitalism, 4. Social classes. 5. State, The. I. Title.
  HB195.M225 1988
  303.6'6–dc 19   87–30914
                                                    CIP

Typeset in 11 on 13pt Sabon
by Cambrian Typesetters, Frimley, Camberley, Surrey
Printed in Great Britain by T J Press, Padstow

Contents

Preface	vii
1 The Autonomous Power of the State: its Origins, Mechanisms and Results	1
2 States, Ancient and Modern	33
3 State and Society, 1130–1815: an Analysis of English State Finances	73
4 Capitalism and Militarism	124
5 War and Social Theory: into Battle with Classes, Nations and States	146
6 The Roots and Contradictions of Modern Militarism	166
7 Ruling Class Strategies and Citizenship	188
8 The Decline of Great Britain	210
Index	238

Preface

Over much of the second half of the twentieth century, social scientists have failed lamentably to address some of the most fundamental problems of modern society. Operating securely within the assumptions of the post-war settlement between the Great Powers of Europe and the United States of America, they narrowed ideological controversy down to that between the two victorious philosophies of capitalism and socialism, and they amicably divided up reality between different academic disciplines. In the West the economy was appropriated by economists, domestic politics by political scientists, history by historians, international relations by a new, as yet nameless, profession and the residual domestic social institutions were given to sociologists. All disciplines have been riven by ideologies ranging from liberal capitalist thought to social democratic and Marxist socialism. Unfortunately these two characteristics have encouraged each other's worst vices. The disciplines have kept insulated within separate compartments social structures that actually and thoroughly interpenetrate one another. And, within each, the ideologies have produced theories that are absurdly pacific, often economistic and, in a rather peculiar way, stateless.

It should be obvious that in the real world, structures of ideological, economic, military, political and geo-political power are in continuous interaction, and that this interaction is continuously changing the nature of each. (If my particular categorization is not quite how you divide up reality, then substitute your own scheme, to arrive at the same conclusion.) Yet most economists study 'the economy' as a thing apart, with its own laws and dynamics, as do all those Marxists, industrial and post-industrial society theorists and others who practise the many different forms of economic determinism and materialism so prevalent in the advanced societies. Most political scientists and political sociologists until recently studied politics as an exclusively domestic discipline, conducted without reference to geo-political relations between states. Theorists of *the* state abound, but they seem not to have noticed that *states* are plural. In fact most sociologists in all fields have come up with peculiarly stateless theories. Their master-concept, 'society', is interchangeably the experience of a particular modern country or some much larger unit like 'capitalism' or 'industrial society'. True, there is one area in which the plurality of states has been noticed – in a further set of sub-disciplinary, insulated compartments known as 'comparative sociology', 'comparative politics' etc. But in these enterprises each state/country is counted as an independent, analogous case, varying from all other independent cases, not as interacting, interpenetrating power actors. Given all this, the final defect, pacifism, flows automatically: without interacting states, there are no modern wars or no militarism to study. Without geo-politics, military sociology settled down into the domestic institutions of armed forces. We won the war, we don't want more. Let's think of other things.

I have exaggerated in one respect, for such things have been thought about – by yet another specialism, international relations. As nuclear weapons developed, these specialists were given the most demanding task of all, 'to think the unthinkable', to avoid yet plan for nuclear geo-politics. Ideological schizophrenia understandably emerged, hard-nosed conservative strategist versus liberal/socialist disarmer – with (power being where it is) the former predominating. But international relations has to cope also with a second fundamental problem, the massive post-war internationalization of the economy. This has been an extremely complex process, for it can be argued that the period has seen a strengthening in all three types of economy and class relations that I distinguish in chapter 5 – the national, the international (relations between national economies and classes) and the transnational (relations proceeding right through the boundaries of states). Their complex interrelation is a clear instance of how the economy has been internally penetrated and shaped by military, political and geo-political power structures (and vice versa). How international relations specialists have coped with these multifarious tasks is a good index of the condition of social science as a whole.

Unfortunately, the answer is again schizophrenia. There have been two main traditions of international relations theory, 'realism' and 'interdependence'. Realism is old-fashioned *geopolitik:* international space is structured by the conflicting interests of states. 'Interdependence' is in many ways the opposite: an economically centred mutuality of interest cuts right across state lines to produce a more harmonious, if more complex world. Interdependence is merely a variant form of the economistic, pacific mainstream, while realism reproduces inverse defects. The international arena is clearly some kind of combination of both these (as well as other) phenomena, and both impact greatly upon domestic societies, states and economies. Yet no one has yet been bold enough to attempt their integration. We need a new, interdisciplinary, integrated theory of modern societies – one that does not neglect states and wars – but we get only limited help from international relations specialists.

I cannot claim that these essays supply such a theory. However, I believe that sociologists, steeped in a classic tradition of broad theory about macro-social development, are likeliest to come up with it. And I can claim personally that over the past few years, along with several other sociologists, I have been working towards such a venture. My *The Sources of Social Power*, vol. I: *A History of Power from the Beginning to 1760 AD* (Cambridge: Cambridge University Press, 1986) attempted a narrative history of the relations between ideological, economic, military and political power in agrarian societies.[1] It will be joined soon by a second volume continuing this history to the present day. The essays contained here fit alongside the two volumes. They are generally more synthetic and theoretical in scope, focusing on three of my four sources of power – with ideology for the moment omitted. My theme is the close interrelations of state (mostly modern states), militarism and war, and the economy (mostly capitalist economies and class relations). If this book has a single point it is to demonstrate that an overall theory of any of the three must involve consideration of them all.

The essays were written over a decade, 1976–86, and so bear

---

1 In my model geo-politics is not a fifth source of social power, but politics, applied externally, normally with a strong dose of military power.

the signs of developing, sometimes changing, ideas. They are presented roughly in the order in which they were written, although the most general, and relatively recent, essay appears first. References to then current events and world leaders also indicate the period in which they were written. I have not sought to bring these references 'up to date'. Let me now comment on each essay individually, indicating how they all fit together, and occasionally how they do not.

The opening essay, 'The autonomous power of the state', was written in 1982–3. It has a slightly over-general title, since it is largely confined to the domestic nature of states, and to the precise nature of the autonomy of states from their civil societies, especially from social classes. It concludes that states are essentially centralized and territorial, and that autonomous state power derives from these twin characteristics. It perhaps needs complementing by another essay (as yet unwritten) on the geo-political role and autonomy of the state – though some of the issues involved in this are discussed in chapter 5.

Chapter 2, 'States, ancient and modern', is the earliest piece, dating from the mid-1970s when so many of us were contemplating the concepts of structural Marxism. Always a critic of that approach (though I hope a not unsympathetic one), I never believed that modes of economic production and class struggle could in the 'last instance' (to use Engels's term) integrate and disintegrate whole societies. The essay extends Herbert Spencer's old distinction between 'militant' and 'industrial' societies, and argues that ancient empires of domination (Rome and China are the examples) were integrated principally by their militaristic states rather than by their economies and class structures. Volume I of my *The Sources of Social Power* supports this view of ancient empires with more detailed analyses of Mesopotamian and Roman cases. Here I contrast empires of domination with contemporary industrial capitalist states and economies in which the mode of production allows for far more extensive organization, especially of social classes. However, the last pages state, in anticipation of my more recent work, that overall integration in the modern West is provided, not by capitalism and classes alone, but by their interpenetration with nation-states.

The only essay to overlap substantially with *The Sources of Social Power* is the third, 'State and society, 1130–1815' being the full time-series data for the material on the English state which is given in chapters 12 and 13 of volume I. The essay shows the predominance of the external military role of the state throughout the medieval and early modern period, as measured by what it spent its money on. Volume II of *The Sources of Social Power* will show this continuing until the late nineteenth century. It was not until 1881 – probably for the first time in world history – that a Great Power (Britain) actually spent more money on domestic civil functions than on its military defence and aggression, and this was not stably the case until after the First and Second World Wars. As a sociologist with a strong preference for empirical over abstract theory, I have a special affection for this proof. All those reductionist theories of the state, from Marxism to pluralism, reducing the functions of the state to economic and domestic ones, are invalidated by these simple financial data.

Chapter 4 is something of a polemic, directed against notions that capitalism has been either especially pacific or especially militaristic when considered in the light of world history. 'Capitalism and militarism' argues that though industrial capitalism revolutionized the means and organization of war, it brought no great change to the militaristic impulse, which is a result largely of geo-political relations left unaltered by the rise of capitalism. It was written in 1981 and was perhaps a little too influenced by the realist conception of geo-politics. I would not now attribute war quite so forcefully to 'the games nations play', even though the conflict between states as articulated by 'statesmen' must remain a substantial part of the explanation. The essay should be read in conjunction with the next, 'War and social theory' which gives a more complex analysis of modern war.

This fifth essay was written in 1985. It is perhaps the core chapter, analysing the close interrelations between classes, nations and state elites in the development of modern warfare. I argue that all three types of actor have contributed their piece toward making the twentieth century such a dangerous place. This and the next chapter both contain normative prescriptions as to what might be done to make the world safer.

Chapter 6, 'The roots and contradictions of modern militarism', tries to understand the sentiments underlying contemporary military ventures as varied as the nuclear confrontation and the Falklands campaign (when it was written). Modern warfare is divided into three phases – periods of limited, citizen and nuclear warfare. Militarism in the nuclear age has transformed certain principles of limited war into what I term 'deterrence-science militarism', a sentiment of statesmen, and citizen participation in war into a 'spectator-sport militarism' of the masses. In the Soviet Union elements of these have fused into 'militarized socialism', which, though often aggressive, has a certain stability and predictability about it. But in the West, especially in the United States under President Reagan, the instability of the relationship between the two has so far been uniquely threatening to peace.

'Ruling class strategies and citizenship', the seventh essay, was originally a lecture given in memory of T. H. Marshall at the University of Southampton in 1986. It reverses the methodology of the three previous essays. Instead of looking at the social causes of war and militarism, it examines the impact of war on social development. I identify five viable strategies for the institutionalization of class conflict in advanced societies, termed liberal, reformist, authoritarian monarchist, Fascist and authoritarian socialist. In explaining their origin and development we should stress the strategies and cohesion of ruling classes and *anciens régimes* rather than those of the rising bourgeois and proletarian classes (as most theory has done). And in explaining their durability we must emphasize geo-politics, especially the two World Wars. If Marshall's vision of three succeeding stages of citizenship is a reasonably accurate view of the overall development of the West, this has been due primarily to the military victories of the Anglo-Saxon powers.

The longest essay in this volume, chapter 8, was originally three lectures given to first-year students at the London School of Economics in 1985. As its title implies, its theme is the decline of *Great* Britain. I argue that we can understand British decline better by comparing it with other cases of Great Power decline and by also by remembering the nature of its past greatness. The British ruling class (like those of other Great Powers before it) institutionalized three structures which had allowed it to become 'Great' in the first place: an essentially commercial form of capitalism, an open economy and a global, if slightly hidden, militarism. Those core British institutions are still in power and are now responsible, in changed conditions, for continuing decline. I thus offer an extended example of the integration of economic, military and political power relations in a narrative history which is the obverse of that contained in *The Sources of Social Power*. The *Sources* discusses only the process and causes of increases in power; this essay explains decline and suggests outline conditions under which it might be reversed.

There is no grand conclusion to this volume. One reason for this is that several of the essays were written in ignorance that other sociologists were beginning to work along similar lines. Their work has ensured that, fairly suddenly, this is no longer neglected terrain — especially Theda Skocopol's modern classic *States and Social Revolutions* (Cambridge: Cambridge University Press, 1979), Caroline Vogler's *The Nation-State: the Neglected Dimension of Class* (Aldershot, Hants: Gower Press, 1985), Anthony Giddens's *The Nation-State and Violence* (Oxford: Polity Press, 1985), John Hall's *Powers and Liberties* (Oxford: Basil Blackwell, 1985) and Randall Collins' *Weberian Sociological Theory* (Cambridge: Cambridge Univesity Press, 1986). Perhaps by digesting these books and (I hope) these essays, plus doing much empirical work and serious thinking, someone may produce the new theory we need.

Michael Mann
London School of Economics and Political Science

1

The Autonomous Power of the State: its Origins, Mechanisms and Results

This essay tries to specify the origins, mechanisms and results of the autonomous power which the state possesses in relation to the major power groupings of 'civil society'. The argument is couched generally, but it derives from my *Sources of Social Power* (1986), a large, ongoing empirical research project into the development of power in human societies. At the moment, my generalizations are bolder about agrarian societies; concerning industrial societies I will be more tentative. I define the state and then pursue the implications of that definition. I discuss two essential parts of the definition, centrality and territoriality, in relation to two types of state power, termed here *despotic* and *infrastructural* power. I argue that state autonomy, of both despotic and infrastructural forms, flows principally from the state's unique ability to provide a *territorially centralized* form of organization.

Nowadays there is no need to belabour the point that most general theories of the state have been false because they have been reductionist. They have reduced the state to the pre-existing structures of civil society. This is obviously true of the Marxist, the liberal and the functionalist traditions of state theory, each of which has seen the state predominantly as a place, an *arena*, in which the struggles of classes, interest groups and individuals are expressed and institutionalized, and – in functionalist versions – in which a General Will (or, to use more modern terms, core values

---

This chapter was first published in the *Archives européennes de sociologie*, XXV (1984), 25, pp. 185–213. We are grateful for permission to reproduce it here.

or normative consensus) is expressed and implemented. Though such theories disagree about many things, they are united in denying significant autonomous power to the state. But despite the existence of excellent critiques of such reductionism (e.g. by Wolin, 1961) and despite the self-criticism implied by the constant use of the term 'relative autonomy' by recent Marxists (like Poulantzas, 1972 and Therborn, 1978), there has still been a curious reluctance to analyse this autonomy.

One major obstacle has been itself political. The main alternative theory which *appears* to uphold state autonomy has been associated with rather unpleasant politics. I refer to the militarist tradition of state theory embodied around the beginning of the century in the work of predominantly Germanic writers, like Gumplowicz (1899), Ratzenhofer and Schmitt. They saw the state as physical force, and as this was the prime mover in society, so the militaristic state was supreme over those economic and ideological structures identified by the reductionist theories. But the scientific merits of these theories were quickly submerged by their political associations — with Social Darwinism, racism, glorification of state power, and then Fascism. The final (deeply ironic) outcome was that militarist theory was defeated on the battlefield by the combined forces of (Marxist) Russia and the (liberal democratic and functionalist) Western allies. We have heard little of it directly since. But its indirect influence has been felt, especially recently, through the work of 'good Germans' like Weber, Hintze (1975), Rüstow (1982) and the anarchist Oppenheimer (1975), all influenced to one degree or another by the German militarist tradition, and all of whose major works have now been translated into English.

I am not advocating a return to this alternative tradition, even at its scientific level. For when we look more closely, we see that it is usually also reductionist. The state is still nothing in itself: it is merely the embodiment of physical force in society. The state is not an arena where domestic economic/ideological issues are resolved, rather it is an arena in which military force is mobilized domestically and used domestically and, above all, internationally.

Both types of the theory have merit, yet both are partial. So what would happen if we put them together in a single theory? We would assemble an essentially dual theory of the state. It would identify two dimensions: the domestic economic/ideological aspect of the state and the military, international aspect of states. In the present climate of comparative sociology, dominated by a Marxified Weberianism, domestic analysis would likely centre upon class relations. And as states would now be responding to two types of pressure and interest groups, a certain 'space' would be created in which a state elite could manoeuvre, play off classes against war factions and other states, and so stake out an area and degree of power autonomy for itself. To put the two together would give us a rudimentary account of state autonomy.

That is indeed precisely the point at which the best state theory has now arrived. It is exemplified by Theda Skocpol's excellent *States and Social Revolutions*. Skocpol draws upon Marx and Weber in about equal quantities. She quotes enthusiastically Otto Hintze's two-dimensional view of the determinants of state organization, 'first, the structure of social classes, and second, the external ordering of the states – their position relative to each other, and their overall position in the world', and she then expands the latter in terms of military relations. Those two 'basic sets of tasks' are undertaken by 'a set of administrative, policing and military organizations headed, and more or less well coordinated by, an executive authority' for whom resources are extracted from society. These resource-supported administrative and coercive organizations are 'the basis of state power as such'. This power can then be used with a degree of autonomy against either the dominant class, or against domestic war or peace factions and foreign states (Skocpol, 1979, pp. 29–31; Hintze, 1975, p. 183). A very similar approach underlies Charles Tilly's work (e.g. 1981, chs 5 and 8). And Anthony Giddens (1981) has argued in similar vein.

Now I do not wish to quite abandon this 'two-dimensional' model of the state – for I, too, have contributed a detailed analysis of English state finances in the period 1130–1815 starting from such a model (see chapter 3 below). All these works advance beyond reductionism. We can develop their insights considerably further, and so penetrate to the heart of state autonomy, its nature, degree and consequences. But to do this we must make a far more radical, yet in a sense peculiar and paradoxical, break with reductionism. I will argue in this paper that the state *is* merely and essentially an arena, *a place*, and yet *this* is the very source of its autonomy.

Defining the state

The state is undeniably a messy concept. The main problem is that most definitions contain two different levels of analysis, the 'institutional' and the 'functional'. That is, the state can be defined in terms of what it looks like, institutionally, or what it does, its functions. Predominant is a mixed, but largely institutional, view put forward originally by Weber. In this the state contains four main elements, being:

1 A *differentiated* set of institutions and personnel embodying
2 *centrality* in the sense that political relations radiate outwards from a centre to cover
3 a *territorially demarcated area*, over which it exercises
4 a monopoly of *authoritative binding rule-making*, backed up by a monopoly of the means of physical violence.[1]

Apart from the last phrase which tends to equate the state with military force (see below), I will follow this definition. It is still something of a mixed bag. It contains a predominant institutional element: states can be recognized by the central location of their differentiated institutions. Yet it also contains a 'functional' element: the essence of the state's functions is a monopoly of binding rule-making. Nevertheless, my principal interest lies in those centralized institutions generally called 'states', and in the powers of the personnel who staff them, at the higher levels generally termed the 'state elite'. The central question for us here, then, is what is the nature of the power possessed by states and state elites? In answering I shall contrast state elites with power groupings whose base lies outside the state, in 'civil society'. In line with the model of power underlying my work, I divide these into three: ideological, economic and military groups. So what, therefore, is the power of state elites as against the power of ideological movements, economic classes and military elites?

---

1 See, for example, the definitions of Eisenstadt (1969, p. 5); MacIver (1926, p. 22); Tilly (1975, p. 27); Weber (1968, p. 64).

Two meanings of state power

What do we mean by 'the power of the state'? As soon as we begin to think about this commonplace phrase, we encounter two quite different senses in which states and their elites might be considered powerful. We must disentangle them. The first sense concerns what we might term the *despotic power* of the state elite, the range of actions which the elite is empowered to undertake without routine, institutionalized negotiation with civil society groups. The historical variations in such powers have been so enormous that we can safely leave on one side the ticklish problem of how we precisely measure them. The despotic powers of many historical states have been virtually unlimited. The Chinese Emperor, as the Son of Heaven, 'owned' the whole of China and could do as he wished with any individual or group within his domain. The Roman Emperor, only a minor god, acquired powers which were also in principle unlimited outside of a restricted area of affairs nominally controlled by the Senate. Some monarchs of early modern Europe also claimed divinely derived, absolute powers (though they were not themselves divine). The contemporary Soviet state/party elite, as 'trustees' of the interests of the masses, also possess considerable despotic (though sometimes strictly unconstitutional) power. Great despotic power can be 'measured' most vividly in the ability of all these Red Queens to shout 'off with his head' and have their whim gratified without further ado – provided the person is at hand. Despotic power is also usually what is meant in the literature by 'autonomy of power'.

But there is a second sense in which people talk of 'the power of the state', especially in today's capitalist democracies. We might term this *infrastructural power*, the capacity of the state to actually penetrate civil society, and to implement logistically political decisions throughout the realm. This was comparatively weak in the historical societies just mentioned – once you were out of sight of the Red Queen, she had difficulty in getting at you. But it is powerfully developed in all industrial societies. When people in the West today complain of the growing power of the state, they cannot be referring sensibly to the despotic powers of the state elite itself, for if anything these are still declining. It is, after all, only 40 years since universal suffrage was fully established in several of the advanced capitalist states, and the basic political rights of groups such as ethnic minorities and women are still increasing. But the complaint is more justly levelled against the state's infrastructural encroachments. These powers are now immense. The state can assess and tax our income and wealth at source, without our consent or that of our neighbours or kin (which states before about 1850 were *never* able to do); it stores and can recall immediately a massive amount of information about all of us; it can enforce its will within the day almost anywhere in its domains; its influence on the overall economy is enormous; it even directly provides the subsistence of most of us (in state employment, in pensions, in family allowances, etc.). The state penetrates everyday life more than did any historical state. Its infrastructural power has increased enormously. If there were a Red Queen, we would all quail at her words – from Alaska to Florida, from the Shetlands to Cornwall there is no hiding place from the infrastructural reach of the modern state.

But who controls these states? Without prejudging a complex issue entirely, the answer in the capitalist democracies is less likely to be 'an autonomous state elite' than in most historic societies. In these countries most of the formal political leadership is elected and recallable. Whether one regards the democracy as genuine or not, few would contest that politicians are largely controlled by outside civil society groups (either by their financiers or by the electorate) as well as by the law. President Nixon or M. Chaban-Delmas may have paid no taxes; political leaders may surreptitiously amass wealth, infringe the civil liberties of their opponents, and hold on to power by slyly undemocratic means. But they do not brazenly expropriate or kill their enemies or dare to overturn legal traditions enshrining constitutional rule, private property or individual freedoms. On the rare occasions this happens, we refer to it as a *coup* or a revolution, an overturning of the norms. If we turn from elected politicians to permanent bureaucrats we still do not find them exercising significant autonomous power over civil society. Perhaps I should qualify this, for the secret decisions of politicians and bureaucrats penetrate our everyday lives in an often infuriating way, deciding we are not eligible for this or that benefit, including, for some persons, citizenship itself. But their power to change the fundamental rules and overturn the distribution of power within civil society is feeble – without the backing of a formidable social movement.

So, in one sense states in the capitalist democracies are weak, in another they are strong. They are 'despotically weak' but 'infrastructurally strong'. Let us clearly distinguish these two types of state power. The first sense denotes power by the state elite itself *over* civil society. The second denotes the power of the state to penetrate and centrally coordinate the activities of civil society through its own infrastructure. The second type of power still allows the possibility that the state itself is a mere instrument of forces within civil society, i.e. that it has no despotic power at all. The two are analytically autonomous dimensions of power. In practice, of course, there may be a relationship between them. For example, the greater the state's infrastructural power, the greater the volume of binding rule-making, and therefore the greater the likelihood of despotic power over individuals and perhaps also over marginal, minority groups. All infrastructurally powerful states, including the capitalist democracies, are strong in relation to individuals and to the weaker groups in civil society, but the capitalist democratic states are feeble in relation to dominant groups — at least in comparison to most historical states.

From these two independent dimensions of state power we can derive the four ideal-types shown in table 1.1

The *feudal* state is the weakest, for it has both low despotic and low infrastructural power. The medieval European state approximated to this ideal-type, governing largely indirectly, through infrastructure freely and contractually provided and controlled by the principal and independent magnates, clerics and towns. The *imperial* state possesses its own governing agents, but has only limited capacity to penetrate and coordinate civil society without the assistance of other power groups. It corresponds to the term

Table 1.1 Two dimensions of state power

Despotic power	Infrastructural coordination	
	Low	High
Low	Feudal	Bureaucratic
High	Imperial	Authoritarian

patrimonial state used by writers like Weber (1968) and Bendix (1978). Ancient states like the Akkadian, Egyptian, Assyrian, Persian and Roman approximated to this type. I hesitated over the term *bureaucratic* state, because of its negative connotations. But a bureaucracy has a high organizational capacity, yet cannot set its own goals; and the bureaucratic state is controlled by others, civil society groups, but their decisions once taken are enforceable through the state's infrastructure. Contemporary capitalist democracies approximate to this type, as does the future state hoped for by most radicals and socialists. *Authoritarian* is intended to suggest a more institutionalized form of despotism, in which competing power groupings cannot evade the infrastructural reach of the state, nor are they structurally separate from the state (as they are in the bureaucratic type). All significant social power must go through the authoritative command structure of the state. Thus it is high on both dimensions, having high despotic power over civil society groups and being able to enforce this infrastructurally. In their different ways, Nazi Germany and the Soviet Union tend towards this case. But they probably traded off some loss of infrastructural penetration for high despotic powers (thus neither attained as high a level of social mobilization during the Second World War as the 'despotically weak' but participatory Great Britain did). Nor is this to deny that such states contain competing interest groups which may possess different bases in 'civil society'. Rather, in an authoritarian state power is transmitted through its directives and so such groups compete for direct control of the state. It is different in the capitalist democracies where the power of the capitalist class, for example, permeates the whole of society, and states generally accept the rules and rationality of the surrounding capitalist economy.

These are ideal-types. Yet my choice of real historical examples which roughly approximate to them reveals two major tendencies which are obvious enough yet worthy of explanation. First, there has occurred a long-term historical growth in the infrastructural power of the state, apparently given tremendous boosts by industrial societies, but also perceptible within both pre-industrial and industrial societies considered separately. Secondly, however, within each historical epoch have occurred wide variations in despotic powers. There has been *no* general development tendency in despotic powers – non-despotic states existed in late fourth millennium BC Mesopotamia (the 'primitive democracy' of the early city-states), in first millennium BC Phoenicia, Greece and Rome, in medieval republics and city-states, and in the modern world alike. The history of despotism has been one of oscillation, not development. Why such wide divergencies on one dimension, but a developmental trend on the other?

The development of state infrastructural power

The growth of the infrastructural power of the state is one in the logistics of political control. I will not here enumerate its main historical phases. Instead, I give examples of some logistical techniques which have aided effective state penetration of social life, each of which has had a long historical development.

1 A division of labour between the state's main activities which it coordinated centrally. A microcosm of this is to be found on the battlefields of history where a coordinated administrative division between infantry, cavalry and artillery, usually organized by the state, would normally defeat forces in which these activities were mixed up – at least in 'high intensity' warfare.
2 Literacy, enabling stabilized messages to be transmitted through the state's territories by its agents, and enabling legal responsibilities to be codified and stored. Giddens (1981) emphasizes this 'storage' aspect of state power.
3 Coinage, and weights and measures, allowing commodities to be exchanged under an ultimate guarantee of value by the state.
4 Rapidity of communication of messages and of transport of people and resources through improved roads, ships, telegraphy etc.

States able to use relatively highly developed forms of these techniques have possessed greater capacity for infrastructural penetration. This is pretty obvious. So is the fact that history has seen a secular process of infrastructural improvements.

Yet none of these techniques is specific to the state. They are part of general social development, part of the growth of human beings' increasing capacities for collective social mobilization of resources. Societies in general, not just their states, have advanced their powers. Thus none of these techniques necessarily changes the relationship between a state and its civil society; and none is necessarily pioneered by either the state or civil society.

Thus state power (in either sense) does not derive from techniques or means of power that are peculiar to itself. The varied techniques of power are of three main types: military, economic and ideoloigical. They are characteristic of all social relationships. The state uses them all, adding no fourth means peculiar to itself. This has made reductionist theories of the state more plausible because the state seems dependent on resources also found more generally in civil society. If they are all wrong, it is not because the state manipulates means of power denied to other groups. The state is not autononmous in *this* sense.

Indeed, the fact that the means used are essentially also the means used in all social relationships ensures that states rarely diverge far from their civil societies. Let us examine what happens when a state pioneers an increase in logistic powers. A characteristic, though slow-paced, example is literacy.

The first stages of literacy in Mesopotamia, and probably also in the other major independent cases of the emergence of civilization, occurred within the state. In this respect, the state was largely codifying and stabilizing two kinds of emergent norms, 'private' property rights and community rights and duties. The first pictograms and logograms enabled scribes at city-state temple-storehouses to improve their accountancy systems, and denote more permanently who possessed what and who owed what to the community. It solidified relations radiating across the surrounding territory and centred them more on itself. Writing then simplified into syllabic cuneiform script still essentially within the state bureaucracy, and performing the same dual functions. Writing was an important part of the growth of the first imperial states, that is of the Akkadian and subsequent Empires of the third and second millenia BC Literacy was restricted to the bureaucracy, stabilized its systems of justice and communications and so provided infrastructural support to a state despotism, though apparently in some kind of alliance with a property-owning economic class.

Yet the general utility of literacy was now recognized by civil society groups. By the time that the next simplifications, alphabetic script and parchment, became common (around the beginning of the first millenium BC) state domination had ended. The main pioneers were now not despotic states but decentralized groups of peasant traders, village priests and trading peoples organized into loose federations of small city- or tribal-states (like the Arameans, the Phoenicians and the Greeks). From then on, the power of such groups, usually with non-despotic states, rivalled that of the despotic empires. What had started by bolstering despotism continued by undermining it when the techniques spread beyond state confines. The states could not keep control over their own logistical inventions. And this is generally the case of all such inventions, whatever period of history we consider. In our time we have instances such as 'statistics': originally things which appertain to the state, later a useful method of systematic information-gathering for any power organization, especially large capitalist corporations.

However, converse examples are not difficult to find either, where states appropriate infrastructural techniques pioneered by civil society groups. The course of industrialization has seen several such examples, culminating in the Soviet Union whose state communications, surveillance and accountancy systems are similar to those pioneered by capitalist enterprises (with their states as junior partners) in the West. In this example what started in civil society continued in state despotism. Infrastructural techniques diffuse outwards from the particular power organizations that invented them.

Two conclusions emerge. First, in the whole history of the development of the infrastructure of power there is virtually no technique which belongs necessarily to the state, or conversely to civil society. Secondly, there is some kind of oscillation between the role of the two in social development. I hope to show later that it is not merely oscillation, but a dialectic.

The obvious question is: if infrastructural powers are a general feature of society, in what circumstances are they appropriated by the state? How does the state acquire in certain situations, but not others, despotic powers? What are the origins of the autonomous power of the state? My answer is in three stages, touching upon the *necessity* of the state, its *multiplicity of functions* and its *territorialized centrality*. The first two have often been identified in recent theory, the third is, I think, novel.

Origins of state power

The necessity of the state

The only stateless societies have been primitive. There are no complex, civilized societies without any centre of binding rule-making authority, however limited its scope. If we consider the weak feudal cases we find that even they tend to arise from a more state-centred history whose norms linger on to reinforce the new weak states. Feudal states tend to emerge either as a check to the further disintegration of a once-unified larger state (as in China and Japan) or as a post-conquest division of the spoils among the victorious, and obviously united, conquerors (see Lattimore, 1957). Western European feudalism embodies both these histories, though in varying mixtures in different regions. The laws of the feudal states in Europe were reinforced by rules descending from Roman law (especially property law), Christian codes of conduct and Germanic notions of loyalty and honour. This is a further glimpse of a process to which I will return later: a perpetual dialectic of movement between state and civil society.

Thus societies with states have had superior survival value to those without them. We have no examples of stateless societies long enduring past a primitive level of development, and many examples of state societies absorbing or eliminating stateless ones. Where stateless societies conquer ones with states, they either themselves develop a state or they induce social regress in the conquered society. There are good sociological reasons for this. Only three alternative bases for order exist, force, exchange and custom, and none of these are sufficient in the long run. At some point new exigencies arise for which custom is inadequate; at some point to bargain about everything in exchange relations is inefficient and disintegrating; while force alone, as Parsons emphasized, will soon 'deflate'. In the long run normally taken for granted, but enforceable, rules are necessary to bind together strangers or semi-strangers. It is not requisite that all these rules are set by a single monopolistic state. Indeed, though the feudal example is extreme, most states exist in a multi-state civilization which also provides certain normative rules of conduct. Nevertheless most societies seem to have required that some rules, particularly those relevant to the protection of life and property, be set monopolistically, and this has been the province of the state. From this necessity, autonomous state power ultimately derives. The activities of the state personnel are necessary to society as a whole and/or to the various groups that benefit from the existing structure of rules which the state enforces. From this functionality derives the potentiality for exploitation, a lever for the achievement of private state interests. Whether the lever is used depends on other conditions, for – after all – we have not even established the existence of a permanent state cadre which might have identifiable interests. But necessity is the mother of state power.

The multiplicity of state functions

Despite the assertions of reductionists, most states have not in practice devoted themselves to the pursuit of a single function. 'Binding rule-making' is merely an umbrella term. The rules and functions have been extremely varied. As the two-dimensional models recognize, we may distinguish domestic and international, or economic, ideological and military functions. But there are many types of activity and each tends to be functional for differing 'constituencies' in society. I illustrate this with reference to what have been probably the four most persistent types of state activities.

1 The maintenance of internal order. This may benefit all, or all law-abiding subjects of the state. It may also protect the majority from arbitrary usurpations by socially and economically powerful groups, other than those allied to the state. But probably the main benefit is to protect existing property relations from the mass of the property-less. This function probably best serves a dominant economic class constituency.

2 Military defence/aggression, directed against foreign foes. 'War parties' are rarely coterminous with either the whole society or with one particular class within it. Defence may be genuinely collective; aggression usually has more specific interests behind it. Those interests may be quite widely shared by all 'younger sons' without inheritance rights or all those expansively minded; or they might comprise only a class fraction of an aristocracy, merchants or capitalists. In multi-state systems war usually involves alliances with other states, some of whom may share the same religion,

ethnicity, or political philosophy as some domestic constituency. These are rarely reducible to economic class. Hence war and peace constituencies are usually somewhat idiosyncratic.

3 The maintenance of communications infrastructures: roads, rivers, message systems, coinages, weights and measures, marketing arrangements. Though few states have monopolized all of these, all states have provided some, because they have a territorial basis which is often most efficiently organized from a centre. The principal constituencies here are a 'general interest' and more particular trade-centred groups.

4 Economic redistribution: the authoritative distribution of scarce material resources between different ecological niches, age-groups, sexes, regions, classes etc. There is a strongly collective element in this function, more so than in the case of the others. Nevertheless, many of the redistributions involve rather particular groups, especially the economically inactive whose subsistence is thus protected by the state. And economic redistribution also has an international dimension, for the state normally regulates trade relations and currency exchanges across its boundaries, sometimes unilaterally, sometimes in alliance with other states. This also gives the state a particular constituency among merchants and other international agents – who, however, are rarely in agreement about desirable trade policy.

These four tasks are necessary, either to society as a whole or to interest groups within it. They are undertaken most efficiently by the personnel of a central state who become indispensable. And they bring the state into functional relations with diverse, sometimes cross-cutting groups between whom there is room to manoeuvre. The room can be exploited. Any state involved in a multiplicity of power relations can play off interest groups against each other.

It is worth noting that one example of this 'divide-and-rule' strategy has been a staple of sociological analysis. This is the case of a 'transitional state', living amid profound economic transformations from one mode of production to another. No single dominant economic class exists, and the state may play off traditional power groups against emergent ones. Such situations were discussed by both the classic stratification theorists. Marx analysed and satirized Louis Bonaparte's attempts to play off the factions of industrial and finance capital, petite bourgeoisie, peasantry and proletariat to enhance his own independent power. This is the 'Bonapartist balancing act', so stressed by Poulantzas (1972) – though Marx (and Poulantzas) rather underestimated Bonaparte's ability to succeed (see Perez-Diaz, 1979). Weber was struck by the ability of the Prussian State to use a declining economic class, the agrarian landlord Junkers, to hold on to autocratic power in the vacuum created by the political timidity of the rising bourgeois and proletarian classes (see Lachmann, 1970, pp. 92–142). All the various groups in both examples needed the state, but none could capture it. Another example is the development of absolutism in early modern Europe. Monarchs played off against each other (or were unable to choose between) feudal and bourgeois, land and urban, groups. In particular, military functions and functions performed in relation to dominant economic classes were different. States used war as a means of attempting to reduce their dependence on classes (as Skocpol, 1979 and Trimberger, 1978 both argue).

These are familiar examples of the state balancing between what are predominantly classes or class factions. But the balancing possibilities are much more numerous if the state is involved in a multiplicity of relations with groups which may on some issues be narrower than classes and on others wider. Because most states are pursuing multiple functions, they can perform multiple manoeuvres. The 'Bonapartist balancing act' is a skill acquired by most states. This manoeuvring space is the birthplace of state power.

And this is about as far as the insights contained within current two-dimensional theory can be expanded. It is progress, but not enough. It does not really capture the *distinctiveness* of the state as a social organization. After all, necessity plus multiplicity of function, and the balancing act, are also the power source and stock-in-trade of any ruthless committee chairperson. Is the state only a chair writ large? No, as we will now see.

The territorial centrality of the state

The definition of the state concentrates upon its institutional, territorial, centralized nature. This is the third, and most important, precondition of state power. As noted, the state does not possess a distinctive *means* of power independent of, and analogous to, economic, military and ideological power. The means used by states are only a combination of these, which are also the means of power used in all social relationships. However the power of the state is irreducible in quite a different *socio-spatial* and *organizational* sense. Only the state is inherently centralized over a delimited territory over which it has authoritative power. Unlike economic, ideological or military groups in civil society, the state elite's resources radiate authoritatively outwards from a centre but stop at defined territorial boundaries. The state is, indeed, a *place* – both a central place and a unified territorial reach. As the principal forms of state autonomous power will flow from this distinctive attribute of the state, it is important that I first prove that the state does so differ socio-spatially and organizationally from the major power groupings of civil society.

Economic power groupings – classes corporations, merchant houses, manors, plantations, the *oikos* etc. – normally exist in decentred, competitive or conflictual relations with one another. True, the internal arrangements of some of them (e.g. the modern corporation, or the household and manor of the great feudal lord) might be relatively centralized. But, first, they are oriented outwards to further opportunities for economic advantage which are not territorially confined nor subject to authoritative rules governing expansion (except by states). Economic power expansion is not authoritative, commanded – it is 'diffused', informally. Second, the scope of modern and some historic economic institutions is not territorial. They do not exercise general control of a specific territory, they control a specialized function and seek to extend it 'transnationally' wherever that function is demanded and exploitable. General Motors does not rule the territory around Detroit, it rules the assembly of automobiles and some aspects of the economic life-chances of its employees, stockholders and consumers. Third, in those cases where economic institutions have been authoritative, centralized and territorial (as in the feudal household/manor of historic nobilities) they have either been subject to a higher level of territorial, central control by the (imperial) state, or they have acquired political function (administering justice, raising military levies etc.) from a weak (feudal) state and so become themselves 'mini-states'. Thus states cannot be the simple instrument of classes, for they have a different territorial scope.

Analogous points can be made about ideological power movements like religions. Ideologies (unless state-led) normally spread even more diffusely than economic relations. They move diffusely and 'interstitially' inside state territories, spreading through communication networks among segments of a state's population (like classes, age-cohorts, genders, urban/rural inhabitants etc.); they often also move transnationally right through state boundaries. Ideologies may develop central, authoritative, Church-like institutions, but these are usually functionally, more than territorially, organized: they deal with the sacred rather than the secular, for example. There is a socio-spatial, as well as spiritual, 'transcendence' about ideological movements, which is really the opposite of the territorial bounds of the state.

It is true, however, that military power overlaps considerably with the state, especially in modern states who usually monopolize the means of organized violence. Nevertheless, it is helpful to treat the two as distinct sources of power. I have not the space here to justify this fully (see Mann, 1986, ch. 1). Let me instead make two simple points. First, not all warfare is most efficiently organized territorially centrally – guerrillas, military feudalism and warrior bands are all examples of relatively decentred military organizations effective at many historical periods. Second, the effective scope of military power does not cover a single, unitary territory. In fact, it has two rather different territorial radii of effective control.

Militaristic control of everyday behaviour requires such a high level of organized coercion, logistical back-up and surplus extraction that it is practical only within close communications to the armed forces in areas of high surplus availability. It does not spread evenly over entire state territories. It remains concentrated in pockets and along communications routes. It is relatively ineffective at penetrating peasant agriculture, for example.

The second radius enables, not everyday control, but the setting of broad limits of outward compliance over far greater areas. In this case, failure to comply with broad parameters such as the handing over of tribute, the performance of ritual acts of submission, occasional military support (or at least non-rebellion), could result in a punitive expedition, and so is avoided. This radius of military striking power has normally been far greater than that of state political control, as Owen Lattimore (1962) brilliantly argued. This is obviously so in the world today, given the capabilities of modern armaments. It is also true of the superpowers in a more subtle sense: they can impose 'friendly' regimes and de-stabilize the unfriendly through client military elites and their own covert paramilitary organizations, but they cannot get those regimes to conform closely to their political dictates. A more traditional example would be Britain's punitive expedition to the Falklands, capable of defeating and so de-legitimizing the Argentine regime, and remaining capable of repeating the punishment, but quite incapable of providing a political future for the Islands. The logistics of 'concentrated coercion' − that is, of military power − differ from those of the territorial centralized state. Thus we should distinguish the two as power organizations. The militarist theory of the state is false, and one reason is that the state's organization is not coterminous with military organization.

The organizational autonomy of the state is only partial − indeed, in many particular cases it may be rather small. General Motors and the capitalist class in general, or the Catholic Church, or the feudal lords and knights, or the US military, are or were quite capable of keeping watch on states they have propped up. Yet they could not do the states' jobs themselves unless they changed their own socio-spatial and organizational structure. A state autonomous power ensues from this difference. Even if a particular state is set up or intensified merely to institutionalize the relations between given social groups, this is done by concentrating resources and infrastructures in the hands of an institution that has different socio-spatial and organizational contours to those groups. Flexibility and speed of response entail concentration of decision-making and a tendency towards permanence of personnel. The decentred non-territorial interest groups that set up the state in the first place are thus less able to control it. Territorial centralization provides the state with a potentially independent basis of power mobilization being necessary to social development and uniquely in the possession of the state itself.

If we add together the necessity, multiplicity and territorial centrality of the state, we can in principle explain its autonomous power. By these means the state elite possesses an independence from civil society which, though not absolute, is no less absolute in principle than the power of any other major group. Its power cannot be reduced to their power either directly or 'ultimately' or 'in the last instance'. The state is not merely a locus of class struggle, an instrument of class rule, the factor of social cohesion, the expression of core values, the centre of social allocation processes, the institutionalization of military force (as in the various reductionist theories) – it is a different socio-spatial organization. As a consequence we can treat states as *actors*, in the person of state elites, with a will to power and we can engage in the kind of 'rational action' theory of state interests advocated by Levi (1981).

The mechanisms for acquiring autonomous state power

Of course, this in itself does not confer a significant degree of actual power upon the state elite, for civil society groups, even though slightly differently organized, may yet be able largely to control it. But the principles do offer us a pair of hypotheses for explaining variations of power. (1) State infrastructural power derives from the social utility in any particular time and place of forms of territorial centralization which cannot be provided by civil society forces themselves. (2) The extent of state despotic power derives from the inability of civil society forces to control those forms of territorial centralization, once set up. Hence, there are two phases in the development of despotism: the growth of territorial centralization, and the loss of control over it. First function, then exploitation – let us take them in order.

Because states have undertaken such a variety of social activities, there are also numerous ways in which at different times they have acquired a disproportionate part of society's capacity for infrastructural coordination. Let me pick out three relatively uncontentious examples: the utility of a redistributive economy, of a coordinated military command for conquest or defence, and of a centrally coordinated 'late development' response to one's rivals. These are all common conditions favouring the territorial centralization of social resources.

The redistributive state seems to have been particularly appropriate, as anthropologists and archeologists argue, in the early history of societies before the exchange of commodities was possible. Different ecological niches delivered their surpluses to a central storehouse which eventually became a permanent state.

The case is often over-argued (e.g. by Service, 1975), but it has often been archaeologically useful (see Renfrew, 1972).

The military route was, perhaps, the best-known to the nineteenth-century and early twentieth-century theorists like Spencer (1969 edition), Gumplowicz (1899) and Oppenheimer (1975 edition). Though they exaggerated its role, there is no doubt that most of the well-known ancient Empires had the infrastructural powers of their states considerably boosted by their use of centralized, highly organized, disciplined and well-equipped military forces for both defence and further conquest. Rome is the example best known to us (see chapter 2 below).

Thirdly, the response of late industrial developers in the nineteenth and twentieth centuries to the interference of their early-industrializing rivals is well-known: a cumulative development, through countries like France, Prussia, Japan and Russia of more and more centralized and territorially confined mobilization of economic resources with state financing and state enterprises sheltering behind tariff walls (classically stated by Gerschenkron, 1962). But it also has earlier parallels – for example, in the history of Assyria or the early Roman Republic, imitating earlier civilizations, but in a more centralized fashion.

Note that in all cases it is not economic or military necessity *per se* that increases the role of the state, for this might merely place it into the hands of classes or military groups in civil society. It is rather the more particular utility of economic or military *territorial centralization* in a given situation. There are other types of economy (e.g. market exchange) and of military organization (e.g. feudal cavalry or chariotry, castle defence) which encourage decentralization and so reduce state power. In all these above examples the principal power groupings of civil society *freely* conferred infrastructural powers upon their states. My explanation thus starts in a functionalist vein. But functions are then exploited and despotism results. The hypothesis is that civil society freely gives resources but then loses control and becomes oppressed by the state. How does this happen?

Let us consider first that old war-horse, the origins of the state. In some theories of state origins, the loss of control by 'civilians' is virtually automatic. For example, in the militarist tradition of theory, the leading warriors are seen as automatically converting temporary, legitimate authority in war-time to permanent, coercive power in peace-time. Yet as Clastres (1977) has pointed out, primitive societies take great precautions to ensure that their military leaders do not become permanent oppressors. Similarly, the redistributive state of the anthropologists seems to have contained a number of checks against chiefly usurpation which makes its further development problematic. In fact, it seems that permanent, coercive states did *not* generally evolve in later prehistory. Only in a few unusual cases (connected with regional effects of alluvial agriculture) did 'pristine' states evolve endogenously, and they influenced all other cases. (This argument is made at greater length in Mann, 1986, chs 2–4.) The problem seems to be that for centralized functions to be converted into exploitation, organizational resources are necessary that only actually appeared with the emergence of civilized, stratified, state societies – which is a circular process.

However, the process is somewhat clearer with respect to the intensification of state power in already established, stratified, civilized societies with states. It is clearest of all in relation to military conquest states. We know enough about early Rome and other, earlier cases to extend Spencer's notion of 'compulsory cooperation' (see chapter 2 below). Spencer saw that conquest may put new resources into the hands of the conquering centralized command such that it was able to attain a degree of autonomy from the groups who had set it in motion. But Spencer's argument can be widened into the sphere of agricultural production. In pre-industrial conditions increasing the productivity of labour usually involved increasing the intensity of effort. This was most easily obtained by coercion. A militarized economy could increase output and be of benefit to civil society at large, or at least to its dominant groups. Obviously, in most agricultural conditions, coercion could not be routinely applied. But where labour was concentrated – say, in irrigation agriculture, in plantations, mines and in construction works – it could. But this required the maintenance of centralized militarism, because a centralized regime was more efficient at using a minimum of military resources for maximum effect.

This would really require considerable elaboration. In other work (Mann, 1986) I call it 'military Keynesianism' (ch. 9) because of the multiplier effects which are generated by military force. These effects boost the despotic power of the state *vis-à-vis* civil society because they make useful the maintenance of centralized compulsory cooperation, which civil society cannot at first provide itself. It is an example of how centralization increases general social resources — and thus no powerful civil society group wishes to dispense with the state — yet also increases the private power resources of the state elite. These can now be used despotically against civil society.

Provided the state's activities generate extra resources, then it has a particular logistical advantage. Territorial centralization gives effective mobilizing potentialities, able to concentrate these resources against any particular civil society group, even though it may be inferior in overall resources. Civil society groups may actually endorse state power. If the state upholds given relations of production, then the dominant economic class will have an interest in efficient state centralization. If the state defends society from outside aggressors, or represses crime, then its centrality will be supported quite widely in society. Naturally, the degree of centralization useful to these civil society interests will vary according to the system of production or method of warfare in question. Centrality can also be seen in the sphere of ideology, as Eisenstadt (1969) argues. The state and the interests it serves have always sought to uphold its authority by a claim to 'universalism' over its territories, a detachment from all particularistic, specialized ties to kin, locality, class, Church etc. Naturally in practice states tend to represent the interests of particular kinship groupings, localities, classes etc., but if they appeared merely to do this they would lose all claim to distinctiveness and to legitimacy. States thus appropriate what Eisenstadt calls 'free-floating resources', not tied to any particular interest group, able to float throughout the territorially defined society.

This might seem a formidable catalogue of state powers. And yet the autonomous power achievements of historical states before the twentieth century were generally limited and precarious. Here we encounter the fundamental logistical, infrastructural constraints operating against centralized regimes in extensive agrarian societies. We return to the greater effective range of punitive military action compared to effective political rule. Without going into detailed logistical calculations here, but drawing on the seminal work of Engel (1978) and van Creveld (1977), we can estimate that in Near Eastern imperial societies up to Alexander the Great the maximum unsupported march possible for an army was about 60–75 miles. Alexander and the Romans may have extended it to nearly 100 miles, and this remained the maximum until the eighteenth century in Europe when a massive rise in agricultural productivity provided the logistical basis for far wider operations. Before then further distances required more than one campaigning phase, or – far more common if some degree of political control was sought – it required elaborate negotiations with local allies regarding supplies. This is enhanced if routine political control is desired without the presence of the main army. So even the most pretentious of despotic rulers actually ruled through local notables. All extensive societies were in reality 'territorially federal'. Their imperial rule was always far feebler than traditional images of them allow for (this is now well-recognized by many writers, e.g. Kautsky, 1982; Gellner, 1983, ch. 2; Giddens, 1981, p. 103–4).

So we have in this example contrary tendencies – militaristic centralization followed by fragmenting federalism. Combining them we get a dialectic. If compulsory cooperation is successful, it increases both the infrastructural and the despotic power of the state. But it also increases social infrastructural resources in general. The logistical constraints mean that the new infrastructures cannot be kept within the body politic of the state. Its agents continually 'disappear' into civil society, bearing the state's resources with them. This happens continually to such regimes. The booty of conquest, land grants to military lieutenants, the fruits of office, taxes, literacy, coinage all go through a two-phase cycle, being first the property of the state then private (in the sense of 'hidden') property. And though there are cases where the fragmentation phase induces social collapse, there are others where civil society can use the resources which the despotic state has institutionalized, without needing such a strong state. The Arameans, Phoenicians and Greeks appropriated, and further developed, the techniques pioneered by the despotic states of the Near East. Christian Europe appropriate the Roman heritage.

My examples are relatively militaristic only because the process is easiest to describe there. It was a general dialectic in agrarian societies. In other words, imperial and feudal regimes do not merely oscillate (as Weber, Kautsky and many others have argued), they are entwined in a dialectical process. A range of infrastructural techniques are pioneered by despotic states, then appropriated by civil societies (or vice versa); then further opportunities for centralized coordination present themselves, and the process begins anew. Such trends are as visible in early modern societies as in the ancient ones from which I have drawn my examples.

Such a view rejects a simple antithesis, common to ideologies of our own time, between the state and civil society, between public and private property. It sees the two as continuously, temporally entwined. More specifically it sees large private property concentrations – and, therefore, the power of dominant classes – as normally boosted by the fragmentation of successful, despotic states, not as the product of civil society forces alone. So the power autonomy of both states and classes has essentially fluctuated, dialectically. There can be no general formula concerning some 'timeless' degree of autonomous state power (in the despotic sense).

But the contemporary situation is relatively unclear. Power infrastructures leaped forward with the Industrial Revolution. Industrial capitalism destroyed 'territorially federal' societies, replacing them with nation states across whose territories unitary control and surveillance structures could penetrate (as Giddens has argued for example, 1981). Logistical penetration of territory has increased exponentially over the past century and a half.

What happens if a state acquires control of all those institutions of control divided historically and elsewhere between states, capitalist enterprises, Churches, charitable associations etc.? Is that the end of the dialectic, because the state can now keep what it acquires? Obviously, in macro-historical terms the Soviet Union can control its provincial agents, and hence its provinces, in a way that was flatly impossible for any previous state. Moreover, though its degree of effective authoritarianism can be easily exaggerated (as in 'totalitarian' theories, for example), its centralization tendencies are novel in form as well as extent. Group struggles are not decentralized, as they are substantially in the capitalist democracies, nor do they fragment as they did in agrarian societies. Struggle is itself centralized: there is something pulling the major contending forces – the 'liberals', 'technocrats', 'military/heavy industry complex' etc. – towards the Praesidium. They cannot evade the state, as agrarian dissenters did; they cannot struggle outside the state, as capitalists and workers often do. Does this authoritarian state exist despotically 'above' society, coercing it with its own autonomous power resources? Or does its authoritarian despotism exist in milder terms, firstly as a place in which the most powerful social forces struggle and compromise, and secondly as a set of coercive apparatuses for enforcing the compromise on everyone else? This has long been debated among theorists of the Soviet Union. I do not pretend to know the answer.

The bureaucratic states of the West also present problems. They are much as they were in relative power terms before the exponential growth in logistical powers began. Whatever the increases in their infrastructural capacities, these have not curbed the decentred powers of the capitalist class, its major power rival. Today agencies like multinational corporations and international banking institutions still impose similar parameters of capitalist rationality as their predecessors did over a century ago. State elites have not acquired greater power autonomy despite their infrastructural capacities. Again, however, I am touching upon some of the central unsolved theoretical issues concerning contemporary societies. And, again, I offer no solution. Indeed, it may require a longer-run historical perspective than that of our generation to solve them, and so to decide whether the Industrial Revolution did finish off the agrarian dialectic I described.

Thus the impact of state autonomy on despotic power has been ambiguous. In terms of traditional theory results might seem disappointing: the state has not consistently possessed great powers — or indeed any fixed level of power. But I have discussed interesting power processes of a different kind. In agrarian societies states were able to exploit their territorial centrality, but generally only precariously and temporarily because despotic power also generated its own antithesis in civil society. In industrial societies the emergence of authoritarian states indicates much greater potential despotism, but this is still somewhat controversial and ambiguous. In the capitalist democracies there are few signs of autonomous state power — of a despotic type.

But, perhaps, all along, and along with most traditional theory, we have been looking for state power with the wrong place. By further examining infrastructural power we can see that this is the case.

Results: infrastructural power

Any state that acquires or exploits social utility will be provided with infrastructural supports. These enable it to regulate, normatively and by force, a *given* set of social and territorial relations, and to erect boundaries against the outside. New boundaries momentarily reached by previous social interactions are stabilized, regulated and heightened by the state's universalistic, monopolistic rules. In this sense the state gives territorial bounds to social relations whose dynamic lies outside of itself. The state *is* an arena, the condensation, the crystallization, the summation of social relations within its territories – a point often made by Poulantzas (1972). Yet, despite appearances, this does not support Poulantzas' reductionist view of the state, for this is an *active* role. The state may promote great social change by consolidating territoriality which would not have occurred without it. The importance of this role is in proportion to its infrastructural powers: the greater they are or become, the greater the territorializing of social life. Thus even if the state's every move toward despotism is successfully resisted by civil society groups, massive state-led infrastructural reorganization may result. Every dispute between the state elite and elements of civil society, and every dispute among the latter which is routinely regulated through the state's institutions, tends to focus the relations and the struggles of civil society on to the territorial plane of the state, consolidating social interaction over that terrain, creating territorialized mechanisms for repressing or compromising the struggle, and breaking both smaller local and also wider transnational social relationships.

Let me give an example (elaborated in much more empirical detail in chapter 3 below). From the thirteenth century onward, two principal social processes favoured a greater degree of territorial centralization in Europe. First, warfare gradually favoured army command structures capable of routine, complex coordination of specialized infantry, cavalry and artillery. Gradually, the looser feudal levy of knights, retainers and a few mercenaries became obsolete. In turn this presupposed a routine 'extraction–coercion cycle' to deliver men, monies and supplies to the forces (see the brilliant essay by Finer, 1975). Eventually, only territorially centred states were able to provide such resources and the Grand Duchies, the Prince–Bishops and the Leagues of Towns lost power to the emerging 'national' states. Second, European expansion, especially economic expansion taking an increasingly capitalistic form, required (a) increased military protection abroad, (b) more complex legal regulation of property and market transactions, and (c) domestic property forms (like rights to common lands). Capitalistic property owners sought out territorial states for help in these matters. Thus European states gradually acquired far greater infrastructural powers: regular taxation, a monopoly over military mobilization, permanent bureaucratic administration, a monopoly of law-making and enforcement. In the long run, despite attempts at absolutism, states failed to acquire despotic powers through this because it also enhanced the infrastructural capacities of civil society groups, especially of capitalist property-holders. This was most marked in Western Europe and as the balance of geo-political power tilted Westwards – and especially to Britain – the despotically weak state proved the general model for the modern era. States governed with, and usually in the interests of, the capitalist class.

But the process and the alliance facilitated the rise of a quite different type of state power, infrastructural in nature. When capitalism emerged as dominant, it took the form of a series of territorial segments – many systems of production and exchange, each to a large (though not total) extent bounded by a state and its overseas sphere of influence. The nation-state system of our own era was not a product of capitalism (or, indeed, of feudalism) considered as pure modes of production. It is in that sense 'autonomous'. But it resulted from the way expansive, emergent, capitalist relations were given regulative boundaries by pre-existing states. The states were the initially weak (in both despotism and in infrastructure) states of feudal Europe. In the twelfth century even the strongest absorbed less than 2 per cent of GNP (if we could measure it), they called out highly decentralized military levies of at most 10 to 20,000 men sometimes only for 30 days in the campaigning system, they could not tax in any regular way, they regulated only a small proportion of total social disputes – they were, in fact, marginal to the social lives of most Europeans. And yet those puny states became of decisive importance in structuring the world we live in today. The need for territorial centralization led to the restructuring of first European, then world society. The balance of nuclear terror lies between the successor states of these puny Europeans.

In the international economic system today, nation-states appear as collective economic actors. Across the pages of most works of political economy today stride actors like 'The United States', 'Japan', or 'The United Kingdom'. This does not necessarily mean that there is a common 'national interest', merely that on the international plane there are a series of collectively organized power actors, nation-states. There is no doubting the economic role of the nation-state: the existence of a domestic market segregated to a degree from the international market, the value of the state's currency, the level of its tariffs and import quotas, its support for its indigenous capital and labour, indeed, its whole political economy is permeated with the notion that 'civil society' is its territorial domain. The territoriality of the state has created social forces with a life of their own.

In this example, increasing territoriality has not increased despotic power. Western states were despotically weak in the twelfth century, and they remain so today. Yet the increase in infrastructural penetration has increased dramatically territorial boundedness. This seems a general characteristic of social development: increases in state infrastructural powers also increase the territorial boundedness of social interaction. We may also postulate the same tendency for despotic power, though it is far weaker. A despotic state without strong infrastructural supports will only claim territoriality. Like Rome and China it may build walls, as much to keep its subjects in as to keep 'barbarians' out. But its success is limited and precarious. So, again we might elaborate a historical dialectic. Increases in state infrastructural power will territorialize social relations. If the state then loses control of its resources they diffuse into civil society, decentering and de-territorializing it. Whether this is, indeed, beginning to happen in the contemporary capitalist world, with the rise of multi-national corporations outliving the decline of two successively hegemonic states, Great Britain and the United States, is one of the most hotly debated issues in contemporary political economy. Here I must leave it as an open issue.

In this essay I have argued that the state is essentially an arena, a place – just as reductionist theories have argued – and yet this is precisely the origin and mechanism of its autonomous powers. The state, unlike the principal power actors of civil society, is territorially bounded and centralized. Societies need some of their activities to be regulated over a centralized territory. So do dominant economic classes, Churches and other ideological power movements, and military elites. They, therefore, entrust power resources to state elites which they are incapable of fully recovering, precisely because their own socio-spatial basis of organization is not centralized and territorial. Such state power resources, and the autonomy to which they lead, may not amount to much. If, however, the state's use of the conferred resources generates further power resources − as was, indeed, intended by the civil society groups themselves − these will normally flow through the state's hands, and thus lead to a significant degree of power autonomy. Therefore, *autonomous state power is the product of the usefulness of enhanced territorial centralization to social life in general.* This has varied considerably through the history of societies, and so consequently has the power of states.

I distinguished two types of state power, despotic and infrastructural. The former, the power of the state elite over civil society classes and elites, is what has normally been meant by state power in the literature. I gave examples of how territorial centralization of economic, ideological and military resources has enhanced the despotic powers of states. But states have rarely been able to hold on to such power for long. Despotic achievements have usually been precarious in historic states because they have lacked effective logistical infrastructures for penetrating and coordinating social life. Thus when states did increase their 'private' resources, these were soon carried off into civil society by their own agents. Hence resulted the oscillation between imperial/patrimonial and feudal regimes first analysed by Max Weber.

By concentrating on infrastructural power, however, we can see that the oscillation was, in fact, a dialectic of social development. A variety of power infrastructures have been pioneered by despotic states. As they 'disappear' into civil society, general social powers increase. I suggest that a core part of social development in agrarian societies has been a dialectic between centralized, authoritative power structures, exemplified best by empires of domination, and decentralized, diffused power structures exemplified by 'Multi-Power Actor Civilizations'. Thus the developmental role of the powerful state has essentially fluctuated – sometimes promoting it, sometimes retarding it.

But I also emphasized a second result of state infrastructural powers. Where these have increased, so has the territoriality of social life itself. This has usually gone unnoticed within sociology because of the unchallenged status of sociology's masterconcept: 'society'. Most sociologists – indeed, most people anywhere who use this term – mean by 'society', the territory of a state. Thus 'American society', 'British society', 'Roman society' etc. The same is true of synonyms like 'social formation' and (to a lesser extent) 'social system'. Yet the relevance of state boundaries to what we mean by societies is always partial and has varied enormously. Medievalists do not generally characterize 'society' in their time-period as state-defined; much more likely is a broader, trans-national designation like 'Christendom' or 'European society'. Yet this change between medieval and modern times is one of the most decisive aspects of the great modernizing transformations; just as the current relationship between nation states and 'the world system' is crucial to our understanding of late twentieth-century society. How territorialized and centralized are societies? This is the most significant theoretical issue on which we find states exercising a massive force over social life, *not* the more traditional terrain of dispute, the despotic power of state elites over classes or other elites. States are central to our understanding of what a society is. Where states are strong, societies are relatively territorialized and centralized. That is the most general statement we can make about the autonomous power of the state.

References

Bendix R. 1978: *Kings or People*. Berkeley, Ca: University of California Press.
Clastres P. 1977: *Society against the State*. Oxford: Blackwell.
Creveld M. van. 1977: *Supplying War: Logistics from Wallenstein to Patton*. Cambridge: Cambridge University Press.
Eisenstadt S. N. 1969: *The Political Systems of Empires*. New York: The Free Press.
Engel D. W. 1978: *Alexander the Great and the Logistics of the Macedonian Army*. Berkeley, Ca: University of California Press.
Finer S. 1975: 'State and nation-building in Europe: the role of the

military', in C. Tilly (ed.), *The Formation of National States in Western Europe*. Princeton, NJ: Princeton University Press.
Gellner E. 1983: *Nations and Nationalism*. Oxford: Blackwell.
Gerschenkron A. 1962: *Economic Backwardness in Historical Perspective*. Cambridge, Mass.: Belknap Press.
Giddens A. 1981: *A Contemporary Critique of Historical Materialism*. London: Macmillan.
Gumplowicz L. 1899: *The Outlines of Sociology*. Philadelphia: American Academy of Political and Social Science.
Hintze O. 1975: *The Historical Essays of Otto Hintze* (ed. F. Gilbert). New York: Oxford University Press.
Hopkins K. 1978: *Conquerors and Slaves*. Cambridge: Cambridge University Press.
Kautsky J. H. 1982: *The Politics of Aristocratic Empires*. Chapel Hill, NC: University of North Carolina Press.
Lachmann L. 1970: *The Legacy of Max Weber*. London: Heinemann.
Lattimore O. 1957: 'Feudalism in history: a review essay', *Past and Present*, no. 12, pp. 47–57.
—— 1962: *Studies in Frontier History*. London: Oxford University Press.
Levi M. 1981: 'The predatory theory of rule', *Politics and Society*, 10, pp. 431–65.
MacIver R. M. 1926: *The Modern State*. Oxford: Clarendon Press.
Mann M. 1986: *The Sources of Social Power*, vol. 1. *A History of Power from the Beginning to 1760 AD*. Cambridge: Cambridge University Press.
Oppenheimer F. 1975 edn: *The State*. New York: Free Life Editions.
Perez-Diaz V. 1979: *State, Bureaucracy and Civil Society: a critical discussion of the political theory of Karl Marx*. London: Macmillan.
Poulantzas N. 1972: *Pouvoir politique et classes sociales*. Paris: Maspero.
Renfrew C. 1972: *The Emergence of Civilisation: the Cyclades and the Aegean in the Third Millenium BC*. London: Methuen.
Rustow A. 1982: *Freedom and Domination: a historical critique of civilization*. Princeton, NJ: Princeton University Press.
Service E. 1975: *Origins of the State and Civilization*. New York: Norton.
Skocpol T. 1979: *States and Social Revolutions*. Cambridge: Cambridge University Press.
Spencer T. 1969: *Principles of Sociology* (one volume abridgement). London: Macmillan.
Therborn G. 1978: *What does the Ruling Class do when it Rules?* London: New Left Books.

Tilly C. 1975: *The Formation of National States in Western Europe*. Princeton, NJ: Princeton University Press.
—— 1981: *As Sociology Meets History*. New York: Academic Press.
Trimberger E. 1978: *Revolution from Above: military bureaucrats and development in Japan, Turkey, Egypt and Peru*. New Brunswick, NJ: Transaction Books.
Weber M. 1968: *Economy and Society*. New York: Bedminster Press.
Wolin S. 1961 *Politics and Vision*. Boston: Little, Brown.

2

States, Ancient and Modern

This essay has a fairly clear overall argument: that the relationship between state and society in large-scale societies changed dramatically with the advent of industrial capitalism. Prior to that development, the state and the state bureaucracy played a substantially autonomous role *vis-à-vis* the class structure of civil society. After that its autonomy has been negligible: indeed, for most analytic purposes the state can be reduced to class structure. Such an argument is by no means original. For example, its outlines were commonplace among eighteenth and nineteenth-century theorists. In this paper I draw somewhat on Karl Marx and Herbert Spencer. For one particular argument I am indebted to the contemporary sinologist Owen Lattimore. The idea of such a dramatic shift in the history of society is nowadays extremely unfashionable, however. Today theorists usually present essentially the same view of state–society relations throughout human history. Most Marxists reduce the state to being contingent upon the 'determining' categories of 'mode of production' and 'class struggle'. Functionalists present a theory of structural differentiation which occurs so early in human evolution that in all recorded history the relationship between, and relative autonomy of, economy and polity are essentially unchanging. Weberians, in arguing for the autonomy of each element of 'the structure of social action', also give a picture of the mutual independence of state and economy throughout history. In all three cases, the caution and specificity of the theory of the 'founding fathers' – Marx, Spencer and Weber – is thrown to the wind.

However, I shall attempt to do more than recreate the

This chapter was first published in the *Archives européennes de sociologie*, XVIII (1977), 23, pp. 262–98. We are grateful for permission to reproduce it here.

descriptive history insisted on by the classic theorists. I will situate this great transformation in a general theory of social structure and social development – 'general' yet actually more concrete than is conventionally the case. If this paper has a claim to originality it lies in its starting-point. I begin by asking *how is it possible for people to establish and maintain social relationships over specified distances* given their existing level of social and technical development? I argue that, prior to the development of capitalist industrialization, large areas and diverse peoples could not be maintained in stable interaction by economic means. Among those societies that nevertheless managed to integrate such areas we must look to immediate military and political causes, and we will also find that the concepts of mode of economic production and social class are of somewhat limited utility in explaining their origins, structure and collapse. By contrast, these must be our key explanatory concepts once capitalist industrialism is established.

The empirical terrain is 'large-scale societies'. I define a society as a network of social interaction at the boundaries of which occur a relative interaction cleavage. This is a conventional definition (see, for example, Parsons, 1971, p. 8). Obviously once we are past a primary group, an important part of this interaction will be indirect, where *A* is linked to *C* only through *B*, and institutionalized, in social structure. By 'large-scale society' I indicate a network of social interaction, with cleavage at its boundaries, extending over several hundred miles. Given the unevenness of actual geography, more precision than this would be misplaced. In the ancient world the societies which extended over such distances are generally termed 'empires' – Rome, Greece, China, India, Mesopotamia and Egypt are all considered to have had empires in ancient times, and in more recent times central and Andean America (Maya and Inca) are similarly labelled. This is a political label and in a sense gives primacy of explanation to the state form. I wish to avoid pre-judging this issue, however, and if I use the term 'empire', it is only to be understood as a label of convenience for this empirical terrain. Though my argument applies in outline to all these cases, I should hasten to add (what will become clear to the reader) that only two cases, the Roman Empire (i.e. not the Republic) and China, are explored in any detail. Furthermore I should make it clear that no primary research has been done: I have complete dependence on the current conventional wisdom of classical scholars and sinologists.[1] At this stage, moreover, 'modern large-scale societies' only enter for certain broad comparative purposes: by this term is to be understood the major capitalist nation-states and Soviet Union.[2] I will not justify empirically the generalizations I make about these societies in this paper.

It is not necessary here to enter into general theories of the state. Only two theorists will be considered in detail, Karl Marx and Herbert Spencer. Spencer conveniently summarizes a theoretical tradition developing in the late eighteenth century through Smith and Ferguson. My concentration is on two issues; (a) how one identifies the key defining structures of society; and (b) the relative autonomy and power of three types of social actor, direct producers (i.e. the subordinate economic class), direct expropriators (i.e. the dominant economic class, landlord equivalents), and the state political elite.

Marxian theory

Central to Marx's theory of the state is the concept of mode of production. Despite all the ambiguities and controversies surrounding this concept, it has a clear explanatory purpose. In the familiar passage from *Capital* which follows, Marx clearly separates the *explanans*, mode of production, from the *explanandum*, the state:

The specific economic form, in which unpaid surplus-labour is pumped out of direct producers, determines the relationship of rulers and ruled... It is always the direct relationship of the owners of the conditions of production to the direct producers... which reveals the innermost secret, the hidden basis of the entire social structure, and with it the political form of the relation of sovereignty and dependence, in short, the corresponding specific form of the State. (1971 edn, vol. III, p. 791).

---

1 I would like to thank Keith Hopkins and J. D. Y. Peel for pointing out my grosser errors with regard to these societies, as well as for their more general comments and criticisms.

2 Two problems of this designation are not faced up to in this paper: (a) the ambiguity between the nation-state and the international capitalist system in terms of basis interaction networks (b) the peculiarities of the Soviet Union and satellites *vis-à-vis* capitalist society.

Indeed, according to Marx (and all subsequent Marxists agree with him in this respect) the state itself only emerges with the separation of the direct producer from his surplus – classless primitive societies did not have states.

The theory is also quite clear with respect to the capitalist state. Private capitalist accumulation requires the enactment of distinctive contract and property law, the restriction of other agents (e.g. monarchs) from entering into accumulation, and an economic infrastructure of a centralized type. Capitalism cannot function efficiently without these conditions. As they are all activities of the state, it follows that if capitalism is to be dominant as a mode of production then there must be corresponding forms of the state. Of course, there are other state activities, which might not be so determined. As Poulantzas has observed, there is nothing inherent in the capitalist mode of production which requires a democratic policy. The political form is free to vary (1972). But of the main functions which most states pursue, dispute regulation (i.e. law in this case) and economic distribution and redistribution are fundamentally determined by the mode of production. This is both a functional and causal statement: a particular mode of production cannot become dominant without transformations in these areas, and if it is dominant its needs must have caused such transformations.

So far, so good. But when we turn to pre-capitalist societies, we discover that Marx left a veritable hornets' nest of problems.

Coercion

The first problem, now well recognized, is that of *coercion*. It is generally traced back to this passage from the same section of *Capital*:

in all forms in which the direct labourer remains the 'possessor' of the means of production and labour conditions necessary for the production of his own means of subsistence, the property relationship must simultaneously appear as a direct relation of lordship and servitude, so that the direct producer is not free . . . Under such conditions the surplus-labour for the nominal owner of the land can only be extorted from them by other than economic pressure . . . (1971 edn, vol. III, pp. 790–1)

States, Ancient and Modern

As all Marxists have equated this type of non-economic pressure as coercion applied *politically*, the state obviously has a different relationship to pre-capitalist modes of production. In capitalism, the state, once captured, institutionalizes private ownership of the means of production. But as the worker is factually separated from these (i.e. he physically leaves them when he clocks off), he would have to take very active steps, including breaking the law, to keep the surplus he has produced. Yet the pre-capitalist producer is in possession of land, tools, and above all, the surplus itself. Now the non-producer has to take active and continuous steps to wrest it from him — hence coercion. Indeed, empirically, there is voluminous supporting evidence for the greater use of direct coercion in pre-capitalist societies. This takes three forms. As Marx says in the above passage, the producer's status is generally unfree — slavery and serfdom are two of the most common ways of tying the producer to the land and to his lord. Secondly, tax and rent gatherers are conspicuously attended by troops in many pre-capitalist societies. In the later Roman Empire, the necessary employment of the regional legionary reserves for tax-gathering severely weakened the defence of the Empire against the barbarians (Jones, 1964, vol. II, p. 686). Thirdly (and as Marx acknowledges in a footnote to the above quote) many of these unfree labour forms actually originated in the conquest of one society by another, especially slavery.

But the evident truth of Marx's remark worsens the conceptual problem. For haven't we now removed the clear distinction between *explanans* and *explanandum*, mode of production and state? One Marxist who accepts the force of this point is Perry Anderson:

The 'superstructures' of kinship, religion, law or the state necessarily enter into the constitutive structure of the mode of production in pre-capitalist social formations. They intervene *directly* in the 'internal' nexus of surplus-extraction, where in capitalist social formations, the first in history to separate the economy as a formally self-contained order, they provide by contrast its 'external' preconditions. In consequence, pre-capitalist modes of production cannot be defined *except* via their political, legal and ideological superstructures . . . The precise forms of juridical dependence, property and sovereignty that characterises a pre-capitalist social formation, far from being merely accessory or contingent epiphenomena, compose on the contrary the central indices of the determinate mode of production dominant within it. (1964a, pp. 403–4; cf. also a passage in 1974b, pp. 542–3)

But if we introduce 'political, legal and ideological superstructures' into our modes of production, is there anything lying outside of it to be determined? Without clear-cut conceptual distinctions between macro-social structures, Anderson's causal accounts of the development of Rome or feudalism or the absolutist state tend to be multi-factor, privileging no possible cause on theoretical grounds – a methodology closer to Weber than to Marx.[3]

Essentially these points have been made by one of the authors (Hirst) of another Marxist attempt to grapple with these problems. Hindess and Hirst (1975) add one excellent point of clarification when dealing with the feudal mode of production. They note that, though in a certain sense the peasant may be 'in possession', the mechanisms of feudal rent nevertheless 'by controlling the size, character and the reproduction of the units of production . . . makes the reproduction of the means of production simultaneously a reproduction of the exploitative production relations' (1975, p. 236). In general, landlords under feudalism control such factors as the size of peasant strips and the provision of specialized services like draught animals, water and pasture land, thereby enmeshing the peasant economically as well as politically in the feudal mode of production. Obviously this form of analysis can be applied to other modes of production – how embedded is the direct producer in the economic exchanges which characterize each mode? I will attempt to answer this question with reference to ancient and modern societies.

However, Hindess and Hirst cannot theorize away the greater use of direct physical coercion in pre-capitalist societies – even if that is not the *sole* reason for their survival, it does at least appear to be more important than in capitalism. Indeed their analysis of mode of production/state relations in their three principal pre-capitalist modes all leave us with problems. In the ancient (Athenian and Roman) mode, appropriation is said to be by political citizenship: citizens exploit non-citizens[4] (we might add

---

3 This may, of course, be a correct methodology – I am at the moment dealing only with the consistency and operational potentiality of the Marxist theory, not its correctness.
4 In this respect, their analysis is superior to another traditional Marxist identification of slavery as the key to the ancient economy.

that later, in the Roman Empire, office-holders exploit others). Empirically they give us a description of the effects of the wars of the Roman Republic and its distribution of booty and slaves. Warfare is therefore crucial to this ancient mode and to its supposed contradictions, and yet it is not theorized. Secondly, the feudal mode is defined and explored functionally, but never causally. Thus the feudal state must legitimate monopoly ownership of land by the landlord class in order for the feudal mode to exist, but we are given no evidence to suggest that 'proto-feudal' production needs actually did lead to the emergence of the feudal state. Scholars generally agree that European feudalism originated in some union of Roman private property and the Germanic warband. Again we would seem to need a theory of the relationship of warfare to economy. Finally, Hindess and Hirst 'abolish' the Asiatic mode of production, because the tax-rent form of exploitation in Asia is merely a variant form of feudal rent. They agree that an important difference remains between Asian and Western European feudal societies: the former had powerful states, the latter did not. They argue that the mode of production cannot explain this difference as it is identical in the two cases (1975, pp. 196–9). Thus state and mode of production seem to have a very substantial autonomy, and their relations are largely untheorized.[5]

In opposite ways, therefore, these Marxian attempts to theorize the relationship between state and mode of production in pre-capitalist societies are in some difficulty. Either the two are merged or they are autonomous. It is clear that this unsatisfactory state of affairs has something to do with the neglect, throughout most of twentieth-century sociology, of warfare between societies. It was the fate of the nineteenth- and early twentieth-century theorists like Spencer, Gumplowicz and Oppenheimer who concerned themselves with warfare to be identified as political undesirables by subsequent generations. But that should not be a sufficient reason for avoiding the whole subject.

---

5 Hindess and Hirst conclude with a throw-away line, 'The only condition that does explain tax/rent is the extension of the rule of already constituted states to previously stateless people', a generalization which is true neither for ancient China nor ancient Sumer (Lattimore, 1962a; MacNeill, 1963).

Mode of production, productive units and classes

The second problem of the Marxian model again concerns a difference between the capitalist mode and the other modes. The mere *definition* of capitalist relations of production presupposes definite relations between productive units. Surplus value depends on exchange between what Marx termed Departments I and II of the economy, between units supplying production goods (means of production) and consumption goods. A capitalist factory cannot exist without other capitalist factories and without exchange between them. Yet no form of economic interdependence is assumed between feudal manors or indeed between ancient estates. They are *similar*, yes, but not necessarily interdependent. Exchange of any kind is not presupposed by either feudal rent or citizenship appropriation. Each productive unit may be self-sufficient; alternatively, it may be involved in exchange only with the state. In fact both of these situations are approximated to in pre-capitalist societies – later on we will see that with the decay of the Roman Empire the latter pattern gives way to the former.

Now this gives rise to a peculiar lack of fit between the geographical boundaries of the economies and polities of ancient Empires, for the extent of the latter considerably outstrip the former. The situation has been reversed with the advent of capitalism: today the political nation-state, even the United States, is embedded in a wider economic system. Indeed *one* of the reasons why the contemporary state's autonomous power *vis-à-vis* the capitalist mode of production is extremely limited is that it cannot control *inter*national capitalist forces. This is particularly clear in the case of Britain which has to clear its political decision-making with the International Monetary Fund. Yet this raises the possibility that in pre-capitalist large-scale societies such a balance of power may have been reversed: that the economy may be 'politically determined' (to use a phrase of Weber's). We will see.

This in turn raises another thorny problem. If the overall economy of a society is made up of a number of largely self-sufficient units of production, economic *interaction* will be extremely limited in geographical scope. And if this is so, how can *classes*, in a societal-wide sense, emerge? Marx himself raised this problem in a well-known passage in *The 18th Brumaire of Louis Bonaparte* concerning the French peasantry. After noting how the

French peasantry were isolated from each other by their mode of production, he continues:

Each individual peasant family is almost self-sufficient; it itself directly produces the major part of its consumption and thus acquires its means of life more through exchange with nature than in intercourse with society. In this way, the great mass of the French nation is formed by simple addition of homologous magnitudes, much as potatoes in a sack form a sack of potatoes.

And Marx concluded that:

In so far as millions of families live under economic conditions of existence that separate their interests and their culture from those of other classes and put them in hostile opposition to the latter, they form a class. In so far as there is merely a local interconnection ... and the identity of their interests begets no community, no national bond, and no political organization among them, they do not form a class. (Marx and Engels, 1968 edn, p. 170–1)

Contrary to many interpretations of Marx, this is not a distinction between 'objective' and 'subjective' aspects of class, for local interconnection is just as 'objective' (and economic) as similarity of condition – though it has political and ideological (i.e. 'subjective') consequences. Can we therefore deduce objectively, according to Marx's second criterion of class, that neither a class of direct producers nor class conflict existed in all such pre-capitalist societies because intra-class interaction was lacking? *Classes can exist only if economic interaction exists.* Thus *if* an empire were built up of a number of self-sufficient production units (estates, manors) it would contain many local, small, similar classes of direct producers, but not a societal-wide producing class capable of enforcing its interests politically. This would constitute a *segmental* class system.

The use of Durkheim's term shows the extent to which I have been exaggerating empirical into hypothetical cases for the sake of illuminating the conceptual problem. For Durkheim (1964 edn, pp. 174–81) used the term 'segmental society' primarily to refer to stateless, loose associations of kin groups at a very early evolutionary stage. The productive units of the civilized societies I am discussing obviously did not possess complete self-sufficiency, but were bound into an empire-wide economy, even if it were rarely reciprocal exchange nor of the commodity form. We can trace two main types of effects of the economic system:

1. Direct or indirect economic interaction: where A exchanges directly with B or where goods pass from A to C through B.
2. Indirect economic *effects*: where the production of production unit A affects that of unit B even though no exchange may connect them. By examining these phenomena we analyse class as interdependence.

The ancient Roman and Chinese economies and class systems

I will begin by describing the main outlines of the Roman and Chinese economies after the development of their centralized, imperial systems and before they had decayed – Rome from the death of Augustus in AD 14 to the early fourth century AD, and China from the formal accession of the Han dynasty in BC 206 to the accession of the Ming dynasty in AD 1368. Naturally, considerable oversimplification must result, and historical changes must be ignored, especially in the case of China (where the latter part of this period saw considerable economic development).

In both Empires around 90 per cent of the population worked as direct producers on the land at just on or above subsistence level. Exploitation was in the dual form of tax paid to the Imperial authorities, and (far less frequently) rent paid to a landlord: similarly non-producers derived their wealth and power either from occupying Imperial office or from being landlord equivalents. Mercantile, trading and artisanal activity was quantitatively small (smaller in China than Rome), interstitial in relation to other class relation, and under considerable Imperial regulation. The boundaries of the Empire were clearly demarcated, and the Imperial authorities regulated, and sometimes prohibited, contact with outside peoples. Thus it constituted a gigantic common market, and was a monetary economy: even peasants paid cash. Its systemic character was thus revealed when Imperial debasements of the coinage caused severe economic dislocation throughout the Empire. Also, Hopkins (1977, p. 5) has shown that an increase in the money supply in one province had immediate effects in other provinces. The economy thus presents two enormous contrasts:

subsistence yet monetary, subsistence yet of a radius of a thousand miles. Exchange relations thus were peculiarly contradictory.

From the point of view of the peasant, the economy was largely *cellular* – that is, his exchange relations were bounded by a 4–5 mile area within which he could reasonably carry his goods for sale or exchange. The technology and costs of transport contributed fundamentally to this. For China Lattimore has calculated that the animals necessary to transport fodder by land would have to eat it up within 100 miles (1962b, p. 479). In Rome, Diocletian's maximum price edict implied that a 1200 lb wagon-load of wheat would double in price in 300 miles (Finley, 1973, p. 128; cf. also Jones, 1964, vol. II, p. 844). When Antioch, the second city of the East, experienced famine in AD 362–3 it required the forcible intervention of Julian and his army to get grain brought from two districts of Syria only 50 and 100 miles away (Finley, 1973, p. 33). As water transport was much cheaper, this cellular structure was probably more marked and more regular in the case of largely land-locked China. Most sinologists place it at the forefront of their analyses (e.g. Balazs, 1964, p. 16; Lattimore, 1962a, p. 41; Stover 1974, ch. 4). Lattimore (1962b, pp. 478–9) notes how from the village a small surplus would go to the district town, 10–20 miles from the next district town. From these a larger surplus would go to the regional city, usually the administrative centre of a region. Only a small surplus would flow from there into national trade. But even the regional city would depend for the greatest part of its produce on its own immediate hinterland. The Roman Empire had a more irregular structure than this, and a greater proportion of inter-regional sea trade. In the two Empires the Mediterranean basin constituted the most developed case of long-distance interdependence. I will discuss its form later. Despite its volume, most Roman cities also depended overwhelmingly on their immediate hinterlands (Jones, 1964, vol. II, p. 714). Even counting such local markets, the volume of trade was low: in the fourth century AD Constantine's new tax on city trade produced only 5 per cent of the land tax, though we cannot be sure of the accuracy of this calculation (Anderson, 1974a, p. 20; cf. Jones, 1964, vol. I, p. 466; but for an account placing rather more emphasis on trade, see Hopkins, 1977.)

That said however, I wish to concentrate on the form of the remaining 5 per cent above subsistence. This is, after all, the economic base of civilization, 5 per cent at the margin of subsistence is also of considerable meaning to the actors themselves! Most trade did not supply the peasant's consumption needs, but rather those of the expropriators. The most profitable form of agriculture in Rome was viticulture, a luxury good. The province which was most intensively farmed for corn was Egypt which supplied the capital (with its upper class and bureaucracy). Trade centres can also be linked to the location of legionary headquarters. The most succinct analysis of the systemic nature of the Roman economy is provided by Hopkins. I quote his conclusion:

> The prime cause of this monetary unification of the whole empire was the complementary flow of taxes and trade. The richest provinces of the empire (Spain, north Africa, Egypt, southern Gaul and Asia Minor) paid taxes in money, most of which were exported and spent, either in Italy or in the frontier provinces of the empire, where the armies were stationed. The rich core-provinces then had to gain their tax-money back, by selling food or goods to the tax-importing regions . . . Thus the prime stimulus to long-distance trade in the Roman empire was the tax-demands of the central government and the distance between where most producers (taxpayers) worked and where most of the government's dependants (soldiers and officials) were stationed. (1977, p. 5)

The peasants' role was either passive and expropriated or as unfree or semi-free labour on large estates. Nevertheless, *some* mass consumption goods were exchanged: metals, pottery, textiles, salt, cheap wines (tea in China). But if we listed the economic benefits to the peasant of membership in such a society, the development of market exchange would only be one, perhaps minor benefit. The benefits were:

1 *Imperial pacification* provided (barely) a security within which interaction between strangers could occur. It also kept in check one prevalent form of non-productive 'labour', banditry. Hopkins (1977, p. 5) notes that Roman ships were far larger and more vulnerable than had been possible in previous, more troubled times. Thus when civil wars interrupted this, trade dropped, with potent effects at that critical margin. Lattimore has noted that even in early twenieth-century China a breakdown in imperial authority dried up the salt trade, with consequent malnutrition (1962a, p. 43).

2 *Imperial technical aids to exchange:* a guaranteed coinage, property and trade law, a literate bureaucracy and military-sponsored communications systems all provided infrastructural support for production and exchange in both Empires. China, additionally, possessed a uniform calendar and weights and measures.

3 *Consumption markets*: the consumption of the bureaucracy, army and the landlord class developed trade and a monetary economy. As non-productive labour, they might appear to be exploitative rather than beneficiary, but we must also note the stimulus their consumption gave to trade.

4 *Intensification of the labour process:* a paradox of the ancient economy was that the most efficient forms of agriculture, and probably the securest levels of subsistence for the producers, were in systems of production that involved non-free labour, especially in large estates and in the small extractive sector (Finley, 1973, p. 106).

Overall, there can be no doubting the level of economic development. The productivity of large Roman estates in Italy appears to have been markedly higher than in contemporary Italy, though there are some grounds for scepticism about yield figures. More reliable is Diocletian's Price Edict which implies a wage distribution to labourers of 1 part in kind to 1½–3 parts in cash. A similar government order in sixteenth-century England envisaged that maintenance would absorb at least half of the wages of labourers. This probably indicates higher living standards in Rome (Duncan-Jones, 1974, pp. 11–12, 39–59). And certainly, at its height, the Empire supported a larger population than existed in Europe for another 700 years after its fall. The fall was part of the relapse from a money to a natural economy which occurred in Western Europe in the Dark Ages (Slicher van Bath, 1963, pp. 30–1). The peasant was better off within the Empire than without it.

But that level of benefit was dependent on a high level of coercion. This is clear from the character of most of the benefits listed above – order itself, a communications system built mainly by soldiers but also by slave or *corvée* labour, the forcible extraction of tax/rent to pay for the consumption of non-producers, and unfree, intensive agriculture. Moreover, the benefits – with the possible exception of the last-named – are all somewhat abstract and indirect. The peasant does not *appear* to be in an exchange relation: his labour and his tax/rent are extorted, and he receives nothing directly in exchange. Only if peasants throughout a region, or even throughout the Empire, all acquiesce in the extortion, then will the benefits accrue to all of them. Finally, the balance could be tipped the other way, *below* subsistence if the state's level of demand for manpower or taxes is increased.

Thus, we may provisionally conclude about the economic relations of the direct producers:

1 Economic-interdependence among direct producers is low because of the cellular nature of the economy.
2 The major form of interdependence between direct producers and expropriators is probably with the state rather than with local landlords (to the extent that is possible to separate the two), except in the case of large estates.
3 That interdependence is abstract, coercive and tenuous.

Let me expand the first point more fully by explicitly drawing the contrast with contemporary capitalism. First, collective organizations of the direct producers now exist. Trade unions have *universally* accompanied the development of capitalism, and in *no* industrial country, capitalist or not, has it proved possible to rule industry without its owners/controllers at least consulting organized groups of workers, either in 'corporatist' or 'oppositional-democratic' structures.[6] Furthermore, in liberal democracies working class political parties have also appeared. The explanation for this is twofold: the essential similarity of subordinate direct producers in the production process, and the interdependence of the workers. The interdependence itself takes two forms: the growth of large productive units (and supportive communities) which concentrate bodies of workers in direct interaction, and the economic effects of different productive units on each other. The latter needs stressing. Given commodity production in capitalism, markets exist for both labour and products. Thus both the wage-rate and the productivity of worker A in Aberdeen affects that of worker B in Brighton, and his productivity also affects that of worker C in California. There is no guarantee that such

---

6 This is not an argument I can justify in detail here. Nazi Germany provides the only exception I know of, and that appeared to need total war to support such a complete repression of working class organization.

competition effects will result in class action – and the intervention of other factors is needed to explain soldiarity (to the extent that it occurs) rather than sectionalism. But there is interdependence. Furthermore, though in a different form, this also exists within other industrial societies. In the Soviet Union and its satellites, productivity and wage-rates of different production units also afffect one another, though here the relationship is mediated by pressure-groups (representing different industries, regions etc.) at the level of the state. Such interdependence was generally lacking in ancient Empires. The first type, interaction, was confined within the economic cells, or within the larger confines of intensive agricultural systems. The second type of economic effect was also generally lacking. The production of peasant A near Antioch did not affect that of peasant B in Bythynia. In the wage-labour sector, wage fluctuations did not result from supply and demand factors (Finley, 1973, p. 23). The only possible economic effect between them would be mediated by the state, i.e. the taxation level of one region has effects on that of others. Not surprisingly, therefore, collective organizations of direct producers barely existed outside of the towns.[7]

This is in no way to deny – despite locality, ethnic and legal status differences – the *similarity* of almost all direct producers when compared to non-producers. The degree of inequality between the mass of the population and a tiny, almost completely urbanized, literate and office-holding elite was enormous. Landholding was extremely unequal and tended to worsen in Rome from the height of the Republic onward. Roman army pay scales give us our most precise data: they embodied a top to bottom ratio of 67: 1, while the division of the spoils among Pompey's soldiers at his triumph embodied the ratio of 500: 1 (Duncan-Jones, 1974, p. 3; MacMullen, 1974, p. 94, and chs 1 and 4 in general). Hopkins (1977, pp. 12–13) goes further and calculates that the income of a Senator was 2000 times that of a peasant family at subsistence level. China contained similar inequality but reinforced it with a greater degree of cultural differentiation, distinguishing linguistically between the *shik*, those trained to serve their rulers, and the *min*, the ruled (Eisenstadt, 1969 edn, p. 321; cf. also Lattimore, 1962a, p. 49). Eisenstadt claims that such a distinction

---

7 With the partial exception of the Chinese secret societies, which did sometimes play a 'class-type' role at a local or regional level (see below).

is common throughout imperial systems. As the poor were illiterate, they have left us no records of how they felt about this. But the wealth was visible, indeed ostentatiously displayed. We must expect that if starvation threatened, they would react with violence against the rich oppressors.

But who were the oppressors? And, in particular, what were the relations between the second and third actors in our model, the immediate expropriators and the political elite? Here we reach a very controversial issue, the degree of autonomy of the state officials vis-à-vis landlord/gentry/noble groups. The argument has evolved around the case of China. At one extreme lies Wittfogel's powerful, idiosyncratic and highly political study of *Oriental Despotism* (1957), some of whose chapter headings speak for themselves: 'A state stronger than society', 'Despotic power – total and not benevolent', 'Total terror'. Wittfogel's argument rested on his conception of a 'hydraulic economy' i.e. large-scale canal and irrigation works which he thought necessitated a centralized imperial 'agro-managerial despotism'. Wittfogel generalized this to ancient empires and draws a parallel with the Stalinist Soviet Union, developing an heretical Marxist analysis of the *economic* foundations of despotic empires. So far as I know, his is the only systematic, consistent attempt to account for the political structure of ancient empires in terms of their economies. However, a closer look at the Chinese economy does not support his argument. Eberhard has summarized the counter-arguments. The Chinese Empire developed its 'oriental despotic' structure before it expanded into the regions of extensive hydraulic agriculture; hydraulic systems were as likely to be developed by local as by central authorities, and if located in the provinces it is not clear they were the responsibility of the central 'ministries'. Eberhard also argues in more general terms that the Chinese state was not 'above' society, that indeed the Empire was a 'gentry society' in which gentry families, living on both the perquisites of office and absentee land ownership, and with different family members as landowners, scholars and politicians, only allowed the imperial authorities despotic power for very short periods (1965 edn, pp. 42–6, 56–83; cf. also Chi, 1936).

This argument represents the other extreme. The state, it is argued, was not 'above' society – rather, it was an instrument of class rule. Actually, though China suited Wittfogel's argument relatively well insofar as hydraulic agriculture was concerned – for other empires tended to have less of it – *politically* it was less suited, for the Chinese gentry was probably the most homogeneous dominant class of all, as Eisenstadt (1969 edn, p. 205) notes. Furthermore, even China exhibited those characteristic politics of imperial or monarchical systems which persisted right up to the modern period over most of the world – the struggle between state bureaucracies/households and landlord classes. Those politics, brilliantly analysed by Eisenstadt, centre on control of two institutions, the army and local civil administration, especially tax-gathering offices. Feudal levy or professional army, centrally appointed offices without tenure, centrally appointed but then hereditary offices, or local tax-farmers? – such were the politics of most pre-industrial societies with states. Naturally, seen from below such conflicts must have seemed trivial. To the peasant it might have seemed one whether his exploiter was an imperial official or a landlord, whether he risked his life as a retainer of his lord or as a mercenary.

Yet despite the economic and cultural homogeneity of the exploiters, their divisions and organizational weaknesses were quite marked. Turning to the economy, we can note the relative lack of economic interaction among the landlord stratum. Unlike the peasantry, it is true, they were substantial producers and consumers of commodities. However, it appears that the two dominant forms of economic transaction did not involve them in economic exchange with each other. The first is represented by the *oikos*, the household economy (which is indeed the root word of our word 'economy'). The landord, resident in towns in both Empires, consumed extensively from his own estates: for example, in the fourth century AD Roman aristocrats took about half of their income in kind. Secondly, the landlord purchased more specialized luxury commodities and also specialized labour from the distinctively urban and interstitial occupations of merchants and artisans. It is rare to find established landlord families engaged in trade, and so again there is little intra-class economic interaction. Now we must not exaggerate: most landlords would sell some of their produce on the market, some also involved themselves in mercantile activities. Such economic activity was not absent, but neither was it dominant. Moreover, it tended to be local and regional – leading in China to the emergence of 'Key

Economic Areas' relatively tightly integrated regional economies which in dynastic crises attained a degree of self-sufficiency from the rest of the Empire – at a cost (Chi, 1936, pp. 5–11). The contrast with capitalist economies is again marked. Capitalists are involved in continuous economic interaction, both direct and indirect, at least at the level of the whole nation-state (and probably outside of it too). And as with the working class, collective organizations have everywhere arisen to control this interaction. Employers' associations, cartels, oligopolies, government agencies of coordination and research are all evidence that the capitalist class is *organized*. There were no comparable collective *economic* organizations of the landlord class in large-scale ancient societies.

Collective organization of a sort did exist, however, most notably in Rome which retained some semblance of its representative political constitution for its entire history. Popular representation had disappeared in the Republic even before the civil wars of the first century BC, but the Senate survived right through the Empire. Of course, it never once successfully challenged the power of an Emperor. There are no real signs that the aristocracy, or indeed landlords as a whole, wanted an active political role. Senators were exempt from the duties of local political office, and repeated attempts by Emperors to rescind this immunity failed. Thus the local city government probably did not involve the greatest landlords – a factor in the loss of power by the city *decurions* (councillors) to the regional officials of the Emperor. Indeed Rostovtzeff assigned to this political weakness of the landlord class (he called it the 'middle class') the decisive role in the decline and fall of the Empire itself (1957 edn, especially ch. 12; cf. also Jones, 1964, vol. II, pp. 722–42). None of this applies to China, of course, where the gentry were without autonomous political representation yet thoroughly penetrated the imperial bureaucracy itself, especially after the introduction of the Confucian examination system. This contrast between Rome and China is instructive, for it may indicate that the only effective form of landlord class organization possible in large-scale ancient societies was through the imperial bureaucracy itself.

The lack of autonomous landlord organization may give the impression of weakness relative to the Emperor. Yet, however much the initiation of policy may be his prerogative, in its implementation he is dependent upon landlords as long as he needs taxes. The peasantry does derive benefit from his rule, but as noted earlier it is abstract and infrastructural. A guaranteed coinage, order and security, and good communications provide an infrastructure for the peasant's economic production but they do not intervene in its form, unless local specialized means of production are under imperial control. Yet such factors as draught animals and their fertilizer, mills and local irrigation were generally controlled by landlords rather than the state in these two Empires.[8] As Hindess and Hirst have noted, such control within the process of production enables the surplus to be extorted partly by direct 'exchange' rather than merely by force, and this puts the landlord in a better position to extort than the imperial authorities. The latter can dispense with taxation under certain circumstances, most notable of which is cheap, successful warfare providing booty, but if he wishes to finance this in the first place he needs taxes — and therefore landlord support.

This completes my static analysis of the imperial economic and class structure. If we identify classes by their *similarity* to the means of production, then we have two: direct producers and expropriators (though *forms* of expropriation vary within the same overall system). However, expropriators are divided into two main groups, landlords and officials, and much politics concerns their conflict. But if we identify classes by their economic interdependence, it is not clear that we have *any*. The alternative is to identify a large number of *segmental* classes. The acid test of this ought to be the nature of the social conflict which ensues from economic crises. Is it *class* conflict?

Class conflict and civil war

When they generalize most shamelessly scholars usually point out a 'surprising' absence of peasant revolts in ancient Empires (Jones, 1964, vol. II, p. 811; MacMullen, 1974, pp. 123–4; Eisenstadt,

---

8 This does not seem to have been the case in the earlier Empires of the Near East where State intervention in production was much stronger. However, when the Sumerian States expanded out of the irrigated river-valleys into the upland pastures, this intervention seems to have declined (McNeill, 1963).

1969 edn; p. 208; Wittfogel, 1957, pp. 329–34). Actually we cannot be really sure whether it is revolts or records that are absent. The literate classes did not seem keen on noticing and chronicling the discontents of their subordinates. Where they did, however, the accounts rarely treat them as phenomena in their own right: they are related especially to the struggles among the expropriating groups. For example, for Spartacus' revolt we learn more about the effect that Crassus' successful suppression of the revolt had on his political ambitions than we do about Spartacus and his followers. In China, accounts are normally linked to accounts of dynastic struggles. This is reasonable given the apparent nature of most revolts. Let us take Rome first.

Severe social conflict was endemic to the Roman Empire as it was to all ancient Empires. In a barely pacified society, away from the main communication routes, those who could afford to fortify their houses did so. Bandits were never actually eliminated from either Empire. In a sense, banditry is a perverted class warfare. Its recruits are generally runaway slaves, peasants and soldiers on whom the burden of exploitation has become intolerable. But they do not resist the rent- or tax-gatherer, they run away from him. And they do not reduce exploitation in the society at large: rather, being non-productive, they increase it.

More organized conflict involving class-type issues and transformational goals is not hard to find either. We can identify three main types. First are the slave revolts, normally by recently enslaved groups and so much less frequent in the Empire than they had been in the Republic. They were aimed at killing (or perhaps enslaving) the estate owners, and re-establishing free cultivation. Unfortunately we know nothing more of the form of production they established. These conflicts were aimed at ending economic exploitation, but they were local and rarely spread to free or semi-free peasants, i.e. they were a 'solution' to the specific relations of production of intensive agriculture (MacMulllen, 1966, pp. 194–9, 211–16; 1974; Thompson, 1952).

Two further forms of conflict achieved wider organizational form, however. One concerns those dynastic civil wars which did appear to have an element of class grievance (obviously a minority of such cases). Rostovtzeff argued that the civil wars of the third century AD are to be explained as the revenge of peasant soldiers on their class enemies in the cities. Though this is nowadays an unfashionable view, we can accept two elements of truth in it: that the army was a main route of upward social mobility, and that for a peasant, booty from the cities might have been the only practicable way of substantially bettering himself. However, in order to accomplish this he must submit to the authority of his commander, almost certainly a rich landowner. The second form of conflict occurs mainly in the later Empire: religious schism. Several of these movements, especially the Donatists of Numidia in the early fourth century appear to have had social and redistributional goals, though this is in some dispute among scholars and in any case co-exists with regional/religious separatist tendencies (MacMullen, 1966, pp. 200–6).

The class elements of these disorders are obviously undercut by another process, the tendency of local producers to place themselves in alliance with local expropriators against the authority of the state. They are dependent on non-economic forms of organization, a pre-existing army or a church/sect. And they tend either to be disintegrative (to seek regional autonomy) or to reconstitute the state unaltered (as in case of a successful dynastic faction). They are not transformative of the state or of the mode of production – unless in a regressive direction.

These processes are exemplified if we examine the fall of the Western Empire itself. It is hardly appropriate for me – with a pretence of authority – to adjudicate centuries of controversy about the 'decline-and-fall' issue. Recently, however, and in support of the general argument of this paper, there has been a swing back to an emphasis on military causes. Traditionally this argument was countered by pointing out that the barbarians who 'conquered' Rome were *never* capable of defeating its armies in the field. Therefore, Rome must have fallen from internal causes. But recent work, especially that of A. H. M. Jones has argued that the low level of military and political organization of the barbarians was precisely their strength. Unlike the civilized enemies faced by Rome (above all the Persians), an orderly process of war, diplomacy, punitive raids etc. could not contain them. They would raid and disappear, living off booty and caring little if the Romans laid waste their homeland. The drain of taxation, needed to finance defence against such persistent enemies, then killed the Empire. Jones has also convincingly observed that the main differences between the Western and the Eastern Empire (which survived for another 1000 years) were in terms of the strength of the enemies they had to face and of the defensibility of their frontiers. By contrast those who look for internal economic causes have had difficulty in specifying any convincing reasons for economic decline before the period of barbarian pressure (Jones, 1964, vol. II, pp. 1025–68; Bernardi, 1970). The nineteenth-century arguments about slavery hindering economic development (reproduced by Anderson, 1974a, p. 27) are no longer accepted by most authorities (Westermann, 1955, p. 120; Finley, 1973, pp. 83–7; Hopkins, 1977, pp. 26–9). Yet there are still several issues which will probably remain unsolved until (if ever) further sources enable us to date more precisely the beginning of economic decay (especially the abandonment of cultivated land, the *agri deserti*) and the extent of the fourth-century recovery. Thus the following is merely an attempt to describe the process of decline once it had started. It may also exaggerate the smoothness of the decline. Whether internal decay and population decline had already begun to weaken the fabric of the Empire, barbarian pressure against the frontiers shook it considerably in the second half of the second century AD. Diocletian's reforms (AD 284–305) saved the Empire but heightened its contradictions. By doubling the size of the army and bureaucracy he increased the burden of taxation. The landowning classes tried to transmit the burden on to their subordinates, but in a near-subsistence economy this policy is soon self-defeating. We know that under the fiscal pressure land went out of cultivation, and we can be virtually sure that people died. Probably as a reaction to the pressure, two major social changes occurred. First, hitherto free men placed themselves under the patronage of local landowners protection, that is from the Imperial tax-collector. As slavery had already declined, this represented, a homogenization of economic positions. The emergence of the 'semi-free' feudal serf (the *colonus*) holding his land as a favour from his lord began to create a 'universal class' within the territories of the Western Empire even before its collapse. Yet this process was undercut by the second development, the decentralization of the economy, as local landowners attempted to increase their independence from imperial power through the self-sufficiency of the household economy (the *oikos*). The decline of inter-provincial trade was hastened by the invasions themselves as communications routes became insecure. Local landowners and *coloni* together viewed the imperial authorities as more and more exploitative. Yet only a few local populations actually welcomed the barbarians as liberators (though many more must have been indifferent). The Imperial system brought benefits if effective. Justinian's reconquest of Italy in the seventh century showed this – he was welcomed as a liberator, despite taxing peasant proprietors at a third of their declared gross product and tenant farmers at an even higher rate (Jones, 1964, vol. II, pp. 773–823, 1043, 1058–63).

The main area of controversy in this description is whether the collapse had quite such drastic effects on the peasantry. Bernardi (1970, pp. 78–80) argues that the peasants did not die, rather, in alliance with their lords, they evaded the harsh taxes. Thus 'the political organization broke down, but not the framework of rural life, the forms of property and the methods of exploitation'. Finley (1973, p. 152) also doubts whether the Roman peasantry could be any more harshly oppressed or hungry than contemporary Third World peasants, who nevertheless breed satisfactorily. Finley's explanation is that the Empire's economy rested 'almost entirely on the muscles of men' who – at subsistence – had nothing to contribute to an 'austerity programme' made necessary by 200 years of barbarian attack. Thus the increased consumption needs of army and bureaucracy (and also the parasitic Christian Church – re-enter Gibbon!) led to a manpower shortage.

But it is the *disintegration* of the Empire that is of interest here. The growth of the *oikos*, the *colonus* and patronage show the decentralizing tendencies, and the way in which local classes, both direct producers and expropriators, united against the state political elite – not to transform it, but to evade it. And in the centuries that followed the collapse of the Empire, these disintegrating tendencies continued as peasants were forced to place themselves under the military protection of a local feudal lord against new barbarian invaders.

These same processes are visible in the better-documented case of China, where *reconstitution* is added to disintegration. The 'dynastic cycle' was almost a regular feature of Chinese history and, of course, peasant rebellions formed a major part of the replacement of one dynasty by another. The initial causes of a dynasty's decay seem to have been varied – expensive and unsuccessful foreign warfare, overpopulation, plainly incompetent

Emperors or quarelling Imperial families. All lead to a tightening of taxation and peasant disturbances. The Emperor is now forced to tax where he can and rely more heavily on local strongmen and their private armies. Uniformity and therefore calculability is broken, trade declines, banditry increases. Out of this turbulence have often arisen radically egalitarian peasant movements, led by 'déclassé intelligentsia', organized through secret societies, and violently directed against gentry and officials alike. However, at this stage they are *local*. As Chesneaux remarks, they did not cross 'the boundaries of the district in which the goods they produced were to be found' (1973 edn, p. 21). They can progress further, nevertheless, and four did so to found new dynasties. But that is the point: to transcend that interaction boundary, they need to take on the imperial form. Moreover, they must recruit the gentry, their private armies and their greater interaction networks. The successful peasant leader, like the founder of the Ming dynasty, chooses the right moment to lessen the messianic emphasis and woo the local gentry (Dardess, 1969–70; cf. also Haeger, 1968–69; Lattimore, 1962, p. 45; Wittfogel, 1957, p. 334; Chi, 1936; Wakeman, 1977).

The general conclusion is now clear: that class conflict in large-scale ancient societies tended towards disintegration in a way that is quite unlike that of capitalist society. When the direct producer reacted to excessive exploitation he might turn against either or both of his exploiters, the landlord or the state official. If only against the latter, he did so in collaboration with local lords in civil wars; if against the landlord, in an overt or disguised peasant revolt at the *local* level. Even these local peasant revolts only happened in conditions of relatively intense agricultural activity (slave estates, coordinated irrigation systems). The crucial difference from capitalist society is the extent of economic interdependence among the society members: especially among direct producers. If the result of such conflict was the reconstitution of the empire – as it was always in China, and was in Rome until very late – this was the result of the imposition by one *regional* 'classless' faction over another after prolonged internecine warfare.

Two further conclusions now emerge: that whatever constituted the defining elements of these societies, whatever made an *empire* possible rather than a smaller territorial unit, was neither class structure nor mode of production. Note the limits of this argument: I am not arguing that classes did not exist (as Finley, 1973, p. 68 does) or that one cannot *describe* Roman or Chinese modes of production; rather that such concepts cannot be used to give an explanation of why these societies were so large in extent and had states of a particular 'Imperial' form. As yet I have not attempted to supply this explanation, but from various hints in the discussion so far we must obviously include *military* factors. So let us now turn to a theory of the state which incorporates military factors.

Herbert Spencer: the militant society

I have taken Herbert Spencer to be the summation of a certain type of social theory prevalent in the eighteenth and nineteenth centuries which commented upon the transformations of the industrial revolution in an essentially complacent way. Peace, progress and freedom had supplanted despotism, barbarism and violence in society. Spencer's clear-cut distinction between *industrial* and *militant* societies may usefully stand for such theories. Spencer set out his theory in the three volumes of *The Principles of Sociology*, published between 1876 and 1896. It is an evolutionary theory. Societies change in terms of growth, aggregation and an increasing differentiation of functions and institutions. Those with a higher 'degree of composition' will better master their environment and – where in competition – other societies. To this classification in terms of degree of composition, Spencer offered a secondary principle of classification 'into the predominantly militant and the predominantly industrial – those in which the organization for offence and defence is most largely developed, and those in which the sustaining organization is most largely developed' (1969 edn, p. 110). Some commentators believe that these 'militant' and 'industrial' societies are merely ideal-types, useful in illuminating societies at any historical epoch – thus the Soviet Union or Nazi Germany are modern approximations to 'militant' cases (Fletcher, 1971, vol. I, p. 284), and indeed Spencer commented that both Bismarck and modern socialists and communists advocated a form of 'compulsory cooperation' reminiscent of ancient militant societies (1969 edn, pp. 519–23; 535–6). But this sits at odds with Spencer's main historical generalization: that human history has seen a shift in more compound societies from the militant to the industrial type. Spencer links the origins of the state to warfare:

> centralized control is the primary trait acquired by every body of fighting men ... And this centralized control, necessitated during war, characterizes the government during peace. Among the uncivilized there is a marked tendency for the military chief to become also the political head (the medicine man being his only competitor); and in a conquering race of savages his political headship becomes fixed. In semi-civilized societies the conquering commander and the despotic king are the same, and they remain the same in civilized societies down to late times ... few, if any, cases occur in which societies ... have evolved into larger societies without passing into the militant type. (pp. 117, 125)

Note that, as a true evolutionist, he is inferring an empirical tendency not a universal law. At times he takes this further, arguing that stratification itself owes its origin to warfare. At any rate in such societies stratification and indeed the economy itself is subordinate:

> the industrial part of the society continues to be essentially a permanent commissariat existing solely to supply the needs of the governmental-military structures, and having left over for itself only enough for bare maintenance. (p. 121)

This militant state-dominated society is governed by '*compulsory* cooperation'. It is centrally, despotically regulated. It has dominated compound societies until recent times. Spencer produces examples indiscriminately from tribal chiefdoms and confederations and ancient Empires. He refers continuously to Rome as a militant society. He can give only one example of a largely industrial society in an earlier epoch, classical Athens. After then, we must wait until the time of the Hanse Towns, the early Dutch Republic and then England. Spencer's causal analysis is sketchy here, and he gives no real explanation of the rise of such 'industrial' societies. They are merely *composed* of an aggregate of a growth in agriculture, manufacture and commerce so that economic exchange relations come to dominate the 'sustaining' organization. Such exchange establishes '*voluntary* cooperation' and interdependence in the economy, and therefore freedom and democracy in the polity. Hence the relationship between state and civil society is reversed, with the latter now dominant.

Such is Spencer's theory. It has a kernel of truth, once we tone down its overstatements and its complacent Victorian glow. Three points must be corrected or added. First, it is incorrect as a theory of the *origins* of the state. Actually, states seem to originate around the world in all kinds of circumstances. If one factor appears more frequently than others, it appears not to be warfare but rather a centralized economic distribution function, the coordination by a chief of exchange between different 'ecological niches' (Service, 1975). However, warfare does appear crucial in understanding the development of two particular kinds of state, the imperial type which is the subject-matter of this paper and the barbarian type which is parasitic upon such empires. This will be explored below. Secondly, Spencer exaggerates considerably the despotism of militant societies as he does the freedom of industrial ones. The power of the central 'militant' state over its peripheral areas could not be complete given ancient communications and was, as we have seen, dependent on the cooperation of the dominant class in civil society. Spencer's view of freedom was decidedly *bourgeois*, blind to the difference in freedom between the economic exchanges of those who own property and those who have only their labour to sell. And what are we to make of the emergence, after his death, of apparently 'militant' industrial societies like Nazi Germany or Stalinist Russia? However – even discounting all this – Spencer nevertheless correctly perceived a shift towards greater democracy in the world (though this is not an argument I will justify in this paper). Thirdly, as I noted, Spencer has no theory accounting for the development of industrial society. This is also outside the scope of this paper.

The origins of empire: military and economic organization

For the purpose of this argument, I make two assumptions which I will in no way justify here: that mankind is restless and greedy for more of the good things of life, and that essentially this is a quest for greater material rewards. However, even on the basis of this rather crude materialist psychology it does not necessarily follow that economic structures are dominant/determinant in human society – it may be, for example, that the most efficient means of attaining material rewards is by military conquest, in which case one must at least consider the possibility that military structures will be determinant/dominant rather than the mode of economic production. I will consider the well-known materialist objection to this later on. For the moment let us note that there are two major ideal-typical ways for an individual or social group to increase his/its material rewards, economically or by physical force. Economically, the process develops through intensification of exchange relations (which may, of course, be highly unequal); militarily, through conquest or the offer of defence for a group menaced by some other group. Naturally the way in which real societies have evolved has normally mixed these processes together along, indeed, with other more minor processes (exchange of women, the growth of cultural homogeneity etc.). I want to consider especially the process by which a group incorporates new peoples and territories into its domain, concentrating on the origin of those ancient large-scale societies I have been describing.

At a very general level of analysis we can distinguish two main phases in the evolution of such societies. In the first place there arise over an area (which may be ecologically uniform or diverse) a number of quite similar small city-states or tribal chiefdoms in each of which a permanent centralized elite organizes economic exchange and redistribution. The state organization comprises essentially a market place, storehouse and management of such intensive agricultural techniques as exist (normally irrigation schemes). It is not necessary here to decide whether the members of this central organization constitute an aristocratic economic class or a political elite (the distinction might not seem a relevant one anyway in this case). The second stage is the extension of the hegemony of *one* of these units over the others. So far as we are able to tell from our sources, this process involved considerable warfare, though this is interspersed with 'voluntary' submissions. The emergence of one unit as hegemonic might appear as relatively steady (as in the emergence of Rome within Italy) or the fortunes of the various units might fluctuate considerably (as in the case of the emergence of the Sumerian city-states as nascent 'empires'). Now, of course, we do not know enough about the cases where the second stage did not follow from the first (obviously, since such societies were unlikely to leave us written records or striking archaeological remains). Moreover, there are at least two cases of societies which are sometimes termed 'empires', and which were certainly large in extent, but which do not fit this model. Both Athens and Phoenicia developed as essentially trading societies (dependent – we may suspect – on the existence of the other cases). Yet this general model applies to the origins of China, to the other civilizations of the Near East and Mediterranean, and to those of central and Andean America (which had recently moved into the second phase when interrupted by the *conquistadores*). We need an explanation for the importance of warfare in their development.

A word of reservation is necessary about the explanation that now follows. Given the paucity of sources it must necessarily be a plausible argument rather than empirically supported proof. However, it emerges out of certain general observations made by Owen Lattimore after a life-time of study of, and participation in, the relationship between China and the Mongol tribes. Lattimore notes that we may distinguish three radii of possible social interaction which remain relatively invariant until the fifteenth century in Europe. The most geographically extensive radius is that of *military action*, itself divisible into two radii of which the inner reaches over territories that, after conquest, could be added to the state, and of which the outer is extended beyond such frontiers in punitive or tribute raids. Hence the second radius, that of *civil administration*, is less extensive and tends indeed to be a mere duplication of regional administrations which become isolated from each other in times of civil and dynastic strife. In turn, this radius is more extensive than the third, that of *economic integration*, which at the maximum is that of the region and at the minimum, the cell. Thus, for a considerable stretch of human history, large-scale integration was dependent on military and not economic factors (1962b, pp. 80–91, 542–51). Thus we are presented with a modern variant of Spencer's militant society.

According to Lattimore this situation came to an end in the fifteenth century when the Portuguese navigational revolution enabled long-distance transportation of staple goods – economic exchange, binding together large areas and diverse peoples, was now possible. This is a little simple and a little technicist: the whole configuration of capitalist development, rather than merely the compass or the stern-post rudder (which in any case China had earlier developed) extended exchange relations. Unfettered commodity exchange, the expropriation of direct producers and their migration to an urban/factory environment and the industrial revolution itself all led to a capitalist mode of production in which economic interaction is paramount.

We must also reduce the evolutionary and teleological tinges of Lattimore's theory by specifying certain preconditions of the situation he describes. He is describing, if not a standing army, then at least a body of armed men which can be called out at any time (and not just when the harvest has been gathered). In turn this presupposes two conditions: a surplus sufficient to support non-productive labour engaged in military activities, and a state which has the authority to call out troops. Thus the second stage of formation of large-scale ancient societies seems to be dependent on the first stage, i.e. the development of the standing army capable of large-scale conquest depends upon the prior existence of the central-place economy and state (which was, for example, largely absent from Africa until colonial times). But once the technique of the latter is present, then all the techniques are available for permanent military organization. The forms of the economy – its warehouses, secretariat and distributional organization – and its surplus can be merely turned over to an army under the same authority. If neighbouring societies appear both vulnerable and tempting, the opportunity for conquest is present. Assuming an evolutionary process in which materially motivated men will tend to seize such opportunities, 'empires' may emerge in such conditions (alternatively, if no one state can attain hegemony, a lengthy period of warring states may ensue). But naturally there is no inevitability about this development.

On one consequence of such warfare, Spencer was essentially correct. Successful booty or conquest warfare tends to heighten the state versus society stratification. This is for two reasons: leadership in emergency situations (of which wars are the clearest examples) needs the speed of authoritarian decision-making, and thus, secondly, booty will be normally distributed by the military-state leadership (see Andreski, 1971, pp. 20–74, for a rather more sophisticated discussion of these issues). The most visible examples of this process are not in the emergence of the empires themselves, but in the development of the state among those barbarian tribes who were able to live off plundering them (for the Germans and Rome see Thompson, 1965; for the Mongols and China see

Lattimore, 1962a). Naturally if the war-leaders wish to maintain their degree of power independent of the classes of civil society, they will seek to continue the wars of conquest – and so develop the characteristic three-way politics of ancient empires I described earlier.

Thus far there is little that Marx would have disagreed with – excepting some of Spencer's and Lattimore's wider generalizations. Marx and Engels both accepted the importance of warfare and conquest in earlier phases of hsitory. However, they always insisted on one central feature of warfare: that it is not productive. Thus in typical polemical vein in *Capital*, Marx comments:

> Truly comical is M. Bastiat, who imagines that the ancient Greeks and Romans lived by plunder alone. But when people plunder for centuries, there must always be something at hand for them to seize: the objects of plunder must be continually reproduced. It would thus appear that even Greeks and Romans had some process of production, consequently an economy, which . . . constituted the material basis of their world. (vol. I, 1970 edn, pp. 81–2)

Except for the last phrase, Spencer would be in agreement. Now it is true that plunder presupposes production; and it is also true that the *character* of warfare is heavily dependent upon the mode of production of a people. Thus pastoral nomads become mobile light cavalry, settled agriculturalists become infantry phalanxes. There is nevertheless a certain autonomous 'military logic' in history, where battles and warfare may be decided not by the level of economic development but by military technology and strategy. The most outstanding example of this appears to have been the superiority in battle of those primitive pastoral nomads over far more economically advanced civiliations. The Chinese Empire was repeatedly conquered by barbarian cavalry able to concentrate its forces quickly, evade enormous infantry armies and strike at the Chinese headquarters. The smallest known group are the Sha-To who, numbering only 10,000 soldiers, conquered and ruled China in the tenth century. Such success apparently also attended the incursions of mounted barbarians in the ancient Near East (MacNeill, 1963).[9] But these conquests are bound to be somewhat

---

9 Rome only rarely faced such enemies. Its barbarians were usually footsoldiers, who were never able to defeat properly equipped and officered legions in the field.

parasitic: how can such a small number of illiterate, half-civilized conquerors without experience of intensive agriculture affect the mode of production itself? Mongol barbarians could not usually displace the existing Chinese bureaucracy/gentry class, for they could not rule without them. Indeed these examples are of a certain *autonomy*, not a determinancy, of military-political factors *vis-à-vis* the mode of production: changes in the composition of the political elite and the form of state may proceed without reference to economic processes, or contrary to their logic. As Marx expressed it in *Capital* (writing about India): 'The structure of the economic elements of society remains untouched by the storm-clouds of the political sky' (1970 edn, vol. I, p. 358). If this is the argument, however, its implications should be fully accepted: that one cannot explain the structure of this form of State, its rises and declines, in terms of the mode of production.

Yet I have presented data which cast doubt on this autonomy of state and economy, indeed which attribute determinancies over certain attributes of economic life to militaristic state structures. Quite contrary to Marx, warfare *is* productive — if it is of a type which leads to the formation of ancient empires. As Spencer pointed out, the form of the ancient state in large-scale societies was 'militant', i.e. it was modelled on the organization of the standing army — centralized, authoritarian and uniform. That was the only way disparate regions and peoples could be held together given the absence of economic interdependence. Spencer claimed that 'civilization' emerged from this route but he never made it clear whether this involved economic growth. Sharing the distaste of most modern intellectuals for such despotism, he was reluctant to attribute functionality to it. Yet it is clear that such a militant state did have important developmental effects upon the extraction of surplus. I described these effects earlier. Three aspects of the militant state seem to have had marked effects on economic development: the heightening of stratification by conquest, the intensification of the labour process that authoritarian forms of labour control allow, and the provision of an infrastructure of order and uniformity.[10] The latter should be particularly stressed, as it was by the imperial authorities themselves. Of the two

---

10 The importance of slavery in the Roman Republic also had economic repercussions peculiar to Rome: the expropriation of free peasants, their migration to the towns and thus the stimulus to urban trade (Hopkins, 1977, pp. 23–31).

empires I have considered in detail, China offered the more sophisticated self-analysis. Hartwell has documented the economic theory of the Northern Sung (i.e. AD 960–1126) financial bureaucrats which laid great stress on active currency and price management by the state as a way of ensuring *predictability* for economic decision-makers. He concludes:

> Internal security against bandits and rebellion, external protection against foreign invasion and conquest, and the development of improved transportation and communications facilities may be ... far more important elements in the history of economic growth ... But if these conditions are met, then 'continuous and consistent' economic policies – taxation methods, maintenance of the monetary system, attitudes toward distributive justice – became essential ingredients in sustained progress. (1970–1, p. 309)

At this point Hartwell refers to Max Weber, noting the illumination which Weber's stress upon formal rationality, calculability and predictability throws upon economic development. My own analysis supports Weber's position. However, insofar as Weber commits himself to a causal explanation of the rationalization process it tends to be in terms of ideological factors, most notably the famous comparison he makes between Eastern and Western religions (as, for example, in the concluding chapter of his *Religion of India*). While I cannot enter into this enormous problem here, and while it might be claimed that I have neglected ideological factors, it seems to me that the conditions of formal rationality are essentially those provided by *pacification*. Furthermore, in both Empires the development of an economic policy embodying formal rationality *followed* the achievement of the pacification process.[11] The chronology is quite clear: military consolidation and pacification – the development of inter-regional economic exchange – the growth of imperial economic policies of uniformity. It is not only the Marxian version of materialism we may oppose to Weber!

Yet as I have noted, economic exchange was never sufficient to replace military control as the major organizational form. Thus the society and its economy remained essentially 'militant' in its organization. Let me illustrate this with the Roman transport

---

11 Though in Rome, Diocletian's introduction of fiscal uniformity followed a period of turbulence which had undermined the earlier pacification of the Empire.

system. First, shipping, the major form of long-distance transport of goods. By the fourth century AD shippers belonged to the guild of *navicularii*, controlled by the provincial prefects of the Empire. Membership was hereditary and compulsory – certain land was burdened by the obligation of *navicularia functio*, and inheritance of this land meant becoming a shipper (though this could sometimes be evaded by bribery). Fees for carrying state goods were fixed by the prefects, and so little free bargaining could occur between the shipper and the merchant possessing the goods. Furthermore, this payment was deliberately inadequate to cover the shipper's cost. He was compensated for this loss by the grant of legal privileges, of which the most important was immunity from civil obligations, that is, from the duties of local government, which were generally compulsory for the middle strata (the *decurions*) of the Empire, and which were costly in both time and money. Over land transport, its control was absolute through actual state ownership, managed directly by praetorian prefects and provinical governors. This *cursus publicus* maintained a vast and costly organization of staging posts, and appears to us to be extremely wasteful of the resources of men, horses, and carts. The amount of long-distance land trade was negligible when compared to the scale of this operation. Some of the more cost conscious Emperors made attempts to reduce its scale, but it remained basically intact until the fall of the Empire (Jones, 1964, vol. II, pp. 827–34).

Such a transport system might seem inefficient to modern eyes. As far as the shipper is concerned, any rational calculation of profit and loss becomes rather difficult, for he has to include the indirect benefits of the legal immunities, as does the prefect in setting what he thinks are reasonable payments. Thus all those concerned have to mix economic and political considerations in their calculations. Finley (1973, pp. 17–23) has noted (exaggerating only a little) that the Roman economy was not a 'differentiated sub-system of action'. It is clear that the government is thinking not in narrowly economic terms, but is combining economic, military and administrative needs. This is particularly so for the *cursus publicus*, which was seen by the government largely as an administrative military necessity. But is the system irrational? The recruitment of the shippers may seem odd, but for achievement to replace ascription as the basis of allocation, a large-scale technical education system would be needed. In fact, without this, hereditary transmission of technical roles is an efficient training mechanism found in most ancient economies. As for the subordination of economic to administrative and military considerations, does not this represent an accurate assessment of the nature of the Empire? For the economic 'spin-offs' are very indirect, especially those flowing from the provision of order itself. Without this, even local exchange relations are precarious, i.e. it is not that the *cursus publicus* develops a large volume of trade (though it develops some) but rather that it provides the pacification whereby all dealings with strangers can be regulated (and where banditry is reduced). The economic necessity of militaristic relations is also clear in the case of the authoritarian control of labour. Agricultural treatises which survive were concerned above all with the direction and control of labour rather than directly with the productivity of labour compared with other factors of production (though they generally date from the Republication period when slavery was more widespread). Finley comments that this shows the viewpoint of the policeman, not the entrepreneur (1973, p. 113). Yet intensive agriculture could *only* be worked with non-free labour. The rationality of the system was militaristic.

In fact this point can be generalized to counter the tendency among writers since Marx and Engels to view the Romans as somehow 'irrational', 'blind to their own doom' or dominated by 'unteachable conservatism' in their failure to develop commodity production. Commodity production did not develop: economic technology (in contrast to military technology) remained essentially unchanged during the Roman Empire (though not during the Chinese); moreover, we might agree that *if* Rome had leaped several technological revolutions toward large-scale commodity exchange, it might not have collapsed. But societies confront the problems of their own time, not those that subsequent generations invent for them. Bandits were never totally eliminated, barbarians were never totally pacified, the political system was never immune from dynastic civil war – the problems *were* military, and authoritarian controls could not be relinquished. The rationality of the system was militaristic. The ancient world, *pace* Marx, did 'live off politics' in one very crucial sense – that its material conditions of existence depended ultimately on structures determined by military-political considerations. In this respect there can be no clear distinction between supposedly 'dominant' and 'determinant' structures.

Conclusion

It is important that I be specific about my argument. It is in no way to be treated as a 'military determinism' of the general kind advocated for the ancient world by Spencer, and, on occasion, for the whole of history by Andreski (1971, p. 26). Over a specific empirical terrain, I have argued that military organization has had important effects upon economic structure. I have not emphasized conquest *per se*, which has had a distinctive and generally non-productive role *throughout* human history (up to perhaps the nuclear stalemate). Modern colonial empires were acquired by force exactly as were ancient ones. The difference lies in processes of consolidation *subsequent* to the conquest. At a definite phase in social development, economic means could not provide this consolidation. They now can do so, and economic imperialism (within, of course, a militarily protected perimeter) has largely taken over. Furthermore a decline has also occurred in non-free forms of labour control as commodity penetration has developed. In ancient empires consolidation, integration, was 'militant' in form, that is centralized, authoritarian and uniform. This had major economic effects: it heightened social stratification, and enabled the first substantial amassing of surplus from nature in human history.

Thus one cannot explain either the political form of the ancient state or its economy without introducing distinctively social Darwinian and militaristic elements into one's theory. The former proposition – the political form – will not be generally contested. It is the latter that is contentious. Let us examine the economic effects a little more closely. It might be asked whether these effects are on 'the productive forces' or 'production relations'. I have emphasized the former: that is, the simple level of economic development. Yet substantial impact on relations can also be observed: heightening of stratification and of authoritarian modes of labour control. I am not sure that it is possible to be more theoretically rigorous about these effects. Now if one takes an extremely general view of a 'mode of production', one could note that none of these changes affect the basic form of expropriation. Tax/rent is the form at the beginning and the end of the imperial state, rent in the successor societies in Western Europe. Hindess and Hirst find these to be essentially the same – one should add *definitionally* the same, given their starting point.[12] That is all very well; but such a position not only fails to explain the state (which they accept), it fails to explain economic effects, which by *any* sociological standards must be regarded as important and worthy of explanation. That enormous societies were raised above subsistence level, contained staggering inequality, and survived, tottered and fell not fundamentally due to class conflict – these are major issues of historical sociology.

Over this empirical terrain, therefore, I have found support for Perry Anderson's position, that a 'mode of production', to be used as an explanatory concept, has to include important non-economic elements, notably 'militant' ones.

What, then, of that most persistent of attacks upon Marxism: that *no* mode of production can be specified without reference to non-economic factors? This argument usually stresses the importance of *norms* in society, i.e. that in order for economic interaction to take place, there must exist prior normative agreements about the rules of exchange. Actually such arguments, by writers such as Plamenatz and Acton, are exactly the same as the much earlier attacks by Rousseau, Burke and Durkheim on contractual, utilitarian theory. In one sense, this traditional argument against varieties of 'economism' is correct. Norms *are* necessary for stable, economic interaction. But the conclusion drawn by all these theorists, that normative consensus must be accorded a privileged causal status in theory, does not follow from this. I have made this argument at greater length elsewhere (Mann, 1977). Here I will merely note the importance of *conquest* in establishing the terms of exchange, the norms in both ancient empires and modern capitalism. Both proceeded by *expropriation*, primarily of conquered peoples, but also of existing subordinate classes. Eventually, within their conquered territories, both systems established uniform rules of exchange and even of the rates of exchange (though these would be affected by further alterations in power relations). Thus these modes of production, and all modes

---

12 I have omitted reference to the so-called 'ancient mode of production' which remains unclear to me.

involving significant territorial expansion, cannot be specified without a consideration of the military state.

However, military factors do not simply lose their importance once territorial conquest is complete. I have shown how the militant state apparatus continues to be necessary to the survival of ancient empires, but a few final remarks are perhaps necessary about the military in the modern world. Though the economy can provide social integration in an industrial society, once pacified, the *international* level of pacification has always been problematic. From its beginnings, expansionist capitalism has been accompanied by devastating wars between nation-states. Norms of international economic exchange (free trade, currency convertibility, peace) have only been clearly established under the aegis of an 'imperial' power: Britain in the nineteenth century, the United States 1945–71 (when President Nixon announced that the United States was abandoning dollar convertibility). The collapse of British hegemony was notably violent, and it conspicuously involved all those modern states which, it might be argued, have exhibited rather more autonomy *vis-à-vis* social classes than my overall thesis allows for – Wilhelmian Germany, the emergence of Fascism and Bolshevism, and Imperial Japan. If in truth these are cases of 'autonomous political power', then we must look to military factors – so long neglected by sociologists – for the major part of our explanation, just as we must in the ancient world. This time, however, 'the problem of the state' is less that of one hegemonic, militant empire, and more of a system of competing nation-states. And if the current demise of US hegemony is likely to be a uniquely peaceful event in world-history, we must also look to two military factors for our explanation. First, the early stages of industrial revolution provided a military technology which makes industrial societies militarily invulnerable to more primitive societies. As Gibbon first noted, unlike Rome or China we cannot be raided by barbarians, and if defence against them were our only external defence requirement, our military budgets would be a minute proportion of our total budgets (again unlike the ancient empires). Secondly, and more recently, a balance of nuclear weapons between the major world powers renders direct warfare of the dominant historical variety unthinkable as a rational strategy of economic appropriation. Within this *pax industria et patria* the economy determines.

References

Anderson P. 1974a: *Passages from Antiquity to Feudalism*. London: New Left Books.
—— 1974b: *Lineages of the Absolutist State*. London: New Left Books.
Andreski S. 1971: *Military Organization and Society*. Berkeley/Los Angeles, Ca: University of California Press.
Balazs E. 1964: *Chinese Civilization and Bureaucracy*. New Haven, Conn.: Yale University Press.
Bernardi A. 1970: 'The economic problems of the Roman Empire at the time of its decline', in C. M. Cippolla (ed.), *The Economic Decline of Empires*. London: Methuen.
Chesneaux J. 1973: *Peasants Revolts in China, 1840–1949*. New York: Norton.
Chi Ch'ao-Ting 1936: *Key Economic Areas in Chinese History*. London: Allen and Unwin.
Dardess J. W. 1969–70: 'The transformation of messianic revolt and the founding of the Ming dynasty', *Journal of Asian Studies*, 24, pp. 539–56.
Duncan-Jones R. 1974: *The Economy of the Roman Empire: Quantitatives Studies*. Cambridge: Cambridge University Press.
Durkheim E. 1964: *The Division of Labour in Society*. Glencoe, Illinois; The Free Press.
Eberhard W. 1965: *Conquerors and Rulers: Social Forces in Modern China*. Leiden: Brill.
Eisenstadt S. N. 1969: *The Political Systems of Empires*. New York: The Free Press.
Elvin M. 1973: *The Pattern of the Chinese Past*. Stanford, Ca: Stanford University Press.
Finley M. I. 1973: *The Ancient Economy*. London: Chatto and Windus.
Fletcher R. 1971: *The Making of Sociology*, vol. 1, London: Michael Joseph.
Haeger J. W. 1968–9: 'Between North and South: the Lake Rebellion in Hunan 1130–1135', *Journal of Asian Studies*, 28, pp. 469–88.
Hartwell R. M. 1970–1: 'Financial expertise, examination and the formulation of economic policy in Northern Sung China', *Journal of Asian Studies*, 30, pp. 281–314.
Hindess B. and Hirst P. Q. 1975: *Pre-Capitalist Modes of Production*. London: Routledge.
Hopkins K. 1977: 'Economic growth and towns in classical antiquity', in P. Abrams and E. A. Wrigley (eds), *Towns and Societies*. London: Cambridge University Press.

Jones A. H. M. 1964: *The Later Roman Empire 284–602*, 3 vols. Oxford: Blackwell.
Lattimore O. 1962a: *Inner Asian Frontiers of China*. Boston: Beacon Press.
—— 1962b: *Studies in Frontier History*. London: Oxford University Press.
MacMullen R. 1966: *Enemies of the Roman Order*. Cambridge, Mass.: Harvard University Press.
—— 1974: *Roman Social Relations*. New Haven, Conn.: Yale University Press.
McNeill W. H. 1963: *The Rise of the West*. Chicago, Chicago University Press.
Mann M. 1977: 'Idealism and materialism in sociological theory', in D. Bertaux and T. Freiberg (eds), *Current Trends in European Critical Theory*. Lexington, Mass.: Heath.
Marx K. 1970: *Capital*, vol. 1. Moscow: Progress Publishers.
—— 1971: *Capital*, vol. 3. Moscow: Progress Publishers.
Marx K. and Engels F. 1968: *Selected Works*. London: Lawrence and Wishart.
Parsons T. 1971: *The System of Modern Societies*. Englewood Cliffs, NJ: Prentice-Hall.
Poulantzas N. 1972: *Pouvoir politique et classes sociales*. Paris: Maspero.
Rostovtzeff M. 1957. *The Social and Economic History of the Roman Empire*. Oxford: Clarendon Press.
Service E. R. 1975: *Origins of the State and Civilization*. New York: Norton.
Slicher van Bath B. H. 1963: *The Agrarian History of Western Europe, AD 500–1850*. London: Edward Arnold.
Spencer H. 1969: *Principles of Sociology* (one-volume abridged edn). London: Macmillan.
Stover L. E. 1974: *The Cultural Ecology of Chinese Civilizations*. New York: Pira Press.
Thompson E. A. 1952: 'Peasant revolts in late Roman Gaul and Spain', *Past and Present*, no. 7, pp. 11–23.
—— 1965: *The Early Germans*. Oxford: Clarendon Press.
Wakeman F. Jr 1977: 'Rebellion and revolution: the study of popular movements in Chinese history', *Journal of Asian Studies*, 36, pp. 201–37.
Westermann W. L. 1955: *The Slave Systems of Greek and Roman Antiquity*. Philadelphia: American Philosophical Society.
Wittfogel K. 1957: *Oriental Despotism*. New Haven, Conn.: Yale University Press.

3

State and Society, 1130–1815: an Analysis of English State Finances

Introduction

In this essay I discuss the relations between state and society in the medieval and early modern period. I am concentrating on the history of England/Britain, though I will be making a few comparisons with other states of the period. The beginning date of 1130 is significant only because certain relevant financial documents of the English state survive from that year onward. The final date of 1815 is rather more significant: it marks the end of the Napoleonic Wars and serves as a rough symbolic watershed between a pre-industrial and an industrial society in Britain. The period covered thus includes some of the major transformations in the recent history of human societies – the transition from feudalism to capitalism: the emergence of social classes as world-historical actors; the emergence of 'the modern state', of 'the national state', and of political democracy; and finally 'the military revolution' induced by the diffusion of artillery.

Obviously I cannot hope to cover all these issues in one essay at an appropriate level of sophistication and depth. I will structure my discussion of them through a fairly simple question: *what are the functions of the state* during this period? 'What does the state concretely *do*, both in its 'feudal' and its early 'capitalist' or 'modern' forms? Despite the recent blooming of interest in the

---

This chapter was first published in Maurice Zeitlin (ed.), *Political Power and Social Theory* (1980), vol. 1, pp. 165–208, Greenwich, Connecticut and London: JAI Press Inc. We are grateful for permission to reproduce it here.

state, especially among Marxists, there has been surprisingly little attention paid to empirical analysis of state activities. The neglect is especially surprising because marvellous source-data exist for a period of no less than 800 years, in the shape of the surviving financial accounts of the English/British state. The main contribution of my essay must therefore be to present these data and to comment upon the empirical trends they reveal rather than to enter the more conceptual and abstract realms of state theory. Only two theoretical points need to be briefly outlined before this can take place.

First, definitional difficulties should be acknowledged. Most state theorists operate with a definition along the lines specified by Max Weber: the state is a centralized, differentiated set of institutions enjoying a monopoly of the means of legitimate violence over a territorially demarcated area. The problem of this definition (apart from the difficult word 'legitimate') is that it embodies both an *institutional* and a *functional* element – the state being recognizable both because its institutions are centrally located and because it undertakes the function of legitimate violence. Difficulties arise when the two characteristics are empirically separable, and European feudalism presents the knottiest example. As we will see, those centralized institutions which we intuitively recognize as 'states' in feudalism – monarchies, duchies etc. – sometimes did *not* possess a monopoly of the means of legitimate violence (either of judicial or military force). Instead they shared these powers with church, local lords and towns. So, the question arises, where was the English feudal state – at Westminster alone, or also in hundreds of church, manorial and civic institutions? The question cannot be answered without a consideration of state theory as a whole, which is outside the purview of this essay. My data relate only to the state at Westminster. Thus the reader should be warned that my operational definition of the state is largely institutional: the state resided at Westminster, in the persons of the monarch, household, bureaucracy and conciliar/parliamentary representatives, with a (sometimes vague) degree of 'ultimate' authority over violence employed within England/Britain. What *this* state undertook, however, is surely not without interest and significance.

Second, I will briefly situate the problem of state functions in relation to previous theories. In fact, state theory has been split into two camps asserting fundamentally opposed views of state functions. The dominant state theory in the Anglo-Saxon tradition has seen the fundamental role of the state as *economic* and *domestic:* the state regulates, judicially and repressively, the economic relationships between individuals and classes located within its boundaries. Writers as diverse as Hobbes, Locke, Marx, Easton, and Poulantzas have roughly operated with this view. But the dominant state theory of the Germanic world has been quite different, seeing the state's role as fundamentally *military* and *international:* states mediate the power relations between different societies and, because these are largely normless, they do so by military force. This view, now unfashionable in the liberal and Marxian era of nuclear stalemate, was once dominant, especially through the work of Gumplowicz, Oppenheimer, Hintz, and – to a lesser degree – Weber.

It is of course absurd to adhere to one of these perspectives to the total exclusion of the other, though this feat is regularly performed by most contemporary writers on the state. Obviously states perform both sets of functions and in relation to both the domestic and the international arena. After establishing the crude historical importance of the two sets of functions I will begin the attempt to relate them in a more theoretically informed way.

The empirical guts of this essay will be an analysis of *state finances* throughout the period. Wherever possible I have attempted to quantify these in statistical presentation of revenue and expenditure accounts. Such an approach has limitations, in terms of both the meaning and internal adequacy of such data. As far as its meaning is concerned, we could not base conclusions as to the importance of different state functions *purely* upon their relative costs. I will make due allowances for this as we proceed. Furthermore, the data have internal limitations. I have not consulted archive sources but am dependent on the good sense of the historians who have published analyses of them. Actually it would be totally beyond the resources of any single scholar to summarize the archival material over the whole period – Steel, for example, appears to have spent two decades examining those of only 120 years. Published research separates itself into two periods, divided by the year 1688. After the date one form of classification is used on a complete annual time-series run of revenue and expenditure accounts. Whatever the imperfections of these data, supplied by Mitchell and Deane (1962), they have the merit of being consistent from 1688 to 1815 (and beyond). For the period from 1130 to 1688, however, we find no consistency of data or of classification technique. I will shortly engage in analysis of their inconsistencies and limitations. Although I emerge with an approximation to a time-series run of revenue from 1155 to 1688, it is less reliable than the subsequent one. In general I will use the post-1688 data to test more fully hypotheses and suspicions derived from the pre-1688 data. And whatever the difficulties encountered in the English material, it is markedly more continuous and reliable than that of any other country.

Despite all limitations of the surviving, published accounts, the rewards in the form of clear, striking, and consistent trends are so considerable as to overcome doubts. The accounts are a gold mine of important data so far neglected by sociologists and generalization-minded historians alike. I claim originality only in the extent of historical coverage attempted here: I express surprise that it has not been previously undertaken. For the justification for such an enterprise was clearly expressed by Schumpeter some years ago:

the public finances are one of the best starting points for an investigation of society.... The spirit of a people, its cultural level, its social structure, the deeds its policy may prepare – all this and more is written in its fiscal history, stripped of all phrases. He who knows how to listen to the message here discerns the thunder of world history more clearly than anywhere else. (1954, p. 7)

Or, as Jean Bodin more succinctly expressed it, fiscal means are the nerves of the state.

Methodology

There are two ways of deducing the quantitative significance of each state function from the financial accounts of the state. The more direct way is to break down expenditure accounts into the main component items. I will do this systematically for the period after 1688. Unfortunately, the earlier expenditure accounts are usually insufficient for this purpose. The earliest account dates only from 1224, and for the next four centuries they permit us only glimpses of state functions. But revenue accounts survive from 1130, and from 1155 they are sufficient for us to attempt to construct a time-series. Thus the second method of assessing state functions is to analyze revenue totals through time, explaining their systematic variations in terms of changing demands made upon the state. This will be my principal method up to 1688. Luckily, the expenditure glimpses and the revenue time-series reveal the same pattern. Every increase in the real financial size of the state up to 1688 is occasioned by two interrelated factors, the onset of war and changing military technology: and the bulk of state expenditure goes to meet these needs.

Four main series of revenue studies cover the period. Those of Ramsay (1920, 1925) cover 1130 to 1485; luckily they are supplemented from 1387 to 1485 by the more recent work of Steel (1954). Then from 1485 to 1640, there are several works by Dietz (1918, 1923, 1928, 1964a, 1964b). Finally, after a gap during the Interregnum, we have a recent study of the period 1660 to 1688 by Chandaman (1975). These studies vary considerably in their methods and accuracy. As research into government records has developed, the older studies have been found wanting in various respects. Many historians indeed consider the results of Ramsay to be unusable, while those of Dietz are also regarded with some scepticism. Without them, of course, we could not construct a time-series or attempt generalizations about secular trends. However, I believe that this can be done, though within certain margins of error which must now be discussed.

The surviving records of revenue transactions are the receipt and issue rolls of the Exchequer and other financial departments of government. All competent researchers have been aware of problems which arise from the incompleteness of record survival and from the changing relations between the departments (at times the Exchequer is virtually the sole financial centre, at other times not). Once these problems are surmounted, however, other more subtle, and only gradually understood, difficulties have arisen. As they illuminate considerably the nature of the early English state, they are worth explaining in detail. They principally concern the use of the *tally* in English finance until the seventeenth century.[1] When a crown official or agent presented himself at the Exchequer

---

1 The following account is taken from Steel (1954, pp. xxix–xxxviii). For its survival into the late seventeenth century see Chandaman (1975, appendix I).

at Westminster with a statement as to his expenditure needs, he may have been paid in cash or with a 'tally'. A tally was a narrow shaft of wood split down the middle on which notches were cut to denote the sum involved – a rather solid cheque, in effect. The Exchequer accountant kept one half, and the official took the other half directly to a local revenue collector named on the tally – a collector of customs or of taxes or a sheriff, for example – where he would be paid in cash. Thus when the revenue collector eventually came to Westminster he would have a mixed bundle of revenue to deliver, cash and tallies (as well as various writs and debentures which often accompanied the tallies). The system was in fact a primitive form of anticipatory drafts on revenue. It is probable that from the twelfth century onward the exchequer of receipt became dominated by tallies rather than cash. From the fourteenth century we can know the exact proportions because marginal notes appear systematically in the receipt rolls. The system makes it difficult to establish annual revenue: if tallies are not immediately cashed, the receipt rolls will not give a reliable guide to revenue in a particular year.

However, a rather more serious problem emerges from a further development of the credit system. Another set of marginal notes is found: *pro* followed by a person's name indicates that the tally has been assigned to that person; but if it is then struck through *(pro)* it denotes that the creditor is marked as paid, but has actually failed to cash his tally. To save trouble with the totals, the Exchequer clerks cancelled the original entry and the amount is recorded again as a new 'receipt' in the form of a loan. If the creditor tried and failed repeatedly to cash his tally, the same amount of money (or perhaps a diminishing amount, if he is partly paid) appears several times over. This is the 'fictitious loan'. If we do not recognize it, then we will overstate total revenue merely by adding up the figures.

The whole system is very revealing of the nature of the state. Its finances were highly decentralized and consisted largely of a set of relations between *persons*. It was more important to the accountants that they set out clearly these relations than that they provide an overall statement of balance. This was what their *accountability* consisted of – i.e., it totally lacked the modern element of the state's accountability to society as a whole or to any organized group who might be said to 'represent' society. The relations

State and Society, 1130–1815

between state and civil society as a whole were non-existent.

To arrive at accurate totals we must laboriously eliminate all fictitious loans – as well as other minor, but similar, transactions. Unfortunately, Ramsay did not do this, though he was not wholly ignorant of these practices. Because of this and other errors (detailed by Steel, 1954, pp. xxiv–xxviii), he probably overstated the revenues during the whole of the period he covered. I say 'probably', because although we can check his figures with those of Steel from 1377, we cannot be sure that fictitious loans and the like prevailed in the whole period. Willard (1927) has shown that they were prominent in 1327–8, and he believes the practice to have been common from the twelfth century (because tallies were), but the marginal notes in the rolls do not start until the fourteenth century. If Ramsay's error is consistent we can introduce a correction factor, based on the post-1377 period. But should we assume this without direct knowledge? Let us see first if his errors are consistent after 1377.

I have calculated average revenues given by both Ramsay and Steel over the following periods: 1377–8, 1389–99, 1399–1410, 1413–22, 1422–8, 1428–54 and 1454–61. The periods are all reigns or parts of reigns for which both historians have given figures and on which the Exchequer rolls are complete. Incomplete years within these periods have been excluded. Steel's figures are what he calls 'real receipts', excluding the bookkeeping devices of real and fictitious loans and *prestitia*, given in his Appendix D, 'C' tables. As the periods are generally quite wide, problems arising for *annual* revenue from the tally system are minimal. The results are as follows: Steel's figures are always lower, being respectively 80, 88, 79, 87, 86, 85 and 42 per cent of Ramsay's in the various periods.[2] Apart from the last period, therefore, the differences are fairly consistent, being in the range 79–88 per cent. The last period, 1454–61, represents the nadir of Henry VI's fortunes during the Wars of the Roses. At that time the revenues apparently collected were negligible, although the Exchequer rolls may be an inaccurate guide to resources during civil war. There is no comparable period of royal collapse in the preceding centuries,

2 Steel's figures for the period 1399–1413 are inconsistent. For other periods his 'C' series of tables appears to include 'loans never repaid' as 'real receipts', but this table (C3) appears not to do this. In the text (p. 105) Steel says that the inclusion of loans not repaid pushes annual revenue to between £90,000 and £100,000 (without such loans, the average is £88,174). I have assumed the correct figure to be £95,000 both here and in table 3.1, but this is, of course, inexact.

with the exception of Stephen's reign 1135–54. As no data survive from then, this need not trouble us. Thus it does seem that Ramsay's errors were of a consistent order.

This returns us to the original problem: are we safe in presuming a consistent error over the earlier, uncheckable period? It is improbable that the error would be any higher then, and actually probable that it would be lower, as the surviving Pipe Rolls of the late twelfth and the thirteenth century are rather simpler and more systematic than the later rolls. In view of this, *I have reduced Ramsay's earlier estimates by 10 per cent*, which leaves a clear margin of error produced by this adjustment of 10 per cent on either side. I will not treat as significant any differences between the revenue of different periods which falls within this range. The place of maximum error is likely to be the 'join' between the two sets of data, around 1377, where the 10 per cent deduction may well be inadequate. I should also point out that the reign of King John is poorly documented, with many gaps in the surviving receipts supplemented by Ramsay's 'estimates'.

With these adjustments, and using Ramsay and Steel together, we can derive a rough time-series from 1155 to 1454. No accurate data are available for the end of the Wars of the Roses.

From 1485 the major problems arise from infrequent surviving rolls, compounded by inaccuracies in the major studies, those of Dietz. Dietz was not unaware of the tally system, though, like Ramsay, he did not allow for the double-counting it might introduce. However, the tally system was in decline from the time of Henry VII onwards. By the reign of Elizabeth redemption of all tallies was contributing only between 10 and 20 per cent to all annual expenses, so that the total amount of double-counting within that must have been very small. It does not seem worthwhile to estimate a correction factor for it. Dietz's main errors lie elsewhere, in his overlooking of duplication in the accounts of the different financial departments. For the reign of Henry VII he overstates considerably total revenue, according to the more recent calculations of Wolffe. During these years we are able to make nearly exact estimates only for the last four years, 1502–5. Here I have followed Wolffe's correction of Dietz's figures (1971, pp. 212–17).

For the reigns of Henry VIII, Edward VI and Mary I have attempted no overall estimates. In any case the decade aggregates

State and Society, 1130–1815

would merely conceal more short-run changes, upon which I will comment later. But the difficulties of this period – sketchy records and a multiplicity of government financial departments – reduce during Mary's reign. During Elizabeth's reign the Exchequer records are very approximate if conservative summaries of overall state finances. Professor G. R. Elton has pointed out to me that they probably underestimate total revenue in a consistent fashion. Revenue apparently received is difficult to trace in Exchequer accounts. If this were added, Dietz's figures relating to traced amounts would have to be increased by perhaps one-third. The figures given for Elizabeth's reign are the 'Grand total of all Revenue received or accounted for at the Exchequer' given in Dietz (1923 pp, 80–90). This is to say, they are the totals provided by the Elizabethan accountants themselves, and not the sum of the individual items (which sometimes vary from this total toward the end of the reign). I am here following current orthodoxy among historians that the accountants' knowledge of their own accountancy practices was greater than ours could be.

The records of James and Charles survive rather less completely, though luckily we have two fairly continuous series, for James from 1604 to 1613 (i.e., ten years) and for Charles from 1630 to 1640, omitting 1632, 1635, and 1639 (i.e., eight years). For all the years used I have added together tallies and cash receipts (given in Dietz, 1928, pp. 136–55), which may result in a small overestimation if 'fictitious loans' still existed.

The Civil War and Interregnum interrupt our data, but finally, a recent study by Chandaman has provided comprehensive figures for the next two reigns, covering 1660–88. I have used his total net income figures (1975, pp. 332–3).

A final note: the financial year ran from Michaelmas to Michaelmas throughout the period. Gaps indicate missing accounts, as for example for Edward II, where the only complete surviving accounts date from the late-middle years of the reign. I have tried to divide the data into even periods, although this is hampered by the uneven length of reigns and by missing data. Most periods include ten to 12 years of accounts.

The results of all these calculations and approximations are contained in table 3.1. So far, however, all I have explained is the basis of the actual revenue figures used, that is of the column 'revenue at current prices'. Yet our interpretation of changes in

Table 3.1 English state finances 1155–1688: average annual revenue at current and constant (1451–75) prices

Reign	Years	Annual revenue in £000		Price index
		Current	Constant	
Henry II	1155–1166	12.2	–	–
	1166–1177	18.0	60.0	30
	1177–1188	19.6	55.9	35
Richard I	1188–1198	17.1	60.9	28
John	1199–1214	37.9	71.5	53
Henry III	1218–1229	31.1	39.4	79
	1229–1240	34.6	54.1	64
	1240–1251	30.3	43.2	70
	1251–1262	32.0	40.5	79
	1262–1272	24.0	26.7	90
Edward I	1273–1284	40.0	40.0	100
	1285–1295	63.2	67.9	93
	1295–1307	53.4	41.1	130
Edward II	1316–1324	83.1	54.3	153
Edward III	1328–1340	101.5	95.8	106
	1340–1351	114.7	115.9	99
	1351–1363	134.9	100.0	135
	1363–1375	148.4	103.8	143
Richard II	1377–1388	128.1	119.7	107
	1389–1399	106.7	99.7	107
Henry IV	1399–1410	95.0	84.8	112
Henry V	1413–1422	119.9	110.0	109
Henry VI	1422–1432	75.7	67.0	113
	1432–1442	74.6	67.2	111
	1442–1452	54.4	55.5	98
Henry VII	1502–1505	126.5	112.9	112
Elizabeth	1559–1570	250.8	89.9	279
	1571–1582	223.6	69.0	324
	1583–1592	292.8	77.9	376
	1593–1602	493.5	99.5	496
James I	1604–1613	593.5	121.9	487
Charles I	1630–1640	605.3	99.4	609
Charles II	1660–1672	1582.0	251.1	630
Charles II	1672–1685	1634.0	268.7	608
James II	1685–1688	2066.9	353.3	585

Sources Revenue: Ramsay, 1925: 1155–1375: with correction factor added (see text); 1377–1452, Steel, 1954; 1502–1505, Dietz, 1964a, corrected by Wolffe, 1971; 1559–1602, Dietz, 1923; 1604–1640, Dietz, 1928; 1660–1668, Chandaman, 1975. Price index: 1166–1263, Farmer, 1956, 1957; 1264–1688. Phelps-Brown and Hopkins, 1956.

current prices is bedevilled by inflation. Accordingly, I have attempted to adjust the revenue totals for inflation by calculating 'constant prices' based on their 1451–75 level. The source for this is the study of the price of a 'composite unit of consumables' needed by building workers conducted by Phelps-Brown and Hopkins (1956) for the period 1264–1954, from which I have only used the earlier part here. Before 1264 I have added two studies by Farmer (1956, 1957), using only his wheat prices for the period 1165–1262, standardizing his figures to those of Phelps-Brown and Hopkins in the subsequent half century for which they both provide prices. Nevertheless an overall price index based on one commodity alone (even if it is the staple) in the earlier period, and on a 'shopping basket' of a non-agricultural group in the later period has its imperfections. I have also consulted another series of price indexes calculated by Thirsk (1967, pp. 846–63) for various agricultural and industrial products during the period 1450–1649. Though her figures for individual years sometimes differ significantly from those of Phelps-Brown and Hopkins, when averaged over the periods distinguished in table 3.1 they are remarkably similar. The methods of aggregation used here are sufficient to reveal overall trends, whatever their imperfections. However, one bit of 'fiddling' should be confessed. The price figures for John's reign, provided by Farmer, are very incomplete but include the three disastrous harvest years of 1201 to 1203. The high prices of these years would over-weight the figures for his reign in a way that does not occur in other reigns. I have therefore omitted these years from all calculations.

However, 'inflation-proof' figures also have limitations in meaning. If prices are rising, the monarch will need to raise additional revenue, and his subjects will doubtless squeal even if in 'real' terms the extraction-rate is unchanged. Thus both sets of figures have real, if partial, significance. That said, we can turn to the main trends of table 3.1.

Trends in revenue totals, 1155–1688

First, what does the price index reveal? Round about 1200 prices began to rise sharply, perhaps almost doubling during John's reign, and only falling back slightly thereafter. Towards 1300 they rose again, this time over almost a 100-year period, again falling slightly thereafter. But in the sixteenth century they rocketed, apparently rising fivefold between 1500 and 1600. Thus 1600 prices were around twenty times higher than 1200 prices. Under these circumstances direct comparison between revenue totals of different periods has its limitations! Let us take separately current and constant price data.

Revenue at current prices shows an obvious upward trend through the period. Ignoring the first decade of Henry II's reign (before he had effectively restored central authority), we can see that the first substantial increase (far greater than our margin of error) occurs during John's reign, after which it falls back slightly until Edward I's accession. Then a steady upward trend ensues for a century until Richard II, after which a decline ensues, interrupted by Henry V, until the Tudors. Revenue then leaps unprecedently in the second half of the sixteenth century and continues through the seventeenth. Those kings apparently requiring large increases in revenue are thus John, the first three Edwards (especially I and III). Henry V, Elizabeth, Charles, I, and Charles II. Henry III, Richard II, Henry IV, and both of the Jameses also manage to maintain most of the rises of their immediate predecessor.

When we switch to constant prices, the overall increase is not so steady, although it is still in evidence. In 'real' terms John's exactions increase, though not as greatly as his money exactions, and they are unmatched until Edward III, whose long reign sees a continuously high rate of extraction. Its maintenance (and increase) during Richard II's reign is something of an artefact in the sense that it is contributed by falling prices rather than an increase in money revenue. Henry V still emerges as a revenue-increasing king, and the low revenues of the kings of the Wars of the Roses are also still evident. But the Tudor pattern has changed. In real terms Henry VII increases his revenue quite substantially, and only during the reign of James I is this real rate of extraction increased. The later Stuarts then increase it again, enormously. In 'real' terms the financial size of the English state reaches a peak in the fourteenth century and does not grow substantially thereafter until the late seventeenth century, when it rockets once again. These are the trends we must now explain in more detailed terms.

The twelfth-century state

There were many European states. From the beginning this was a multi-state system. The Roman Empire was eventually succeeded by an astonishing variety of geographical units, some of which had clearly defined political centres ('states') and some of which did not. Some corresponded to natural economic or geographic areas, some had a clearer relationship to militarily defensible space, and some covered a terrain whose only logic seems to be that of dynastic accretion. However, most were monarchical or quasi-monarchical in form, and shared two characteristics. First, the formal authority of the prince rested in one of the variant forms of a feudal, military contract: the vassal swore homage and gave military service in return for protection and/or the grant of land. Second, the monarch did not possess clear and agreed-on rights of access to the population as a whole. Whatever functions he might fulfil for the society at large, they were exercised *through* other autonomous power actors. His ritualistic functions were shared with a transnational church: his judicial authority was shared with church and local manorial courts: his military leadership was exercised only at times of crisis over retainers of other lords: and he had virtually no fiscal or economically redistributive powers. This weakness of the early feudal state sets it apart from both ancient and modern states. Indeed, in some ways it is misleading to call any of them 'states', so decentralized were political functions.

Thus a modicum of international economic regulation already existed in the Roman and Christian legacy. All Christians were considered to be human beings – looting, pillaging, or raping them carried moral opprobrium and the danger of retribution. Weber's 'internal ethic' applied *outside* of the boundaries of 'states'. Ownership rights of private property were already established through the inheritance of Roman law and institutions. International institutions, including trading houses and guilds, merely needed reviving. Feasible patterns of greater regional exchange and division of labour were present as memories. No imperial power liable to tax, confiscate and prohibit now existed. No single state had sufficient power to interfere internationally with the distribution of property, or with the considerable autonomy of transnationally organized merchants.

The separation of economic and political structures is regarded by most commentators as a crucial part of capitalism. However the separation of the *state* from economic activities had actually been established *before* the development of capitalism. The essence of the landed property relationship (and of the feudal mode of production itself, according to Marx) was the extraction of surplus labour through rent. Without taxation, no part of this rent accrued to the state (other than on its own estates). Ultimately, of course, the state eventually provided a legal and coercive back-up to the monopoly ownership rights of the lords. But the state intervened barely at all in the extraction process itself, in contrast to both the ancient and modern state. And if we shift our attention from land to trade, the state was at first similarly uninvolved in economic relations. The separation between 'economic' and 'political' was thus accomplished in both production and circulation spheres long before capitalism.

Indeed – quite contrary to conventional wisdom – capitalism helped accomplish the *reintegration* of economic and state structures, as we will see later. If the gap had remained, we would have lived right up to the present in a different world, one whose boundaries were set by the end of the twelfth century, one without significant state boundaries and with transnational economy and classes.

All this is slightly less true of the English state than of any other, however. Because of the Norman conquest and the subsequent lack of outside threat, the English state was probably the most centralized in Europe. Only clerics and those vassals with estates outside as well as inside the Anglo-Norman domains owed ultimate allegiance to any competing source of authority; over all other persons the king of England's sovereignty was universal. The growth of royal power had occurred earlier and was more complete than in other countries. Yet the growth was as uneven as elsewhere. By the mid-twelfth century the king had established his legal sovereignty over all lay freemen, but not yet over dependent villeins (still subject to the manorial court) or over the clergy (though Henry II effectively remedied this, at least in their secular affairs). The other two main areas of subsequent state growth, the economic and the military, were only slightly more advanced than in other countries. No general power of taxation, no extensively levied customs dues, and no professional army yet existed. Thus the financial accounts which we will examine now pertain to the most developed state in Europe, yet one that by modern standards was puny indeed.

Revenue and expenditure, King John to Henry V (1199–1422)

The first substantial increase occurred in the reign of King John. His average annual revenue more than doubled over the receipts of Henry II. Controlling for inflation makes the increase seem much less dramatic (though still greater than the margin of error), but it is the increase at current prices that John actually extracted from his subjects. He did so principally through taxation, which contributed over half his revenue and which was increasingly levied in a uniform way over most of the population. Why the increase?

John's conflict with the church (which provided all the chroniclers of the period), and his unattractive personality and habits, ensured that he should receive the most unsympathetic treatment from historians of any English king. Yet two totally extraneous factors at the beginning of his reign, disastrous harvests and galloping, little-understood inflation, set him labouring under an insupportable burden. Unfortunately for John he could not weather these storms by simply muddling through a period of mounting debt and reduced state activity (as his successor Henry III did). His French possessions were under attack from the resurgent French crown, and they were indeed for the most part lost by him. In the twelfth century princes usually requested not monies, but service in person – the feudal levy. Throughout the twelfth century, however, several tendencies undermined the military effectiveness of the levy. Complex inheritance patterns, especially the fragmentation of holdings, made assessment of military obligation increasingly difficult. Regional variations throughout the Anglo-Norman Empire meant that some lords lived in peaceful surroundings, and their levies were increasingly found to be militarily useless. In the late twelfth century the character of warfare also changed as the space of Europe became filled with organized states – now campaigns were larger, involving especially prolonged siegework. In England, the feudal levy was obliged to serve without pay for two months (and only 30 days in peace time): after that, their cost fell upon the king. Thus at the end of the twelfth century, princes began to need more money for warfare at the same time that some of their subjects were less willing to turn out in person. *Ad hoc* taxes such as scutage (a payment in lieu of providing one's own 'shield'), and tallage (levied on the less warlike urban groups) were the compromise result. Thus John's need for funds to pay his troops was the precipitant of increased revenue, as indeed it was for all thirteenth-century kings (and those of subsequent centuries, as we shall see). As I noted earlier the accounting system laid many pitfalls for analyzing annual revenues and their fluctuations. However, the fluctuations in Ramsay's thirteenth-century data are very consistent. In 1224–5 revenue apparently trebled over the previous year; in 1276–7 it doubled; in 1281–2, it trebled; in 1296–7 it doubled – all occasioned by the onset of war. Such pressures were not unique to England. By the late twelfth century over Europe as a whole the number of knights (and their retainers) equipping themselves was equalled by mercenary knights requiring payment. In fact England (except for John's reign) was relatively unique in sticking largely to the national levy until the sixteenth century. Financial strain was felt by the government of thirteenth-century Flemish towns (Verbruggen, 1977), by the Commune of Siena from 1286 (Bowsky, 1970, pp. 43–6), by fourteenth-century Florence (de la Roncière, 1968; Waley, 1968) and by France in the thirteenth to fifteenth centuries (Hennemann, 1971; Rey, 1965; Strayer, 1970, Wolfe, 1972). From the end of the twelfth until the sixteenth century, European armies combined professional with levy elements, and they were in the field for longer periods of time. After that they became fully professional – England's included. And during the thirteenth century, their size, and their size relative to the population, increased dramatically.[3] Such warfare necessitated cash. Loans from Jews and foreign bankers and merchants were resorted to by all the princes, but these could be only temporary expedients. Sooner or later, systematic taxation would be required. By the reign of Edward I taxation was normal, as table 3.2 reveals. These figures are Ramsay's, unadjusted. The

3 Sorokin estimated that the increase in army size relative to total population between 1150 and 1250 was between 48 per cent and 63 per cent (according to which population estimate is accepted) over four European countries (1962, pp. 340–1).

Table 3.2 Average annual sources of revenue in three reigns, 1272–1307 and 1327–1399

	Edward I 1272–1307 (%)	Edward III 1327–1377 (%)	Richard II 1377–1399 (%)
Hereditary crown revenues	32	18	28
Customs	25	46	38
Lay taxation and subsidies	24	17	25
Clerical taxation and subsidies	20	18	9
Total %[a]	100	100	100
Average annual total £ (current prices)	63,442[b]	105,221	126,068

[a] Columns do not total exactly 100 per cent because of rounding.
[b] In this year I have excluded an additional £4000 p.a. deriving from Irish revenue, which is not broken down into component types.
Source: Ramsay, 1925, II, pp. 86, 287, 426–7. Totals unadjusted.

grand total is not of primary interest at this point, only the approximate relative contribution of the different sources.

The most obvious trend is the overall increase in revenue, doubling through a hundred years. But substantial changes have also occurred in sources of income. The first of these categories, 'hereditary revenue', is rather heterogeneous, the two major components being rents from crown lands and the profits of justice — from the modern point of view the former are 'private' and the latter 'public', though contemporaries did not know the distinction. What is clear, however, is that the hereditary revenues remained stable in volume and declined in proportion of the total receipts, as customs revenue and taxation increased. In 1275 Edward I first established an export duty on wool, and other customs and excise duties were soon added. This was a substantial step, not only toward adequate state financing, but also toward the emergence of the *territorial* state. Exports were taxed so that — in line with the current economic theory — English resources should not be drained away abroad at a time of war. A second cause of such duties was the recognition by merchants that their international activities needed military protection. The revenue was supposed to be used for naval purposes and could not be counted as part of the king's 'own' hereditary resources. Neither sentiment could have resulted in customs duties if traders had not recognized a collective *national* identity, an identity that had not existed two centuries earlier. Other states were not able to follow England in developing extensive customs revenues. What they shared, however, was a close fiscal relationship with merchants. The French crown depended heavily on taxes and loans from the merchants of Paris, as well as on taxes on highly visible objects of trade (like the infamous *gabelle*, the salt tax). The Spanish crown had a special relationship with the *mesta* (the sheep-herders' guild). The weaker German states exploited internal tolls, with a consequent proliferation of internal customs barriers.

Direct taxation formed a substantial and well-established part of fourteenth-century revenue, as table 3.2 reveals. If we add it to the indirect customs taxes, we see that over half of the English crown's revenue was now derived from taxation. Almost invariably taxes were voted for military purposes, though we must note that military considerations had widened into the aggressives economic theory just mentioned.

So we see two trends: the escalation of total revenue and the growing role of taxation, both precipitated by the more costly nature of warfare. Note that table 3.1 reveals the jump in revenue at the beginning of the Hundred Years War to be a real one. Once again the size of armies and their size relative to the population was increasing (Sorokin, 1962, pp. 340–1). More importantly, the character of warfare underwent great changes. The knights of four major powers – Austria, Burgundy, the Count of Flanders and England – were defeated by the largely infantry armies of the Swiss, Flemish and Scots in a series of battles between 1302 and 1315. This was followed by the massacre of Crecy in 1346 in which more than 1500 French knights were killed by English (i.e., Welsh) bowmen. These unexpected reverses did not lead to massive changes in the international balance of power because the major powers were swift to react. Henceforth their armies combined infantry, bowmen and cavalry in increasingly complex formations. Infantry with a new, independent role on the battlefield needed more drilling than the medieval infantry cast

State and Society, 1130–1815

merely in a supporting role to knights. A state which sought to survive had to participate in this tactical race, which therefore escalated war costs for all concerned.[4]

Expenditure data enable us to gain a more complete picture, though the picture is not easy to interpret. Modern uses of these accounts would have been barely comprehensible to the men who drew them up. They did not distinguish between 'military' and 'civil' functions or between the king's 'private' household expenses and more 'public' ones. At times we are uncertain which 'department' has primary responsibility for expenditure – and remember that the two principal 'departments' were originally the *chamber* in which the king slept and the *wardrobe* where he hung his clothes. Nevertheless surviving thirteenth-century accounts reveal that throughout the century the expenses of the royal household remained in the £5000–£10,000 bracket, while extraordinary, foreign, and military expenses might add figures ranging from £5000 to £100,000 per annum according to the situation of war of peace. 'Inflation' seems to have been confined largely to military costs! More systematic accounts survive from the next century. Some of the most complete are contained in table 3.3.

These three subheadings are the ancestors of those modern categories 'civil', 'military', and 'debt repayment' which will figure throughout my analysis of expenditures. What can explain the great variations in total volume and type of state expenditure? The answer is simple. In 1335–7 Edward III was at war, personally conducting a campaign in the Netherlands for most of the period: for part of the period 1344–7 he was again at war, in France: and in 1347–9 he was at peace in England. Now these figures do not allow us entirely to separate 'military' from 'civil' expenditure. Though the bulk of household expenses are 'peaceful', in the sense that they continue when the king is at peace, nevertheless his household follows him abroad on campaign and is more costly there (as the figures reveal). Similarly, 'foreign and other' expenses are mostly but not entirely warlike – for example, bribes paid to wavering vassals for their allegiance or alms distributed while on campaign are difficult to categorize. Debt repayment, of loans granted for the most part by merchants and bankers, might also seem to straddle the distinction between civil and military, but

---

4 For the military developments of this period, see Finer, 1975, Howard, 1976, pp. 1–19; Verbruggen, 1977.

Table 3.3 Annual averages of expenditure accounts in periods 1335–7, 1344–7 and 1347–9 (current prices)

	1335–7 (£)	(%)	1344–7 (£)	(%)	1347–9 (£)	(%)
Household expenses	12,952	6	12,415	18	10,485	40
Foreign and other expenses	147,053	66	50,634	76	14,405	55
Prests (debt repayment)	63,789	28	3,760	6	1,151	5
Total	223,794	100	66,809	100	26,041	100

Expenditure figures for the period 1224–1399 derived from Tout (6 vols, 1920–33), supplemented by other sources quoted later. As yet the annual figures are not sufficiently reliable to test systematically for the impact of war and peace, as I can do later for the post-1688 figures.

actually these loans were invariably incurred to pay for extraordinary military expenses. Finally, if we wish to estimate the total financial 'size' of the state in this period we should actually add the *profits* of state activities, notably the judiciary, to expenditure.[5] These would add around £5000 to £10,000 to the cost of 'civil' functions. When due allowance is made for these difficulties, we can estimate that, as in the previous century, the civil activities of the state remained fairly stable in volume, still not greatly exceeding the leading baronial households, while its total outlay was enormously inflated by the onset of war. In peace-time the state's 'civil' activities might comprise between one-half and two-thirds of all finances, but in war they normally shrank to around 30 per cent and they could go as low as 10 per cent.[6] If we add the

[5] Financial totals also understate the 'size' of the state's activities by ignoring labour services, of which the most obvious was military service. However, they were also required by various states for peaceful purposes – the building of roads, fortresses, bridges and canals. We have no knowledge of the real extent of these practices. Payment in kind was also frequent, especially before 1150 when the unfavourable balance of trade with the East perpetuated a shortage of coinage in Europe. Indeed in the Duchy of Burgundy, significant payments in kind did not end until the fourteenth century (probably a century later than in England). Nevertheless, both labour services and payment in kind were both in general decline from the mid-twelfth century as coinage circulated more widely.

[6] The highest proportion of expenses accounted for by the king's household and domestic departments during this period appears to be two-thirds, in 1362–4 and the lowest is around 10 per cent during Edward I's campaigns in Gascony in 1288–90 and from 1294 (Tout, 1920, pp. 76–83, 115–19; Tout and Broome, 1924, pp. 404–19; Harris, 1975, pp. 145–9, 197–227, 327–40, 344–5, 470–503).

fact that perhaps half those peaceful activities were essentially 'private', concerning the king's own household, we can see that the functions of the state *for society* were largely military in nature. If a king waged war frequently, his functions became *overwhelmingly* military. Thus at the beginning of the next century, Henry V, who was more or less continuously at war, during the decade 1413–22 spent about two-thirds of his English revenues plus all his French revenues on warfare (Ramsay, 1920, I, P. 317). Fairly clear answers are thus emerging from this analysis of the finances of the medieval state: that it was predominantly fulfilling external *military* functions and that the growth in the financial size of the state at both current and constant prices was a product of the growing costs of warfare.

Even so these functions would hardly loom large in the life of the English population as a whole. In the Hundred Years War the largest army – and it was exceptional – accounted for about 1 per cent of the population of England and Wales. As McFarlane concludes (1962, p. 5), this would occasion no dislocation in the labour market. The impact of war was highly uneven, affecting lords, merchants and their households disproportionately (unless the war was being fought over one's land, of course, which it was for many of the French). And the peace-time state, far smaller in volume, could not have had much salience for the mass of the population. After all, the revenue at constant prices, in table 3.1, reveals that the 'real' increase in the financial size of the state, from the twelfth to the fourteenth century, is only a doubling from a rather small base. The most salient aspect of the state to the people of England was probably still the person of the king, accompanied in his perambulations by the pageantry of his household. And what proportion of the population would even see the monarch during its lifetime?

Table 3.3 also reveals the beginnings of a trend that was subsequently to play a major 'smoothing' role in state finances – debt repayment. From the fourteenth to the twentieth centuries, states that have borrowed heavily to finance wars have seen a consequent reduction in the fluctuations of their expenditure, for debts were normally repaid over a number of years extending beyond the duration of the war. Thus peace-time expenditure seems not to return to pre-war levels. The state is increasing, albeit slowly, its 'real' bulk. In contrast to previous reigns, both receipts and expenses in the reigns of Edward III and Richard II (1327–99) fluctuated less (except for a trebling in 1368–9). The sheer cost of war meant that the repayment of debts could hardly be financed out of the monarch's private or hereditary revenue. Taxation in peace-time was the almost-inevitable consequence. Furthermore all these fiscal methods increased the machinery of finance itself. The costs of collection became an important and a near permanent item. As much as possible the English crown minimized the political costs of taxation by deciding the rate of assessment through *ad hoc* consultation with the taxpayers themselves, and indeed in an age where wealth was impossible to determine no other system was ultimately practicable. But in a relatively centralized system, such as that of fifteenth-century France, the costs of collection could add up to 25 per cent or more of all revenue (Wolfe, 1972, p. 248). Thus did military costs spill over into a greater 'civil' administration.

Revenue and expenditure: Henry VII to James II (1485–1688)

Passing over the disruptions – to the country and to the records – of the Wars of the Roses, we arrive at the Tudor and Stuart period. Table 3.1 revealed that Henry VII more or less restored the level of state finances, at both current and constant prices, to that enjoyed by Henry V. Then the figures up to the Civil War show two trends: an enormous price inflation which rockets actual state finances, and a levelling-off in revenue level if we control for inflation. The latter trend is quite surprising, for most historians see a great development of the state occurring under Tudor rule. Even if we add an extra third to expenditure during Elizabeth's reign (as suggested by Professor Elton), the overall trend would be unchanged. Elizabeth would then have raised revenue only a quarter higher than Henry VII's level, an increase dwarfed by the post-1660 rise. The 'real' growth in state finances did not occur until after the Restoration in 1660, when – for the first time – revenue at constant prices rises (indeed doubles) over the late medieval level. Let us examine these trends in more detail.

Though some of the details of Henry VII's finances are obscure or controversial, the overall contours are discernible. Bothered by neither inflation nor long-lasting wars, he had the means to balance his books and even to accumulate a surplus. His revenue came in roughly equal proportions from three main sources: the rents from crown lands, customs duties and parliamentary taxation. Despite his financial reorganizations, his state – in overall size and main functions – was essentially medieval. Paying the expenses of his household, buying the political advice of a few counsellors, administering supreme justice, regulating trade across territorial boundaries, issuing a coinage, and waging occasional wars with the help of his loyal barons – that was the sum of state functions, almost certainly involving less than 1 per cent of national wealth, and being marginal to the lives of most of its subjects.

In the course of the next two centuries this state was significantly changed by three forces, two of which were traditional and one relatively novel. Both escalation in the costs of warfare and inflation we have repeatedly encountered: an increase in the role of the state as the *coordinator* of civil society, though already hinted at, was not yet generally felt. I will discuss all three in turn.

The first change was entirely predictable on medieval experience: the consequences of the accession of a more warlike king, Henry VIII. We don't know the exact details of his finances, but table 3.4 is clear enough. It contains Treasury cash expenditure totals during the first years of Henry VIII's reign. At this time the Treasury was the main, though not the sole, disbursing agency, so the figures are indicative of nearly all expenditure. These figures take no account of the tally system, of course. I am using them only to demonstrate the general impact of war.

Look at the fourfold increase in 1512, the year he began his French wars, and the almost threefold increase the following year, as the campaign intensified. And note that the increases are *entirely* due to military expenses. Exactly as in the three previous centuries, it is still war that makes the state substantial. Such jumps at the onset of war reach right up to our own times. But the height leaped now begins to diminish. Henry's French Wars have increased expenditure tenfold in the two years 1511 to 1513. His French and Scottish Wars of 1542–6 increase expenditure around fourfold, if Dietz's figures (1918, p. 74; 1964, I, pp. 137–58) can be relied on. Fourfold increases seem to be the norm through the next century, though after 1688 – as we shall see – they diminish

Table 3.4 Cash expenditure of the English Treasury, 1511–20

Year	Total expenses (£)	Military expenses (£)	Aid to foreign allies (£)
1511	64,157	1509	—
1512	269,564	181,468	(32,000 gold florins)
1513	699,714	632,322[a]	14,000
1514	155,757	92,000	—
1515	74,006	10,000	—
1516	106,429	16,538	38,500
1517	72,359	60	13,333
1518	50,614	200	—
1519	52,428	—	—
1520	86,020	—	—

Source: Dietz, 1964a, pp. 90–1
[a] Plus 10,040 crowns

still further. It is not that the state changed its spots and waged war more moderately; it is rather that *peace-time* military expenditure has risen. Actually table 3.4 concealed that this was already being prepared in Henry VIII's early wars. Its figures are an incomplete guide to total military expenditure, for at least one item of military expenditure was paid out of a separate account – the upkeep of the garrison at Tournai in France cost £40,000 a year between 1514 and 1518 (when it was surrendered). Now, throughout most years of the sixteenth century, garrison expenditure at Berwick, Calais, Tournai and in Ireland, absorbed sums almost as great as the whole of the rest of the expenditure in *peacetime* put together. The 'permanent war state' was arriving.

Garrison costs were, in fact, the tip of an iceberg of changes in military organization occurring roughly in the period 1540–1660. To these changes many historians, following Roberts (1967), have given the label 'The Military Revolution'. Firearms were naturally at the core of the revolution. Their introduction in Europe in the late fifteenth century was slow, and they made little initial impact on armies' tactics. To the 'battles' or 'battalions' of pikemen which had dominated since the early fourteenth century, handguns were merely added. Larger artillery guns had a greater effect, especially on naval warfare, for they involved investment on a scale that was

State and Society, 1130–1815

out of reach of the provincial nobility. Only the king could afford artillery, and so he could batter down the castles of the feudal nobility. Actually, the centralizing consequence of the gun seems worldwide — its introduction in Europe, Japan, and various parts of Africa has enhanced central state power (Brown, 1948; Kiernan, 1957, p. 74; Stone, 1965, pp. 199–223; Goody, 1971, pp. 47–56; Bean, 1973; Law, 1976, pp. 112–32). But, paradoxically, in Europe the gun led eventually to the triumph of a new type of defensive land warfare, the bastion or *trace italienne*, elaborate star-shaped low fortifications behind which musketeers could mow down besiegers, even before they reached the main castle walls. Reducing such bastions with heavy artillery or starvation took longer, prolonged campaigns, and cost more. Added to this were the mobile tactical innovations of generals like Maurice of Nassau and Gustavus Adolphus who realized that the reintroduction of battle *lines*, made obsolete in the fourteenth century by the Swiss and Flemish, could improve the fire-power of infantry armed with muskets. But lines needed far more drilling than battalions. Professionals were needed more than ever. Thus guns increased the centralization of military organizations and ensured the dominance of mercenaries. Additionally, the size of armies relative to the population increased again in the sixteenth century, by at least 50 per cent (Sorokin, 1962, pp. 340–1; Parker, 1972, pp. 5–6 argues that army size went up tenfold in the century in some instances; cf. also Bean, 1973). To this we must add a considerable naval presence for the more westerly powers from the mid-sixteenth century. At first specialized warships were rare, but even converted merchantmen and merchant seamen required refitting and retraining, while the conversion process required considerable planning. Cannonry used in naval warfare eventually led to considerable investment in men-o-war. All these changes led to a greater role for *supplies*, and therefore for centralized, orderly administration and capital accounting. The first appearance of 'capitalistic' methods in Elizabeth's navy and Wallenstein's army has often been commented upon. These forces not only increased the costs of warfare, they ensured their permanence. War *or* peace, military costs were now considerable.

In one paragraph I have compressed a period of military history which covers, let us say, the two hundred years from the first regular, paid artillery company formed by Charles VII of France in

1444 to the deaths of Maurice of Nassau and Wallenstein in 1625 and 1634, respectively. It is therefore necessary to emphasize that military developments constituted a 'revolution' not because of their suddenness but because of their prolonged, cumulative effect. The technology of guns, the tactics and strategy, and the forms of military and state organization evolved over the whole of this period. Only right at the end was the transformation completed, perhaps symbolically at the deaths of those two great entrepreneurs of death. Now, as Otto Hintz expresses it, 'The colonels ceased being private military entrepreneurs, and became servants of the state' (1975, p. 200). The monarchs of Europe moved gradually, if unevenly, toward total control of the war machine, with Spain and Sweden in the van, England and Austria bringing up the rear. The changing pattern of the sixteenth century is documented for Spain by Parker (1974, pp. 560–582), who concludes that the severe sixteenth-century increase in state expenditure in Europe as a whole was due mainly to escalating military costs and to the evolution of more permanent debt repayment systems (cf also Ladero Quesada, 1970; Parker, 1970).

England brought up the rear because the costs of its main armed force, the navy, did not really escalate until well into the seventeenth century. At first converted merchantmen were adequate for most naval purposes, and in the Elizabethan period England's naval activities were largely handled by privateers, that is by private enterprise. Only when England and Holland, began to supplant parasitic private activity with their independent empire-building activities and encountered each other's naval power, did their states really take off. The three Anglo-Dutch naval wars date this precisely to the 1650s, 1660s and 1670s. From the mid 1660s for the next 200 years, the navy was the largest single item in English state expenditure, except in those few years when either land forces or the repayment of war loans overtook it in cost. By comparing Dietz's figures for the reigns of Elizabeth and the first two Stuarts with Chandaman's for the reigns of Charles II and James II, we can easily see a change. In the former period combined military expenses can descend to around 40 per cent of all expenses in years of peace, but in the latter they never fall below 50 per cent and are in addition bolstered by a heavier debt repayment burden (Dietz, 1923, pp. 91–104; Dietz, 1928, pp. 158–1; Chandaman, 1975, pp. 348–6). The permanent war state arrived in England in two stages. Though the Tudor garrisons were its first harbingers, Repys' navy constituted its main thrust.

This idea is reinforced if we look at the second traditional disrupter of the state, inflation. It can be seen from table 3.1 that only after 1660 does the state's financial size increase substantially in real terms (in fact the jump probably occurred during the undocumented period of the Commonwealth in the 1650s). This is largely a growth in military and debt-repayment expenditures. Yet, of course, inflation is worthy of study in its own right. Tudor inflation had an innovating impact on the state, as it had done traditionally. Now the effect was heightened by the sheer extent of the price rise. In England prices rose sixfold in the 100 years following 1520 and this was probably close to the Europeanwide figure. It was then historically unprecedented for European states (though our own century looks likely to exceed it). Real wealth was, of course, expanding throughout the period, so that higher prices could, in general, be borne. But inflation would tend to affect adversely some sources of crown revenue, especially rents from lands, while most types of revenue would have to be increased, either by negotiation or arbitrarily. Pressured by inflation and the growing current costs of war, the governments of Henry VIII, Edward VI and Mary resorted to all kinds of non-repeatable manoeuvres – expropriation of the Church, debasement of the coinage, the selling of crown lands, wholesale borrowing. Additionally, under Henry VIII one important and permanent development occurred: peace-time taxation. From around 1530 it cannot be assumed that taxation was occasioned by the onset of war (Elton, 1975) though the grants of taxation were still almost entirely devoted to remedying inflation and bearing military costs. Nevertheless, some authorities believe that these years mark an important shift. Schofield, for example, notes that in 1534 the preamble to the parliamentary grant of taxation contains for the first time a reference to the necessity of maintaining the general civil benefits of the king's government. This appears to refer largely to pacification needs in Ireland and to fortifications and harbour works. Schofield none the less considers it 'revolutionary', because rather general references to the king's 'greatness and beneficence' now begins to dot parliamentary language (1963, pp. 24–30). So what about the 'civil functions' of the Tudor and

Stuart state? Were they widening? This will raise the third innovator, the increase in the coordinating role of the state.

If we look merely at financial size, an increase in 'civil' functions is not really discernible in the sixteenth century. The rise in household expenses between Henry VII and Elizabeth's last years is about fivefold, according to Dietz (1932), and this is just about the same as the rise in prices through the period. No other non-military expenses appear to rise further. Yet with James I a change occurs, for his civil expenses apparently rose to about 25 per cent above Elizabeth's level, at a time of price *de*flation. If we examine the detailed figures given in Dietz's earlier (1928) study, we find three apparent contributing factors. First, unlike Elizabeth, James was married and had children; therefore his household costs were correspondingly greater. Second, he was undoubtedly extravagant, as his opponents claimed: £15,593 on Queen Anne's child-bed showed amazing prodigality! But the problem with 'extravagance' is that it merged into a third type of expense, which was becoming increasingly integral to all states of the period, the rewarding of noble officeholders. The fees and grants used by James to buy the loyalty and service of his magnates partly stemmed from his own insecurity as a foreigner on the throne. But they could hardly be stemmed by subsequent monarchs, and they became increasingly common throughout Europe even under supposedly stronger kings than James. (Before James, they were in evidence during the reign of the boy-king Edward VI under whom the spoils system had also developed.) The cost of this was not extraordinary, being still dwarfed by other forms of expenditure. But its significance is rather greater than its cost, for it seems to herald an extension in state functions.

Let us first view the 'spoils system' from the recipients' point of view, that is from the perspective of the nobility and gentry. The whole issue of whether the nobility, gentry, or factions of the one or other were 'rising' or 'declining' in the period, and whether they were dependent on office-holding for this wealth, is too controversial and unsettled to be commented on. But one point is clear: as *individual households*, the great families of the time were far less great than their predecessors had been. Several historians have attempted to calculate the revenues of late Tudor and early Stuart noble families (Finch, 1956; Batho, 1957; Stone, 1973). Their figures differ widely, but all of them are tiny in relation to crown revenues. This had not been so in the medieval period, though we have little evidence as to the timing of the change. The 'magnates' were now great *as a class* rather than as a handful of individual families and their households.

It follows, of course, that the medieval conciliar form of government – the king in his council of about 20 great men – was no longer appropriate as a means of consultation. A coordinated office structure and representative assemblies were both more appropriate methods – and these were the 'absolutist' and 'constitutional' paths of the period, to be discussed later. It also follows that the great men cannot be involved in the traditional *personal* lord–vassal relationship. To impress a much larger number of men with his power and worth, the monarch now becomes more *public*, displaying his quality with ostentatious pomp and pageantry. At its extreme this became bizarre, as we can see from Poggi's description of Louis XIV:

> The king of France was thoroughly, without residue, a 'public' personage. His mother gave birth to him in public, and from that moment his existence, down to its most trivial moments, was acted out before the eyes of attendants who were holders of dignified offices. He ate in public, went to bed in public, woke up and was clothed and groomed in public, urinated and defecated in public. He did not much bathe in public; but then neither did he do so in private. I know of no evidence that he copulated in public; but he came near enough, considering the circumstances under which he was expected to deflower his august bridge. When he died (in public), his body was promptly and messily chopped up in public, and its severed parts ceremoniously handed out to the more exalted among the personages who had been attending him throughout his mortal existence. (1978, pp. 68–9)

Perhaps now we can appreciate what a court was actually like.

The great men as a class were equally useful to the state. Though their autonomous military resources were now less necessary, the monarch required part of their wealth. They were also in control of local administration and justice in most countries, and thus controlled the wealth of their neighbours. Their powers of passive resistance against the state, especially against the tax collector, were still considerable, and no monarch could govern without them. Therefore, they were drawn increasingly into central state offices, both military and civil. Not the household but the *court* was now the focus of activity, and *offices* the focus of hopes. The number of offices increased, though in different ways in different countries. Everywhere, the favour of the monarch, the 'extravagance' of James I, 'the spoils system', increased in scope and quantity, now *centralizing* the historic social solidarity of the monarch with the landed nobility and, therefore, also centralizing their conflicts. It is at the beginning of this process, in the sixteenth century, that centralizing tendencies begin once again to make state finances an incomplete guide to the activities of the state. Neither the financial benefits nor the costs of the spoils system were enormous, yet the *coordinating* role of the monarch had grown very considerably. The political implications were great, inaugurating a set of conflicts between 'court' and 'country' parties, which was an important step in the development of symmetrical, state-transforming class struggle, forcing the nobility, and reinforcing the merchants, towards a state-bounded role.

The sphere of social legislation is a good example of these trends. The English state had long accepted responsibility, like most states of Europe, for ultimate control of wages, prices and mobility in crisis conditions. Edward III's Statute of Labourers of 1348 is an example of a state's response to crisis, that of post-Black Death labour shortages. Under the Tudors and Stuarts the legislative scope widened. A secular trend of economic and population expansion produced turbulent and visible social effects. Outstanding among these were the forcible enclosures that caused so much Parliamentary discussion, and a threefold and destabilizing growth in the population of London between 1558 and 1625. Fear of public disorder and charitable sentiments combined to develop the Elizabethan Poor Law. Formally, the scope of the new laws was vast. Local taxes would pay for a dual system that provided money and work materials to those who wanted to work and punishment and correction for the idlers. Local JPs would administer the system under the overall control of the Privy Council. The Poor Law itself was not even seen as the main thrust of the legislation, but rather as a 'back-up' to a wide range of statues which sought to regulate wages and conditions of employment, control labour mobility and provide food to the poor in times of famine. This apparently represents a significant widening of the functions of the state: no longer merely a war machine and law-court of last resort, but an active controller of class relations.

Nevertheless the reality was a good deal less revolutionary than this. We don't know exactly how the Poor Law was enforced, but it was uneven and under local control. The JPs were, of course, the local gentry. The taxes levied were small, almost certainly much less than the amount of private charity given for similar purposes (except during the Interregnum), which probably exceeded the total expenditure of the Tudor state on civil functions, if we exclude household and court expenses. Tudor *claims* were all encompassing – positively to enforce the welfare and the morality of their citizens and to expand industry and trade. But, apart from the particularities of Henry VIII's break with Rome, they were not carried into practice. And the reason was finance: inflation, warfare and the private needs of the household and court dominated expenditure. 'Virtually nothing was spent by the state toward the realization of the social ends envisaged by the contemporary publicists', concludes Dietz (1932, p. 125). Nevertheless, the change in state ideology is interesting. The language of the legislation is a good index of the change. As all the legislation of the period was filled with charitable exhortation, it appears that the state was less expressing a sense of *its own* duties (as the modern welfare state does in its legislation) than of giving voice to the common sentiments of the dominant classes, previously voiced by the church. The administrative apparatus appears merely as an offered technical aid to local charity and control of the poor. That aid was not usually needed. The social legislation was an example not of greater state powers *over* society but of greater collective organization, greater *nationalization*, of the dominant groups in society.

So far, then, the significance of the development of the state in the sixteenth and early seventeenth century seems to lie less in its overall bulk than in its growing role of coordination. It was still tiny in size. Indeed, as a proportion of national wealth at a time of general economic expansion, its revenue and expenses must have been declining rather substantially, though we have no reliable figures on national income until much later.[7] It is worth remarking here the apparent painlessness of tax extraction in Tudor England.

7 Bean (1932, p. 212) confidently asserts that less than 1 per cent of national income was spent on warfare by states in the medieval period, over 2 per cent in the sixteenth century, and 6 to 12 per cent in the seventeenth century. This is pure guesswork, but assuredly wrong. For it to be true, national income would have to be in decline in the sixteenth and seventeenth centuries, an impossible assumption.

The sums extracted were lump sums, assessed on local communities' net wealth by themselves and collected over a very short period of time. Schofield has also demonstrated that the sums granted by Parliament were invariably forthcoming. The contemporary state could not maintain its level of tax extraction in this way – I could not produce one-third of my income at such short notice! The sums required by the Tudor state must have been a far lower proportion of personal and national resources. In terms of its resource-requiring functions, the Tudor and early Stuart state was late medieval – to its main, traditional activity of making war it had merely added a more regular administrative and fiscal machinery which, none the less, still served military ends. Even when the state begins to grow formidably in size, under the Commonwealth and then the later Stuarts, it is still almost entirely along these tracks hallowed by the centuries. If we wish to talk of a 'Tudor Revolution in Government' (to quote the title of G. R. Elton's classic work) then we are describing a social and administrative reorganization of existing resources, a *condensing* of social relationships at the level of the state.

State expenditure and warfare: 1688–1815

So far the analysis of state finances has had to depend on figures that undoubtedly contain errors. Though I have tried to allow for inconsistency and inaccuracy wherever these become evident, it is impossible to arrive at totally reliable estimates of state income or expenditure before 1688. But the data brighten up considerably after 1688. From that year we have a published, reliable and unbroken annual set of accounts for the central government of Great Britain, neatly collected and standardized by Mitchell and Deane (1962) and Mitchell and Jones (1971). Though the figures contain discrepancies and classification changes, they are nevertheless substantially accurate and comparable. Conveniently, the 1690s also mark the beginning of a 'long century' (until 1815) of a fairly regular succession of periods of peace and major war in Europe. Utilizing expenditure data for this period we can systematically test the hypotheses already suggested for earlier periods. The chronology is straightforward. After William III's initial Irish campaigns and naval battles, peace lasted from 1697 until 1702. During this period, in 1694, the foundation of the Bank of England placed English borrowing and debt repayment on a regular basis, which has lasted until the present day. Then the War of the Spanish Succession, involving repeated campaigns by the Duke of Marlborough, lasted from 1702 until 1713, followed by a largely peaceful period until 1739. Then began 'the War of Jenkins' Ear', which soon became 'the War of the Austrian Succession' and lasted until 1748. A period of uneasy peace was ended by the Seven Years War, 1756–63. Then peace until the American War of Independence merged into prolonged naval wars between 1776 and 1783. Then peace again until 1792 when the French Revolutionary Wars and Napoleonic Wars lasted more or less continuously until 1815, though with a short-lived lull at the beginning of the century, sealed by the Peace of Amiens in 1801. This is a much more regular sequence of war and peace than in the nineteenth or twentieth centuries, and, as it also predates the influence of industrialization on state expenditure, it gives us a convenient test for the pre-industrial period.

I have presented the main results in graph form in figure 3.1, separating total expenditure and its three components, military, civil and debt-repayment expenses. The graph is of 'real' expenditure, i.e., controlled for inflation by using once again the price index of Phelps-Brown and Hopkins (1956). I have controlled for prices at their 1690–9 level, the beginning of the period. Thus these figures are not comparable with those of table 3.1, which presented current prices and constant prices at the level of 1451–75. When assessing the price level in each of the subsequent specified years, we must overcome one problem, however. Annual expenditure figures are now a reliable guide to the expenditure actually incurred in that year (unlike previous centuries). But the price level relevant to that year is not only the prices of the year itself, but also of previous years in which the state began to draw up its provisional estimates. Accordingly, I have estimated the price index at the average of the expenditure year *and* the two previous years. This will also have the effect of smoothing the effects of a single unreliable price figure. It will be recalled that previously the price index has been averaged over whole decades. The expenditures at current prices, together with the price index itself, are given in table 3.5, which follows the graph. I must confess that I have controlled for inflation in this graph, not only

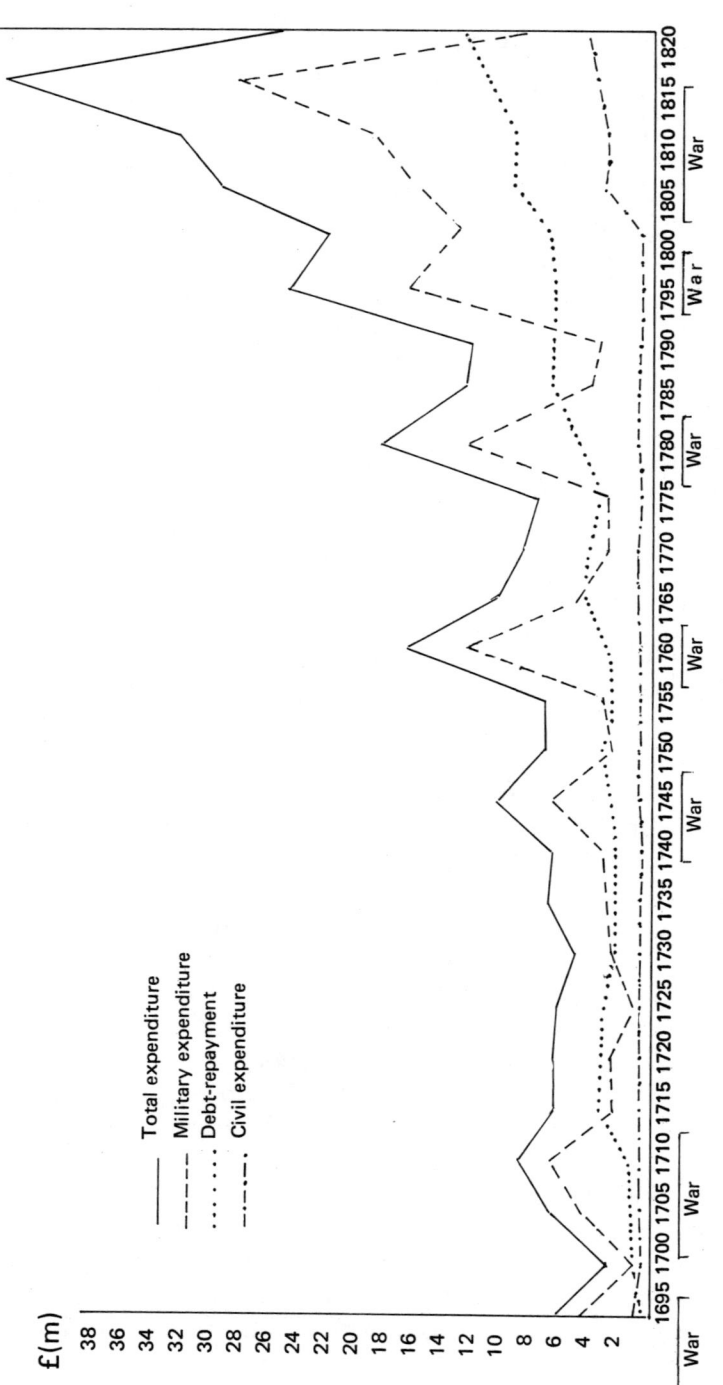

Figure 3.1 British state expenditure 1695–1820 (at constant prices: 1690–9 = 100)

Table 3.5 State expenditure, 1695–1820, Great Britain (£m): current and constant (1690–9) prices

Year	Price index	Military expenditure		Debt-repayment		Civil expenditure		Total expenditure	
		Current	Constant	Current	Constant	Current	Constant	Current	Constant
1695	102	4.9	4.8	0.6	0.6	0.8	0.8	6.2	6.1
1700	114	1.3	1.1	1.3	1.1	0.7	0.6	3.2	2.8
1705	87	4.1	4.7	1.0	1.2	0.7	0.8	5.9	6.8
1710	106	7.2	6.8	1.8	1.7	0.9	0.8	9.8	9.2
1715	97	2.2	2.3	3.3	3.4	0.7	0.8	6.2	6.4
1720	94	2.3	2.4	2.8	3.0	1.0	1.0	6.0	6.4
1725	89	1.5	1.7	2.8	3.1	1.3	1.5	5.5	6.2
1730	99	2.4	2.4	2.3	2.3	0.9	0.9	5.6	5.6
1735	82	2.7	3.3	2.2	2.7	0.9	1.1	5.9	7.1
1740	90	3.2	3.6	2.1	2.3	0.8	0.9	6.2	6.8
1745	84	5.8	6.9	2.3	2.7	0.8	1.0	8.9	10.6
1750	93	3.0	3.2	3.2	3.5	1.0	1.1	7.2	7.7
1755	92	3.4	3.7	2.7	2.9	1.0	1.1	7.1	7.7
1760	105	13.5	12.8	3.4	3.2	1.2	1.1	18.0	17.1
1965	109	6.1	5.6	4.8	4.4	1.1	1.0	12.0	11.0
1770[a]	114	3.9	3.4	4.8	4.2	1.2	1.1	10.5	9.2
1775	130	3.9	3.0	4.7	3.6	1.2	0.9	10.4	8.0
1780	119	14.9	12.5	6.0	5.0	1.3	1.1	22.6	19.0
1786[b]	131	5.5	4.2	9.5	7.2	1.5	1.2	17.0	13.0
1790	134	5.2	3.9	9.4	7.0	1.7	1.3	16.8	12.5
1795	153	26.3	17.2	10.5	6.8	1.8	1.2	39.0	25.5
1801[c]	230	31.7	13.8	16.8	7.3	2.1	0.9	51.0	22.2
1805	211	34.1	16.2	20.7	9.8	7.8	3.7	62.8	30.0
1810	245	48.3	19.7	24.2	9.9	8.8	3.6	81.5	33.3
1815	257	72.4	28.2	30.0	11.7	10.4	4.0	112.9	44.0
1820	225	16.7	7.4	31.1	13.8	9.8	4.4	57.5	25.6

[a] Between 1770 and 1801 the detailed items fall short of the total given by about £500,000. No reason for this is given in the source.
[b] 1785 figures follow an idiosyncratic budgeting system.
[c] 1800 figures are incomplete.

because it seems more meaningful to do so, but also because otherwise the graph would look rather unbalanced. The inflation of the Napoleonic War years causes actual money expenditures to rocket, making all previous variations difficult to perceive on a graph. Mitchell and Deane provide figures for every year; I have selected those for every fifth year.

The graph offers clear support to several of the arguments made concerning earlier historical periods. Note first the upward trend in the financial size of the British state: between 1700 and 1815 real expenditure rises fifteenfold (and the increase at current prices is thirty-fivefold!). This is easily the fastest rate of increase we have seen for any century. And we can guess that state expenditure has also increased as a proportion of gross national income. In 1688, using Deane and Cole's (1962) calculations based on Gregory King's famous contemporary account of national wealth, we can estimate state expenditure as comprising about 8 per cent of gross national income (but see Deane, 1955, for details of the method of calculation; by 1811 it had risen to 27 per cent. These figures are not very reliable, but the magnitude of difference is none the less impressive.

But the upward trend in the graph is not steady. The total is rocketed up suddenly six times, and – it will come as no surprise by now – all but one of these is at the beginning of a war, and all six are due primarily to a large rise in military expenditure. Furthermore debt-repayment, used exclusively to finance military needs, rises towards the end of each war and is maintained in the first years of peace. The patterning is beautifully regular: shortly after the end of all six wars, the rising debt-repayment line crosses the military line coming down, exceeding it by an increasing margin each time. This has the effect of flattening the impact of war. Looked at year by year, the biggest increase in total expenditure at current prices over the previous year was only just over 50 per cent (in both 1710–11 and 1793–4), which is much lower than the 200–1,000 per cent increases we saw prevalent at the onset of wars right up to the early years of Henry VIII. And in peace-time it is now largely military expenditure (and especially the navy) and debt-repayment which keep up the relative level. A 'permanent war state' has arrived with a vengeance, and civil expenses are remarkably steady and small. They do not rise above 23 per cent (occurring in 1725 after a decade of peace) in any year over the entire period. During the Napoleonic Wars there appears a slightly new trend, however. The civil expenses, having remained static over the previous century, begin to rise after about 1805. The industrial revolution is about to begin to change the nature of the state. The permanent war state also means that after each war state expenditures do not fall back to the pre-war level, even in real terms. In mid-century the poet Cowper expressed this in a simple couplet:

War lays a burden on the reeling state.
And peace does nothing to relieve the weight.

These figures confirm every hypothesis made for previous centuries on the basis of sketchier data. State finances are dominated by foreign wars. As warfare developed more professional and permanent forces, so the state grew both in overall size and (probably) in terms of size in relation to its civil society. Each new war led to a larger state in two stages: an initial impact on military expenses and a delayed impact upon debt-repayment. As yet the functions of this state – a 'constitutional' state, let it be remembered – are overwhelmingly military. Other functions are largely 'spin-off' from its wars.[8]

I have not the space here to discuss other states of the period. Systematic, time-series data are available only for two other countries, Austria and the United States, and only from the 1790s. They confirm the British figures over this period in almost every respect. Sketchy data from various scattered years in the seventeenth and eighteenth centuries exist for Prussia, and stray annual figures can be found for France, the Netherlands, Russia and Spain. None deviates significantly from the British pattern.

No doubt each side had its peculiarities, but the overall pattern is clear. A state that wished to survive had to increase its extractive capacity to pay for professional armies and/or navies. Those that did not would be crushed on the battlefield and absorbed into others – the fate of Poland, of Saxony, of Bavaria in this and the next century. No European states were continuously at peace. It is impossible to escape the conclusion that a peaceful state would have ceased to exist even more speedily than the militarily inefficient actually did.

One aspect of the militarization of the state needs further comment. So far I have treated its military functions as being synonymous with its *external* functions. But – it might be objected – is not its force used for domestic repression, and is it not then integrally linked to internal class relations? Obviously there is some force in this objection. In every European country the army was used periodically for internal repression. Standing armies were seen everywhere as an instrument of both naked class exploitation and of despotism. The employment of military force for internal repression is characteristic of every state in every period of history

---

8 One exception exists to this. By the end of the eighteenth century, the Poor Law financed locally (and not appearing in these figures) but arguably a 'function of the state', was costing quite large sums, though the sums are still tiny in relation to military expenditure. If we add its costs to civil expenditure their combined total does not exceed 20 per cent of the new grand total. If we further add all local government expenses (available from 1803), the total is still below 25 per cent until 1820.

— it is part of the very *definition* of the state. But internal repression cannot be the causally determining factor in the growth of state finances. In the first place, as I have repeatedly shown, the growth of the state's size is occasioned throughout the whole period by warfare between states and only marginally by internal developments. Second, the growth of the necessity for internal repression organized by the state (rather than by local lords) is usually occasioned in the first place by the state's need to raise money for warfare. Third, variations between different countries in the degree of internal repression can be explained in relation to war finance needs. Perry Anderson notes the importance of this in Eastern Europe (1974, pp. 197–217). If the poorer states of that region were to survive they would have to tax more intensively, which needed a higher level of repression. At the other extreme, a rich trading country like England could maintain great power status without reaching a high level of tax extraction and, therefore, without a standing army. To this we might add the military-strategic consideration – that naval powers have difficulty anyway in using their forces for internal, dry land, repression. The overall argument still stands: that the financial growth of the modern state up to the early nineteenth century is not explained in domestic terms, but in terms of international relations of violence.

Conclusion: three theoretical implications

We can now answer the questions posed at the beginning. From an analysis of state finances, the functions of the state appear overwhelmingly military and overwhelmingly international rather than domestic. For over seven centuries, somewhere between 75 per cent and 90 per cent of its financial resources were almost continuously deployed on the acquisition and use of military force. And though this force might also be used for domestic repression, the chronology of its development has been almost entirely determined by the incidence and character of international war. For several centuries, the state grew only fitfully and in small degrees, though each 'real' growth was the result of war developments. Most of its growth before the seventeenth century was actually due to inflation, disappearing when we examined finances at constant prices. But in the seventeenth and eighteenth centuries, the state's real financial size grew rapidly. Before then it was tiny in relation to the resources of the economy and marginal in relation to the life experience of most of its inhabitants. By 1815 – a year of major war, of course – it loomed large over civil society. The 'modern state' had arrived, the product of the developments often called the 'military revolution' – artillery-induced professional, permanent armies and navies. Even as late as 1815 its civil functions were negligible in financial terms.

This is not to argue for a 'military determinism'. The character of military technology is largely determined by that of the mode of production, and became more so during this period as industrialization became a prerequisite of military strength. The purposes of warfare also became more clearly economic, as the expansion of the European economy became more entwined with the military conquest and retention of land and markets. I have, of course, fed in the European economic expansion as 'given' in my argument, though it greatly influences the development of the state. Rather I am seeking to integrate military and economic factors in a theoretically determinate way. I can only here point out certain directions for this integration, concentrating on three implications of the empirical findings outlined above. These concern the issues of for whom is the state functional, the absolutist or constitutional form of the state and the national segmentation of capitalism.

For whom is the state functional?

Marxist theory asserts that, ultimately, the state is functional for the owning class in the dominant mode of production. Liberal and functionalist theory assert that it is functional for the whole society. Both rivals share the assumption that the state's main functions are economic. But I have shown this assumption to be false over this historical terrain; and so both assertions are also likely to be false. If external warfare dominates the state, we must ask in whose interests is warfare? And the answer is three main groups who cannot be summed up as either the dominant economic class or the whole society. Obviously the 'war party' was mixed, and it varied from country to country. However, three main groups can be identified.

First, single-son inheritance systems established a continuous demographic pressure through land-hungry younger sons of the nobility, gentry and yeoman groups. Such systems pre-dated both the feudal and capitalist modes of production and cannot be reduced to them. We may add other minor nobles periodically impoverished by changing economic trends. Both were nurtured by the militaristic culture of the noble class in general, a characteristic of feudalism.

The second group was composed of those interested in foreign trade – let us call them merchants, even though they might actually be major barons or clerics engaged in commercial ventures. The medieval autonomy of merchants, to which I referred earlier, carried certain disadvantages. Pacification between states was weaker than that within their core areas, so merchants were vulnerable to being plundered when abroad. Furthermore, the pacification and protection function of the state can be subjected to economies of scale. The circumference and the radius of a space do not increase at the same rate as its total area. The state's pacification function in pre-industrial societies was concentrated on the frontiers (circumference) and main communication routes (radii), and so the costs of protection over an area policed by one state would be much less than those over the same area if policed by several states. Naturally, this is dependent on the large state possessing the technique and resources to pacify such an area. Through the twelfth to fourteenth centuries, the techniques were largely recovered – the church provided literate bureaucrats, coinages were standardized and Roman law or its equivalent was established. Whether the state also possessed the resources in money and manpower depended on its ability to tax. As merchants had an interest in the pacification function, this could be arranged. Thus both military technique and economic expansion favoured the consolidation of larger territorial states and the alliance of king and merchants.

The third warlike interest group was the monarch and his state bureaucracy. From about the fourteenth century, successful international warfare undertaken for either land or trade required state direction. The military aim of the state was truly functional, and so could be exploited for private state ends. The development of permanent fiscal machinery and mercenary armies provided opportunities for the enhancement of monarchical power. Sorting out the power relations within this war party is a complex task, but it is clear that the war party is not simply reducible to dominant economic classes. Furthermore the interest in warfare was not totally confined to these groups.

It is ultimately impossible to decide precisely who benefited from war. Doubtless substantial sections of the peasantry remained largely unaffected by the expansion of trade. However, warfare – *provided* it did not take place over one's own terrain – was not noticeably harmful to any of the civilian population. It was largely fought by professionals and was not costly in terms of social wealth as a whole. *Successful* warfare was obviously to no one's disadvantage in the victorious state (unless very heavily taxed), and (probably) to the benefit of the majority. The people of England were the major gainers, for no wars were fought over their terrain and they generally enjoyed the fruits of victory. For them it is not fanciful to talk of some common benefits of warfare, though the benefits of imperialism were so unequally distributed that mass living standards were not significantly affected until as late as the 1860s. In short, the dominant military aim of the state was functional for an assorted *congerie* of groups, in some respects wider than the dominant economic class(es) and in some senses narrower, but in all real senses far narrower than society as a whole. Marxist, liberal, and functionalist theories alike are thus in need of some revision.

Absolutist and constitutional regimes

The second major implication concerns the political *form* of the state. I have demonstrated that the state was marginal to domestic social life in general but central to international warfare. Therefore it seems probable that the *form* of the state would be more affected by the latter than by the former. I shall in fact argue this with respect to the problem of absolutism.

Absolutism has two principal components.

1 The monarch is the sole human source of law, although, as he is subject to the law of God, some residual right of rebellion exists if he transgresses 'natural law'. But absolutism is characterized by an absence of representative institutions. At the close of the medieval period all European monarchs governed with the concurrence of small, informal, but in some sense representative, assemblies of orders privileged by law – the clergy, the nobility, a

third estate of burghers and sometimes a fourth estate of peasants. This is usually known as the *Ständestaat*, which, if we attempt a literal translation, comes out as 'Estates State' (see Poggi, 1978, pp. 36–59 for a description of this form of state). But in many European countries these were suppressed in the following period. For example, assemblies met for the last time or the next-to-the-last time in Aragon in 1592, in France in 1614, in the Spanish Netherlands 1632, and in Naples in 1642 (Lousse, 1964, pp. 46–7). The regimes that supplanted them are generally termed absolutist until representative assemblies began to re-emerge at the close of the eighteenth century. This criterion fairly clearly demarcates 'constitutional monarchies' ('the king *in* Parliament') like England and Holland from most Continental, 'absolutist' regimes.

2 The monarch governs with the aid of a permanent, professional, *dependent* bureaucracy and army. The officers, civil and military, have no significant autonomous power or social status from that conferred by their office. Traditionally this had not been so, for the king had governed and made war with the aid of magnates who had significant independent resources in land, capital, military power and church institutions. In 1544 the state officials of the Spanish crown's Milan possessions were asked to give a part of their wealth to the crown, as had been traditionally required by their personal oath of loyalty. But they refused, on the grounds that their earnings from office were necessary reward for services rendered, not a gift from the crown. This, according to Chabod (1964, p. 37), is a precise example of the emergence of a new 'bureaucratic' conception of state office, one that is necessary to absolutism. On the military side, a consequence of the change is a 'standing army' that – whatever its necessity for defence of the realm as a whole – can also be used to repress internal dissent and enhance the monarch's power over his civil society. It is with this second criterion that most of the historical problems arise, for this is less effective at distinguishing apparently different types of regime, as we will see in a moment. First, however, the general theories.

Using these two components it is reasonable to distinguish between two different forms of regime in Europe of the fifteenth to eighteenth centuries: on the one hand the 'constitutional' monarchies and republics, principal among which were England and Holland, and on the other hand 'absolute monarchies' like Austria, France, Prussia, Russia, Spain, Sweden and the Kingdom of the Two Sicilies.

The theories of absolutism I will consider relate its rise in the latter set of countries to some determinate state of civil society as a whole, and especially to class relations. There are actually three competing versions: that absolutism is to be explained by the survival of the *feudal* mode of production, that it is associated with the rise of the *capitalist* mode, and that it is a product of *transitional* class structure where neither the one nor the other is dominant. Thus, Anderson (1974, pp. 17–40) argues that the expansion of production and exchange relations meant that feudal serfdom could no longer be politically supported by compartmentalized manorial authority – dependent class relations now require a centralized authority. And the feudal nobility were the main prop of absolutist regimes. Wallerstein (1974) and Lublinskaya (1968) argue that emerging capitalist relations required a 'strong' state in the core areas of Europe to legitimize its social revolution and to protect its foreign expansion. Mousnier (1954) argues that absolutism arose in a transitional period where the monarchy could play off emerging bourgeoisie and traditional nobility the one against the other. Each of these theories has merit, and each is notably better at explaining some states than others (Eastern Europe = late feudalism; Spain = emerging capitalism; France = transitional).

In the light of what we have seen so far of state finances, each of these theories seems rather too *reductionist*, failing to grant to politics sufficient autonomy from class structure. It is not, however, that states had an autonomy because of their *strength* and power. Quite the reverse, for we have seen that they were rather puny structures, marginal to domestic social life in general and perhaps not even essential were it not for international violence. This is surely the point. The economic functions of the state, even the Tudor and Stuart state, were feeble. Dominant classes possessed a sufficient monopoly of force over the as yet cellular and unorganized peasantry to be able to repress them without calling in a central state. Late feudal landlords could surely have enforced dependency themselves. Early capitalists had the added bonus of Roman law and forms of capital accounting and enterprise organization that derived from the tiny city-states and duchies of Italy. Why would capitalism 'require' a powerful territorial state to enforce its form of expropriation? It is perfectly true that the 'absolutist' regimes did increasingly undertake these functions, but so too did the 'constitutional' ones. And as we have already seen, the tendency for magnates to lose some of their economic and military autonomy was general throughout Europe, occurring in the 'constitutional' as well as the 'absolutist' regimes. The conversion of 'magnates' into 'officers' does not necessarily lead to absolutism.

The fact that each of the three views has a different degree of plausibility in different cases is inherently suspicious. If we start from the realization that these states were tiny, we can begin to appreciate the idiosyncrasies of their development. The essence of absolutism is that the monarch acquires a measure of financial autonomy from his more powerful and organized subjects. Yet the sums involved were not particularly large. Actually, if the monarch eschewed foreign wars and could live on his own, he could generate a small surplus, acquire a professional army, repress representative assemblies and then raise more money by arbitrary means (though this had limits). Prussian and Russian absolutism certainly had their origins in the extensive private estates of their rulers. Elizabeth could have dispensed with Parliament were it not for the Irish adventures. Charles I was proceeding exactly along this path when, unfortunately for him, he acquired a *Scottish, Puritan* army which did not prove to be amenable to his particular type of absolutism. Spanish absolutism was founded upon the gold and silver of the New World; French absolutism on the delaying, divisive strategy of the sale of offices. Accidents, especially of foreign policy, and financial expediency could steer one state toward absolutism, another to constitutionalism.

There is one fairly systematic variable at work, however. The association of a profesional army with absolutist regimes is genuine, but perhaps it is more peculiar than has been implied so far. It is really cheating to specify a standing *army*. That effectively excludes England and Holland, of course. But if we included 'standing *navies*', that would let in both these countries, especially in the period when they were thoroughly constitutional, after 1660. Armies can be used for internal repression, navies cannot.

Thus the English Parliament never feared the professional navy the way it feared standing armies. Rather specific military/geographical factors clearly have a lot to do with the development of constitutional and absolutist regimes. Only Spain could not fit such a generalization (being unchallengeably absolutist, yet a mixed land/naval power). When states' main functions are warlike, it makes more sense to explain their variety in terms of war than in terms of relatively minor functions like class regulation.

But by the same token the marginality of the state to social life must reduce the strength of absolutism itself. Ideology claimed divinity for the monarch; he was subject to divine, not human, law. But he was no ancient emperor – in reality he was not the sole source of law, of coinages, weights and measures, economic monopolies and the rest of the panoply of ancient economic infrastructure. He *owned* only his own estates. Private property in the Roman sense (full rights of alienation) was deeply embedded in European social structure. It had been bequeathed by the transnational Roman/Christian legacy, and the small states could hardly have overturned it had the thought even occurred to them.

What was the state to do with enhanced power? As we have seen, war appears to have been its main function and desire. Unfortunately, however, war had become immensely expensive. The genuinely autonomous and absolute monarch could probably build splendid palaces, entertain lavishly and repress his own internal rivals, but he could not easily raise the vast sums to take on his fellows abroad. When Louis XII asked the mercenary Trivuke how the success of his invasion of Milan could be assured, he received this reply: 'Most generous King, three things are necessary: money, money and still more money' (quoted by Ardant, 1975, p.164). Even a standing army cannot in itself ensure the extraction of that money. In a pre-industrial society it is no easy matter even to assess where the wealth is, let alone extract it. Both activities require the cooperation of the wealth holders or local persons who can assess and extract the wealth of their neighbours. In practice all regimes depended on assistance from other groups. Returning to our constitutional and absolutist regimes, we can see that they are distinguishable in the forms of assistance offered to the crown. England and Holland relied on taxation of the rich with their consent, the absolutist regimes on taxation of the poor, with the consent and repressive help of the rich. In most absolutist regimes, unlike the constitutional ones, the landed nobility were generally exempt from taxation, while the merchants and urban bourgeoisie were not. These are, of course, *class* differences, very much in line with the type of theory of absolutism I have been criticizing. Thus we cannot explain absolutism without *any* reference to class structural differences. But they only emerged in this form because of the *military* functions of the state: a pacific monarch would have needed neither representative assemblies nor the recruitment of the nobility. And type of warfare once again plays an important causal role: landlocked powers hoped for territorial gains and attracted the group more interested in landholding, the nobility (especially its younger sons); sea powers hoped for trade gains, and attracted those with realizable capital, 'merchants'.[9]

The national segmentation of capitalism

But perhaps the most enduring legacy of these puny, yet militaristic states is the way they succeeded in 'structuring the social space' of emergent capitalism. The economy of the medieval period was significantly transnational: state boundaries were not boundaries to economic interaction (nor were they to ideological interactions either). Furthermore, the feudal mode of production and the capitalist mode of production are also transnational concepts — they imply nothing about national-state boundaries. And yet we have witnessed a growth in the coordinating role of the state over the economic relations existing within its own territories. This important role emerged, as it were, in the interstices of the financial accounts, for it was relatively costless. In England the widening of the legislative scope of the state occurred before the great increase in its financial size — that is, under the Tudors instead of under the Stuarts. And this is almost certainly the case in other countries, too. This particular, and major, aspect of the rise of the 'modern state' — the monopolization of legislative and judicial powers by *one* central state — cannot be attributed directly and immediately to military transformations. If we ask, to what was it due then, the answer probably lies in the extension of class

---

9 The Spanish Empire is an intermediary case, founded on both army and navy, using its ships to conquer a land empire, and therefore attracting the interest and support of the younger sons.

State and Society, 1130–1815

relations over a wider geographical terrain through the transition from feudal to capitalist productive processes. But there is nothing inherent in either the feudal or the capitalist mode of production to lead to the development of class systems each one of which is actually *bounded* by the territories of a state. We have been witnessing the emergence of *many* systems of production, a *segmental* series of class struggles which had no prior historical parallel.

Thus by the time of the Industrial Revolution, capitalism was already contained within a system of competing geo-political states, whose relations constituted an unstable mixture of trade and warfare, neither of which were indeed seen as being mutually exclusive by the powers. Transnational organizations, except in the field of banking, had almost disappeared. Economic interaction was largely confined within national markets, supported by imperial dominions. Each geo-political state approximated to a self-contained economic system. International economic relations were significantly mediated by states. Ownership regulation and class organization thus developed over a series of geographical areas shaped by existing geo-political units. This can only be explained by the peculiar and dialectical relationship which existed between economic gain and warfare.

The classes of capitalist society were shaped by the necessity for the regulation of basic ownership rights by states. Merchant and landlord capitalist entered a world of warring states. This need for state regulation both internally and externally, and the state's need for finances, pushed classes toward a national form of organization, eventually toward a British, a French, a Dutch etc., bourgeoisie, between whom economic interaction was small. The geo-political states were *systems* of production between which economic relations were only *ad hoc*. These national parameters were set *centuries* before we may legitimately talk of the second major class of the capitalist mode of production, the proletariat. This was the world which the proletariat entered. Furthermore, these geo-political parameters imply warfare between rivals in a way that the capitalist mode of production, as a 'pure type', does not. If we were to continue the historical narrative, we could see that warfare had major implications for the subsequent development of the bourgeoisie and the proletariat.

Thus, in the development of capitalism, the state has exercised a major role which cannot be reduced to its relationship to pre-existing classes or to civil society as a whole. Nothing in the capitalist mode of production (or the feudal mode if that is defined economically) leads of itself to the emergence of many capitalist *systems* of production, divided and at war, and of an overall class structure which is nationally *segmental*. It is an extraordinary paradox that the puny, marginal state of the late feudal and early modern period had such a decisive role in system-integrating the world in which we live today.

We have seen that modes of production and classes as actual historical entities and forces cannot 'constitute themselves' without the intervention of military and political structures. The same obviously applies in reverse to states and political elites. As always in sociology, our analytic constructs are ultimately precarious — actual modes of production, classes and states depend for their existence upon the totality of social experience. Neither 'economic determinism' nor 'political' or 'military determinism' would take us very far in any analysis. However, in the present context, a combination of the three would seem to offer an extraordinarily powerful explanation of the parameters of the modern world — until, that is, another military revolution at last renders warfare totally irrational as a means of economic appropriation or of domination in general. But this analysis has stopped a long way short of 6 August 1945.

References

Anderson P. 1974: *Lineages of the Absolutist State*. London: New Left Books.

Ardant G. 1975: 'Financial policy and economic infrastructure of modern states and nations', in C. Tilly (ed.), *The Formation of National States in Western Europe*. Princeton, NJ: Princeton University Press.

Batho G. R. 1957: 'The finances of an Elizabethan nobleman: Henry Percy, 9th Earl of Northumberland (1564–1632)', *English Historical Review*, 9, 433–50.

Bean R. 1973: 'War and the birth of the nation-state', *Journal of Economic History*, 33, 203–21.

Bowsky W. M. 1970: *The Finances of the Commune of Siena, 1287–1355*. Oxford: Clarendon Press.

Brown D. M. 1948: 'The impact of firearms on Japanese warfare, 1543–98', *Far Eastern Quarterly*, vol. 7.
Chabod F. 1964: 'Was there a renaissance state?' in H. Lubasz (ed.), *The Development of the Modern State*, London: Collier-Macmillan.
Chandaman C. D. 1975: *The English Public Revenue 1660–88*. Oxford: Clarendon Press.
Coleman D. C. (ed.) 1969: *Revisions in Mercantilism*. London: Methuen.
Deane P. 1955: 'The implications of early national income estimates', *Economic Development and Cultural Change*, vol. 4.
Deane P. and Cole W. A. 1962: *British Economic Growth 1688–1959*. Cambridge: Cambridge University Press.
de la Roncière C. M. 1968: 'Indirect taxes or 'Gabelles' at Florence in the 14th century', in N. Rubinstein (ed.), *Florentine Studies*. Evanston, Ill.: Northwestern University Press.
Dietz F. C. 1918: 'Finances of Edward VI and Mary', *Smith College Studies in History*, vol. 3.
—— 1923: 'The Exchequer in Elizabeth's reign', *Smith College Studies in History*, vol. 8.
—— 1928: 'The receipts and issues of the Exchequer during the reign of James I and Charles I', *Smith College Studies in History*, vol. 13.
—— 1932: 'English public finance and the national state in the 16th century', in E. F. Gray (essays in honour of), *Facts and Figures in Economic History*. Cambridge, Mass.: Harvard, University Press.
—— 1964a: *English Government Finance 1485–1558*. London: Cass.
—— 1964b: *English Public Finance 1558–1641*. London: Cass.
Elton G. R. 1975: 'Taxation for war and peace in early-Tudor England', in J. M. Winter (ed.), *War and Economic Development*. Cambridge: Cambridge University Press.
Farmer D. L. 1956: 'Some price fluctuations in Angevin England', *Economic History Review*, vol. 9.
—— 1957: 'Some grain price movements in 13th century England', *Economic History Review*, vol. 10.
Finch M. E. 1956: *The Wealth of Five Northamptonshire Families, 1540–1640*. London: Oxford University Press.
Finer S. E. 1975: 'State and nation-building in Europe: the role of the military', in C. Tilly (ed.) *The Formation of National States in Western Europe*. Princeton, NJ Princeton University Press.
Goody J. 1971: *Technology, Tradition and the State in Africa*. London: Oxford University Press.
Harris G. L. 1975: *King, Parliament and Public Finance in Medieval England to 1369*. Oxford: Clarendon press.
Henneman J. B. 1971: *Royal Taxation in Fourteenth Century France*. Princeton. NJ: Princeton University Press.

Hintze O. 1975: *The Historical Essays of Otto Hintze* (ed. F. Gilbert). New York: Oxford University Press.
Howard M. 1976: *War in European History*. London: Oxford University Press.
Kiernan V. G. 1957: 'Foreign mercenaries and absolute monarchy', *Past and Present* no. 11.
—— 1965: 'State and nation in Western Europe', *Past and Present*, no. 31.
Ladero Quesada M. A. 1970: 'Les finances royales de Castille à la veille des temps modernes', *Annales*, vol. 25.
Law R. 1976: 'Horses, firearms and political power in pre-colonial West Africa', *Past and Present*, no. 72.
Lousse E. 1964: 'Absolutism', in H. Lubasz (ed.), *The Development of the Modern State*. London: Collier-Macmillan.
Lublinskaya A. D. 1968: *French Absolutism: the Crucial Phase, 1620–1629*. Cambridge: Cambridge University Press.
McFarlane K. B. 1962: 'England and the Hundred Years' War', *Past and Present*, no. 22.
Mitchell B. R. and Deane P. 1962: *Abstract of British Historical Statistics*. Cambridge: Cambridge University Press.
Mitchell B. R. and Jones H. G. 1971: *Second Abstract of British Historical Statistics*. Cambridge: Cambridge University Press.
Mousnier R. 1954: *Les XVIe et XVIIe siècles*. Paris: Presses Universitaires de France.
Parker G. 1970: 'Spain, her enemies and the revolt of the Netherlands 1559–1648', *Past and Present* no. 49.
—— 1972: The Army of Flanders and the Spanish Road 1567–1659. Cambridge: Cambridge University Press.
—— 1974: 'The emergence of modern finance in Europe, 1550–1730', in C. M. Cipolla (ed.), *The Fontana Economic History of Europe*, vol. 2. London: Fontana.
Phelphs-Brown E. H. and Hopkins S. V. 1956: 'Seven centuries of the price of consumables', *Economica* vol. 23.
Poggi G. 1978: *The Development of the Modern State*. London: Hutchinson.
Ramsay Sir J. H. 1920: *Lancaster and York*. Oxford: Clarendon Press.
—— 1925: *A History of the Revenues of the Kings of England 1066–1399*. 2 vol. Oxford: Clarendon Press.
Rey M. 1965: *Les finances royales sous Charles VI*. Paris: SEUPEN.
Roberts M. 1967: 'The military revolution 1560–1660', *Essays in Swedish History*. London: Weidenfeld and Nicolson.
Schofield R. S. 1963: 'Parliamentary lay taxation 1485–1547', unpublished PhD thesis, University of Cambridge.

Schumpeter J. 1954: 'The crisis of the tax state', in A. Peacock et al., *International Economic Papers: Translations Prepared for the International Economic Association*, New York: Macmillan.
Sorokin P. A. 1962: *Social and Cultural Dynamics*, vol. III. New York: Bedminster Press.
Steel A. 1954: *The Receipt of the Exchequer 1377–1485*. Cambridge: Cambridge University Press.
Stoney L. 1965: *The Crisis of the Aristocracy 1558–1641*. London: Oxford University Press.
—— 1973: *Family and Fortune: Studies in Aristocratic Finance in the 16th and 17th Centuries*. Oxford: Clarendon Press.
Strayer J. R. 1970: *On the Medieval Origins of the Modern State*. Princeton, NJ: Princeton University Press.
Thirsk J. (ed.) 1967: *The Agrarian History of England and Wales*, vol. 4, 1500–1640. Cambridge University Press.
Tout T. F. 1920–1933: *Chapters in the Administrative History of Medieval England*, 6 vol. Manchester University Press.
Tout T. F. and D. Broome 1924: 'A national balance-sheet for 1362–3', *English Historical Review*, vol. 39.
Verbruggen J. F. 1977: *The Art of Warfare in Western Europe during the Middle Ages*. Amsterdam: North-Holland.
Waley D. P. 1968: 'The army of the Florentine republic from the 12th to the 14th century', in N. Rubinstein (ed.), *Florentine Studies*. Evanston, Ill.: Northwestern University Press.
Wallerstein I. 1974: *The Modern World System*. New York: Academic Press.
Willard J. F. 1927: 'The crown and its creditors 1327–1333', *English Historical Review*, vol. 42.
Wolfe M. 1972: *The Fiscal System of Renaissance France*. New Haven, Conn.: Yale University Press.
Wolffe B. P. 1971: *The Royal Demesne in English History*. London: Allen and Unwin.

4

Capitalism and Militarism

Introduction: three theories

The aim of this essay is less to write a history of the relationship between capitalism and militarism than to analyse their present relationship in the light of history. More specifically, I seek to answer the questions: what difference, if any, has capitalism brought to the nature and degree of militarism in modern society? And to what extent, if any, is the threat of militarism which, in its nuclear form, leans so terrifyingly over our society, to be blamed upon capitalism?

I define capitalism later. *Militarism is here defined as an attitude and a set of institutions which regard war and the preparation for war as a normal and desirable social activity.*

To these questions, social theory gives three types of answer. The first, which I shall call *the theory of militaristic capitalism*, asserts that whatever militaristic tendencies lay in earlier societies they were boosted considerably by the advent of capitalism. The second, *the optimistic theory of pacific capitalism*, asserts on the contrary that capitalism (or often, industrial capitalism) is inherently pacific and, as it is also *the* central structure of modern (Western) society, we can be optimistic about the likelihood of militarism declining. The third, *the theory of geo-political militarism*, argues that militarism is due fundamentally to other, more permanent aspects of the international relations of states, to which capitalism has brought little change. I shall criticize all three but argue that the last, suitably amended, has most to commend it.

Of course, these are not just theoretical questions. They have

This chapter was first published in Martin Shaw (ed.) *War, State and Society* (1984). London: Macmillan. We are grateful for permission to reproduce it here.

great bearing upon contemporary politics (and, indeed, upon our very survival). Hence the theories, or popularized versions of them, have had great impact upon political movements and world leaders. This is necessarily so: in order to make the world safer, we have to decide which fundamental elements of our social structure contribute to militarism. Then, perhaps, we can reform or overthrow them.

It is particularly important to clarify the role of capitalism in militarism. For there is a clear political carry-over between attitudes to the two. Those active in peace movements, who are probably more concerned than anyone else about militarism, tend to be anti-capitalist. Sometimes explicitly, more usually implicitly, they tend to blame capitalism for nuclear militarism, because they tend to blame it for the other ills of society. Political activists all over the Western world denounce capitalism and militarism not as separate, but as essentially conjoined, enemies.

Such political denunciations are usually supported by the theory of militaristic capitalism. Capitalism is the keystone of our society and it is fundamentally militaristic, it is argued. Hence militarism cannot be eliminated unless we eliminate capitalism. Naturally, to this argument must be added a specific explanation of militarism in the Soviet Union which I will not enter into here. Indeed this theory has many particular strands which cannot be discussed in a paper of this length. I will not discuss the 'military-industrial complex' variety associated particularly with C. Wright Mills and American radicals. Nor will I enter into the controversy started by radical economists arguing that militarism in the form of high military expenditure is functional for the capitalist economy. A third strand not discussed here is that militarism is useful in diverting the attention of the working class from the facts of their exploitation by capital. A fourth emphasizes that militarism is necessary to keep down the even more exploited peoples of the Third World. These two last-mentioned generally unite in the Marxist theory of imperialism, associated with some of Marx's successors, especially Hilferding and Lenin. I will discuss this, albeit briefly. Nevertheless, all these detailed controversies can, to an extent, be bypassed by a more general historical analysis inquiring what difference capitalism seems to have made to the contours of militarism.

But blaming capitalism has been a minority tradition in

mainstream social science theory. In economics and sociology, and in liberal and some social-democratic political rhetoric, the second theory, the optimistic theory of pacific capitalism, has predominated. Like the radicals, this has seen capitalism, or often industrial capitalism, as the keystone of modern society, but it is a pacific keystone because it is *transnational*. It brought to an end the militaristic states of previous historical epochs. Whatever else divided such theorists as Adam Smith, Bastiat, Carey and Schumpeter or St Simon, Comte, Spencer, Marx himself and Durkheim, on one prediction they united. Contemporary militarism between states was 'archaic', the declining residue of an earlier epoch (to which they often gave a militaristic name; for example Spencer's militant society or Bastiat's, Carey's and Schumpeter's age of imperialist plunder). The modern era was to be pacific, because its keystone, industrial capitalism, was transnational.

These views, prevalent in the nineteenth and early twentieth century in England, the United States and France, did not go unchallenged. Writers like Gumplowicz, Ratzenhofer, Schmitt, Hintze, Mosca and Pareto stressed the continued vitality of militaristic currents in contemporary society. But several of them seemed actually to approve of militarism. And as, ironically, they all belonged to the defeated powers of the two world wars, their memory was largely suppressed. By and large the Anglo-Saxon and Gallic victors in the West preferred to forget their ideas. The dominant liberal, and a surprising proportion of the Marxist–socialist tradition, have continued to believe that capitalism and industrialism are pacific – often struggling heroically against the overwhelming evidence of modern history to do so. Here, for example, is Perry Anderson, struggling more than most Marxists to understand warfare, discussing the prevalence of war in about every year in the sixteenth and seventeenth centuries. He concludes, 'that does not correspond to a capitalist rationality: it represents a swollen memory of the medieval functions of war ... Such calendars are foreign to capital, although ... it eventually contributed to them (Anderson, 1974, pp. 31–3). After 95 million dead in two world wars, almost all of whose protagonists were mature capitalist powers, this is a little difficult to believe!

But in both post-war periods, liberals and socialists alike seem to have decided that it would be best to wish militarism away by ignoring it. For example, in the Marxist tradition, in the 1960s and 1970s came a flurry of theories of the state. Dozens of books and hundreds of articles have poured forth on 'the capitalist state'. Almost none has contained a single word about what has been one of the principal activities of most capitalist states — preparing for, and conducting, wars (see, for example, the review article by Jessop, 1977).

More or less the same would be said of liberal theory, in which pluralist theories of the state have competed in silence on militarism (Mills' 'elite theory' crops up again here as the principal opponent which does deal with militarism).

However, in quite recent times changes have been occurring, especially among Marxists. E. P. Thompson has most notably broken with orthodoxy in his suggestion that we are now confronting a new, post-capitalist 'exterminist mode of production' which unites capitalism and the Soviet system (1980a and b). Militarism is at the centre-stage but it is not necessarily connected to capitalism, he argues. Unfortunately, it is not clear what it does relate to. Thompson is better at demolishing traditional leftist slogans concerning the nature of what he calls 'the logic of exterminism', than he is at constructing his own theory.

Thompson's sensitivity to contemporary militarism has been paralleled by Martin Shaw. He has also moved considerably between his 1974 article on the state, which largely maintained the then normal silence on militarism in Marxist state theory, and his article of 1984 which calls for a new Marxist theory of militarism. Neither of these writers, starting *theoretically* from a belief in the centrality of capitalism in modern society but then noting *empirically* the importance of militarism, has yet been able to locate the essential causes and nature of militarism today.

This is not surprising because capitalism and militarism are both core features of our society but they are only contingently connected. In contrast to both these traditional views on the relation between capitalism and militarism, I will make the following three points:

1 Militarism *is* a central part of modern society.
2 But its centrality does not derive principally from either capitalism or industrialism.

3 Instead militarism derives from geo-political aspects of our social structure which are far older than capitalism.

Thus any argument is initially congenial to the third theoretical tradition, *geo-political militarism*. In academe, the traditional home of this theory has been in political science and more recently in departments of international relations. Within sociology, Raymond Aron's notable contributions to this theory (ably discussed by John Hall, 1984) have been largely ignored. But the major impact of the approach has been felt outside academe, in the rather more important power relations of militaristic states themselves. Thus, for example, the author of an academic book on Metternich, which was written entirely from this viewpoint, became an actual successor of Metternich in the geo-political arena – Henry Kissinger (1964).

On the other hand, this tradition has an obvious weakness: it is so obsessed with geo-political relations that it takes the existence and future destinies of states as the only significant actors upon the stage as 'givens'. But states are not the only collective actors in societies, and their influence waxes and wanes in the historical process. I ask here how and why the modern geo-political system arose, and, more specifically, to what extent it was a part of the rise of capitalism.

On this basis I will add three further points to the three listed above.

4 Militarism became contingently associated with the rise of capitalism.
5 This association had the effect of greatly increasing both technically and socially the menace of militarism.
6 But in the twentieth century both menaces became the general property of expansionist industrial societies and are no longer specific to capitalism.

To demonstrate all six points, I proceed in two stages. First I will take various indices of militarism and examine their secular tendencies. Have they noticeably altered in the period of capitalism's emergence and development? On that basis I turn to the second stage, to see whether there is a causal relationship between capitalism and the changes that do emerge.

Secular tendencies in militarism

Have war and militarism been a constant in human experience: the reflection, perhaps, of our own aggressive natures and/or of the essence of social cooperation? Such a view is often found, especially as a kind of pessimistic base for geo-political theory. But studies of war among primitive peoples enable us to refute these notions in two ways. It is perfectly true that the vast majority of all known societies engage routinely in war-like activities. But, first, the mere fact that a minority do not (in Otterbein's 1970 study four out of 50 primitive peoples) silences the fear that war is *essential* to our individual or social natures. Secondly, most warlike activity does not actually involve systematic killing: in most primitive societies a ritualized brandishing of weapons and ferocious intent sufficiently deters further escalation. In these 'wars' it is considered disastrous if anyone does get killed – which happens perhaps once in a generation (see also Brock and Galtung, 1966; Moore 1972; Divale and Harris, 1976).

We of the nuclear age should look longingly at even this second level of pacific primitivism – let Ronald Reagan annually drive a (disconnected) ICBM to the East German border, there to make rude gestures at Yuri Andropov! The causes of *dangerous* militarism do not lie in our inevitable natures, but in historical developments, which are therefore potentially reversible.

Yet the emergence of systematic warfare happened very early in our history and has become nearly universal among more civilized peoples. Thus it is ultimately impossible fully to explain it. A number of inter-connected factors appear to have been involved.

1 When the surplus extracted from nature increased, the spoils of plunder became more desirable. Some could live without working.
2 Associated with this was an increase in territorial fixity of the surplus and of the human labour invested in it. This made it impossible to run away with one's resources if threatened (as hunter-gatherers could). One stayed to fight.
3 Also associated with this was an increase in the fixity of social cooperation as labour was invested in cooperation with a

particular and permanent social group with whom one then fought in cooperation.
4 All these tendencies encourage the rise of organized, centralized social cooperation, territorially and socially fixed – that is, the state.

The consequence is clear: where we find socially and territorially fixed groups with states and surpluses, we find systematic killing in organized wars. Not all such killing is undertaken by states – though it is rare to find a situation where none of the combatant groups is state-organized – but all states undertake such killing. Geo-political factors are essential to an understanding of historical militarism.

Indeed, though states have other purposes too, they have been *principally* concerned throughout recorded history with warfare. This is revealed in relatively advanced states in their financial accounts. In chapter 3 I showed that in the period 1130–1815 the English state spent the bulk of its revenue (and normally between 75 per cent and 95 per cent of all revenues spent on public functions) on war and preparations for wars. In this, it was typical of the European states of these centuries, as well as of states in classical Greece, Rome, imperial China and indeed throughout recorded history. So militarism is largely the province of – and the largest province of – the state. Capitalism arrived so late on this scene that it might seem that the mould was relatively firmly set.

So let us now examine the incidence of war. Has it greatly changed in the period of the emergence and development of capitalism? Here we can turn to the various compilations made by social statisticians. The first great study was Sorokin's *Social and Cultural Dynamics*, vol. III (1962 edn; originally published in 1937). For the nineteenth and twentieth centuries, especially outside of Europe, I have supplemented Sorokin with Singer and Small (1972) and have checked the main trends against those reported in Wright (1942) and Richardson (1960).

Throughout the whole history of the West from 500 BC to the present day, the average state has been engaged in at least one open, organized war with another state in about 50 per cent of years. No states have a predominantly peaceful history: unexpectedly, Germany/Prussia has been the most peaceful modern state on this measure, engaged in war in only a third of the years from

1651 to the present day. But the fluctuation between states is only between one-third and just less than two-thirds (between Prussia and Spain, from 1476 onwards). A century of peace is unique to the case of Holland: 1815 to 1914. Since 1815, non-European states have enjoyed slightly more peace than the European states. There has been no tendency for the incidence of war to either increase or decrease throughout the period. In fact, measured just by the frequency of war, the eighteenth century was unusually war-like, the nineteenth century unusually peaceful and the twentieth century just about average so far. Apparently, warfare has been a normal way of conducting international relations throughout recorded history. But *always* in conjunction with peace: war and peace succeed each other as the characteristic instruments of inter-state relations. These are therefore carried on in relatively rational, calculative forms, with an eye to the particular advantages in any situation of either war or peace. To these historic patterns of diplomacy, capitalism cannot have contributed much, one way or another.

A further sign of this is the recurrence of certain basic patterns of diplomacy enduring right through the period in which capitalism emerged. I will mention two such patterns. The first is found where no one state predominates in a multi-state system. In self-defence, and with an eye to its own potential aggressions, each power becomes embroiled in a fluctuating alliance system which is invoked particularly when one power seeks to attain hegemony. Thus certain characteristics of the diplomacy and wars which greeted the advent of Charles V and Philip II, of Napoleon and of Hitler were very similar. This is despite the many social-structural changes occurring between the early sixteenth, nineteenth and twentieth centuries, including the emergence of capitalism. The end result was the same of course: the humiliation of the would-be hegemonizer.

But it is an example of a second pattern which threatens us today: the rise and confrontation of two super-powers. Here we must go back further for close parallels – to Rome and Carthage, or to Greece and Persia. In such cases, the two rivals hegemonize their neighbours until no neutral space is left between them. Then they encourage subversives in each other's domains and client-states, claiming, of course, that they stand for certain eternal verities – individual freedom against despotism, citizenship against oligarchy, progress against reaction, order against anarchy (of the four classical cases we lack only the Carthaginian version of the justice of their cause). Indeed, the final conflagration is part thrust upon, part provoked by the super-powers, normally through the agency of the disorderliness of the subverted client-states (the revolt of some of the Greek colonies of Asia Minor against Persia; or faction fighting in Greek and Carthaginian city-states of Sicily). This is still the probable way in which the world will end – the contradiction of the uncontrollable clients. It is difficult to see in the modern version of the pattern much of a contribution from capitalism (or indeed from socialism). Imperialism, yes – but that is as old as the well-ordered state.

There are many other patterns besides these two. They are the staple diet of the theory of geo-political militarism. They are also part of the consciousness of state elites themselves. They are, as the title of one academic text puts it, *Games Nations Play* (Spanier, 1972). They are the *same* games as we can see played out in the rather older texts of Herodotus and Polybius (which concern the two earlier cases mentioned of super power confrontation). In these respects little has changed.

In the sphere of war, the metaphor of 'the game' may seem in rather bad taste, like black comedy. One reason why the comedy keeps repeating itself is that the victors survive to dominate the next period, and usually to write history. When states neglect their militarism they perish: where are the Burgundies and Bavarias of yester-year? The consequence is that at any one point in time, the major states are almost certain to have benefited considerably from militarism. It is asking a lot of the United States and the Soviet Union to abandon their nuclear arsenals when their super-power status emerged through two world wars which finished off their rivals. Thus the militaristic patterns are actually self-fulfilling prophecies. That is the main force of the theory of geo-political militarism, one that still endures today.

But not all our militarism is patterned by such a long time perspective. In certain respects the geo-political struggle *has* been revolutionized in our modern era. This is obviously true of the techniques of war and diplomacy. Here capitalism provided one of the major initial impetuses. No one would dispute this. In the past few centuries successive revolutions have occurred in the technology of weapons. More precisely this has led to an exponential growth in what military specialists call 'lethality indices'. Until the development of gunpowder, the capacity of armies to kill did not greatly increase through recorded history. The first jump, attributable to artillery in the fifteenth to eighteenth centuries, was not caused principally by the emergence of capitalism. But when capitalism pioneered industrialism, it proved capable of generating repeating rifles, heavy bore field guns, high explosives, tanks, ironclad battleships, fighter and bomber aircraft, submarines, rockets and nuclear weapons. In the century from the 1870s to the 1970s, the lethality of weaponry increased a *billion-fold*, according to Robinson's (1977) estimates. Luckily, the last and major part of this rise is still only potential. But in actual warfare casualty rates have nevertheless rocketed, though this tended to occur in two stages, rising almost threefold in both the seventeenth century and the twentieth century. As we are nowadays well aware, the arsenals of the super-powers are now sufficient to kill everyone on the planet in a matter of hours. Because of this we live in fear. Without capitalism's historical contribution we would probably not live in fear, but in poverty, in poor agrarian societies incapable of destroying each other.

In addition, by penetrating the whole globe, capitalism revolutionized international diplomacy. Nowhere is now outside of the diplomatic system or the military striking range of the super-powers; and they have nowhere to expand which does not bring them into contact with each other. The entire world is a client-state system, threatened as a single entity by militarism. And again, without capitalism's historical contribution, this would not be so. Israelis and Arabs, black and white southern Africans, Cambodians and Vietnamese, would be threatened only by each other (plus, perhaps, the activities of any greater power adjacent in territory to them).

Third, these two changes have had an impact on the culture of militarism. It is a necessary part of militarism to value highly whatever qualities are thought useful to military efficiency. For most of history, these qualities centred upon martial physical valour. Thus physical violence was glorified. The fact that this no longer occurs to any significant extent should not blind us to the continued existence of high regard for military efficiency. Our sports may not be dominated by chariot races, gladiatorial combat or races in full battle gear, but our culture is permeated by the desirability of team discipline, of mathematically precise logistical planning, of split second timing: all qualities which are most closely paralleled in our society by the requirements of warfare. Similarly, as Randall Collins (1974) has brilliantly demonstated, the era of trigger and push-button warfare has fostered the development of different emotional supports: from *ferocity* and *cruelty*, useful for killing people in physical combat, to *callousness*, useful for remote control killing. Our militarism is impersonal, not in the service of gods against devils, but in the service of rational necessity.

Fourth, the capitalist era has directly implicated not just military personnel but the whole population in its militarism. Indeed, the military figures alone conceal this. Historical statistics exist as to the proportion of the size of the army to total population — the military participation ratio (MPR) (see Andreski, 1971). For what it is worth, the MPR in the West appears high in classical Greece, highest of all in the Roman Republic and Empire, and varies in the subsequent historical period — lowest in the twelfth century, growing considerably from the twelfth to the fourteenth, dropping in the fifteenth, rising in the sixteenth and seventeenth, dropping slightly in the eighteenth, greatly in the nineteenth, and then rising again in the first half of the twentieth century (but only back to the level of the thirteenth). Throughout the period from the twelfth to the twenieth century, the highest century's ratio (the seventeenth) is about three times that of the lowest (the twelfth). Variations in militarization thus seem erratic and not attributable in simple fashion to the emergence and development of capitalism. Nevertheless this conceals two trends.

The first concealed trend is that if we were also able to include in the MPR 'civilian participation' through armament industries, then industrial capitalism would have a far more pronounced effect, especially in war-time. Here the only rivals would be ancient ones, some Greek city-states and the later Roman Republic and the Roman Empire. The second concealed trend is that the degree of total resource mobilization (not just manpower) for militarism is also higher in the modern period than in previous European history. Even in peace-time, though our states today spend only half the proportion of their budgets on defence as their medieval counterparts did, as a proportion of Gross National Product it is assuredly far higher. What is often forgotten is how

Capitalism and Militarism

puny the medieval states were, and how marginal they were to the lives of most of their inhabitants. Not until the seventeenth century would any of them have spent as much as 2 per cent of estimated GNP; not until the Napoleonic Wars were they up to 10 per cent. Now they disburse anywhere between 30 per cent and 50 per cent of GNP. And in the two major twentieth century wars, the major combatant states actually spent this proportion of GNP on war alone.

With these two corrections made, there is only one historical period whose level of militarization of social life in general approaches our own. It is the classical age; from the rise of Sparta and Athens to the triumph of Rome, especially the latter. Obviously even then a far higher proportion of total social resources than today would be spent on mere subsistence rather than on a 'luxury' like militarism. But in another sense their militarism exceeds ours – in its relentless stability. For around six centuries the Roman state spent about 75 per cent of its annual resources on its legions and navies, geared its 'class' structure, its citizenship, its political offices, its conception of virtue and honour to military exigencies. If our militarism has the potentiality to so endure until AD 2500, it will assuredly destroy the world beforehand.

To even begin to regard our militarism as comparable to Roman militarism is to draw attention to its extraordinary strength and threat. For there is a similarity between our militarism and theirs which is most profound and terrifying – their capacity for popular mobilization. In between these two eras, war was a matter for state elites and their clients and their clients' dependants – it was not diffused to the whole population. The citizen army, the mobilized economy, are to be found *only* then and now. (The exceptions are the armies of a few small city-states or tribal groupings. It is equally sobering to reflect that the only comparable pre-classical quasi-citizen army may have been the Assyrian. Read the Old Testament or visit the British Museum to catch the two main available glimpses of the terror *that* inspired.) The modern version of this level of mobilization is *the nation-state*. This is the infrastructure of modern militarism which requires explanation.

We have found militarism to be highly traditional in society, probably caused by factors connected with the initial rise of the state and soon taking on patterns which have endured right through history up to today. Nevertheless, there are some modern characteristics of militarism. It mobilizes the population as a whole – as it did previously only in classical Rome and to a lesser extent in classical Greece. And the techniques of militarism now encompass all populations everywhere. Thus something requires explanation from outside of the theory of geo-political militarism. It seems to concern the relationship between the nation-state and capitalism. I turn to the second stage of the argument.

Militarism necessary for capitalism

It is time to define capitalism. The capitalist mode of production contains three main interrelated elements.

1 *Commodity production* – every factor of production is treated as a means, not as an end in itself, and is exchangeable with every other factor. This includes labour.
2 *Private possession of the means of production* – the factors of production, including labour-power, belong formally to a private class of capitalists (and not to the state, the mass of labourers, the community, God or anyone else).
3 *Labour is free and separated from the means of production.* This is implied by (1) and (2) above. Labourers are free to sell their labour-power and withdraw it as they see fit; they receive a wage but have no claims over the surplus produced.

The definition itself contains nothing about states or militarism – and nor does any other definition of which I am aware. But do these characteristics presuppose militarism?

It is not difficult to see why these elements would have implications for states and militarism. First, commodity production presupposes a set of universal rules defining the terms under which values are to be established and exchanged. The flow of commodities cannot be interrupted by numerous local rules and customs assigning fixed values to things. Thus, an unusual degree of long-distance political regulation backed up by force is required by capitalism. Second, private possession of the means of production and the full separation of labour are, in historical terms, extremely unusual. It is normal to find a multiplicity of overlapping individual, familial and communal rights to the means of production. Specifically, free hired labour is rare (and often confined to soldiers and foreigners). We should also note that full private ownership of the means of production runs counter to common sense. A large enterprise is worked cooperatively by workers, by those with managerial or scientific expertise and by those who provide risk capital (to say nothing of also presupposing others who work in educational, communications and health infrastructures). Thus it is positively bizarre to regard those who provide the land or the capital as the sole proprietors! It is surely a safe bet that capitalism would need a large degree of political and military support to be introduced into regions where multiple property rights existed. It presupposes wholsesale expropriation by military force.

Yet have these two functional requirements led capitalism to a higher level of militarism than any other historic form of imperialism? This seems doubtful. *Any* conquest requires the imposition of rules – whether relatively universalistic, as in the case of capitalist imperialism, or particularistic, as in most previous cases – and the expropriation of property. It is not capitalism's form that particularly encourages militarism, but its *success*. The European capitalist powers have provided the world with imperialism on a global scale – and extremely rapidly. Is this the source of the similarity with Rome, which had hitherto provided the most successful and rapid conquests in Western history?

But there is a problem confronting this analogy. Unlike Roman imperialism, capitalism, once institutionalized, seems to require relatively *little* maintenance by force. If basic rights to property are established then value can be set by the operation of supply and demand in markets. Furthermore, once capitalism entered its industrial phase, two other cases of force common in pre-industrial societies diminished. First, in agrarian societies increasing economic productivity usually meant increasing the intensity of labour. The usual means was to step up the level of coercion through slavery, serfdom or *corvée* labour. Through industrialization, machinery increased the quality of labour and this did not usually entail coercion. Second, in agrarian societies the local peasantry is 'in possession of' the means of subsistence. If non-producers extract the surplus from them, this requires coercion. But after industrialization, with an extensive division of labour and exchange of commodities, very few local groups are potentially self-sufficient. Extensive interdependence generally replaces local coercion (as Marx noted). In both respects, industrial capitalism diminished the significance of a form of militarism that had so far escaped my notice – local, non-state militarism. It is true, of course, that like any form of expropriation, capitalism will be defended by force if necessary by its dominant classes. Nowadays that is largely force wielded by the state. But in this respect it differs only from a wholly non-exploitative system of production. 'Class militarism' is not specific to capitalism – indeed it is less evident there than in most historic societies.

This combination of tendencies has led to the 'core–periphery' differences so typical of the development of capitalism. In each phase of its development, capitalism has contained an institutionalized, relatively non-coercive core and an expropriated, militaristic periphery. Its core has widened from the 'Home Counties' around the capital of countries like England, France and Spain from the late fourteenth to the sixteenth centuries; thence to the 200–400 mile diameter 'national' extensions of such counties, and to the 'Home Counties' of their client-states and imitators in the sixteenth to the early nineteenth centuries; thence to their entire national territories and to wider cores of their clients, imitators and 'white' colonies in the nineteenth and early twentieth centuries; thence to neo-colonial enclaves all over the world in the mid-twentieth century; and thence, most recently, to the emerging 'middle class' countries of South East Asia in the 1970s and 1980s. All the while, more and more of the globe has been caught up in the transition from 'backwardness', through an era of massive expropriation, coercive labour forms and military violence, to a more institutionalized integration into capitalism and free wage labour. The earlier phases of this movement have all been thoroughly charted by Wallerstein (1974, 1979). But it still continues today.

Thus we can begin to appreciate why capitalism has been regarded so variously as militaristic and pacific. It all depends where you look, and at what point in that locality's history. Furthermore, the unevenness has been heightened by particular military and geo-political chronologies. As European capitalism expanded, it tended to encounter less and less advanced peoples (though the penetration of the Far East does not fit such a chronology). And simultaneously its own weapons were becoming exponentially more lethal. The military superiority of the core over the periphery became more and more pronounced. Quite small numbers of troops, ships and colonial garrisons were sufficient to dictate the terms of trade and expropriate property rights and labour, either directly or through local native elites. Thus militarization of the periphery did not usually have major repercussions on the core. No European power required a high level of military mobilization to sustain the capitalist part of its global imperialism. This cannot be the source of our society's closest resemblances to Roman imperialism.

Militarism necessary to the multi-state system

We must now discuss a second aspect of the militarism of the capitalist era. So far I have discussed the expansion of capitalism as if there were a 'one-to-one' relationship between capitalism, the state and military force. But there were, of course, *many* capitalist states. The overwhelming mass of military activity was not directed outwards by one capitalist state. Nor was it even directed by many capitalist states outwards against peripheral areas and states. Instead it was directed by capitalist states against each other. Why should this be so?

One point must be made clearly – there is nothing in the capitalist mode of production which itself 'requires' a multi-state system. The two are contingent. Indeed, the requirements for political regulation and military expropriation mentioned above would be met more efficiently by a single, universalistic state, at first European-wide, then global in scope. It is true that many historians argue that the multi-state system encouraged the competitive dynamism of capitalist development; that is competition between states, as well as enterprises, encouraged growth. I accept this argument. But if so, this was an empirical fact, not a functional requirement. This multi-state system was in place well before capitalism emerged. So, too, were the cores of about half the actual major powers of mature capitalism. And though the process of capitalist industrialization encouraged the disintegration of some, and the growth of others, the personnel change among the leading powers was not noticeably greater or slower in the period of capitalist development and domination than it had been earlier. The multi-state system cannot be reduced to the requirements of industrial capitalism. Nor, therefore, can the fact of warfare between them, which we also saw earlier was a constant right through European history.

This point is rarely denied by the theory of militaristic capitalism. Instead it is ignored. Versions of this theory start with the individual geo-political state as a given. They note, often correctly, the influence of capitalism upon its foreign policy and so conclude that war is inherent in the structure of capitalism. But that is only if we first assume that capitalism is structured by the boundaries of states. For example, the Marxist theory of imperialism argues that inter-capitalist rivalry under certain economic conditions will take a militaristic turn and precipitate wars, like the First World War. Regardless of the correctness of the economic arguments — which are usually disputed by historians — there is one large gap in the argument. Why should rivalry between capitalists be between 'national' blocs of capital? Not a word in Marx, in Hilferding, in Lenin or in the rest of the orthodox Marxist tradition serves as an explanation of these factors. The most important point of all in the conflagration of 1914–18 — that it was fought between nation-states: Germany, Austria-Hungary and allies against Britain, France, Russia (and later the United States) and allies — is not explained at all. Nation-states are *presupposed* in the Marxist theory of imperialism.

Where do they come from? They need explaining, after all, for they were not there in medieval Europe. If we take, for example, the twelfth century states of Henry I in England, or Louis VII of France, or Frederick Barbarossa in Germany, we are not dealing with states with clearly defined territorial boundaries, with monopolistic powers over their people, or indeed with *any* direct relationship to the people as a whole. They were 'feudal' or 'patrimonial' states existing by virtue of particularistic, voluntaristic contracts made between sovereigns and lords, only reaching the people *through* such lords. Yet over the next centuries, through slow, unsteady and variable rhythm, they gradually became 'modern states' in Max Weber's sense, possessing universalistic, rule-making powers, backed up by a monopoly of the means of legitimate violence over a given territorial area. This territorial area began to be known in the sixteenth to nineteenth centuries as a 'national' area, and in the seventeenth to twentieth centuries the core people inhabiting them became a nation. (Obviously, the exact relations between 'nations' and 'states' have been complex and varied; some became multi-national rather than national; in other cases 'nations' existed before states.) These nation-states are the perpetrators of our era's extraordinary militarism.

Chapter 3 above discussed the rise of these states. There seem to have been two main, connected causes of their emergence and dominance up to the early nineteenth century: developments in military technology, and an economic expansion that became increasingly capitalistic in form. The feudal state gradually became obsolete in the later middle ages as first mercenaries, then trained mixed infantry/cavalry/archery armies, and finally armies with guns, successively wasted the lords' levies. Professionals, training and equipment required more central organization and, above all, more money. States – hitherto puny – that happened to be around became strengthened, if they could master the additional resources. This depended upon economic expansion, the second factor. Economic expansion disproportionately increased realizable wealth, that is, trade and money visibly entering market-places, and river and road toll-gates. It could be taxed more easily than could land itself. The persons involved in such trade also needed protection, especially when operating abroad, and increasingly only the state could supply this. A symbiotic fiscal–military relationship grew up between states and dominant economic classes, cemented by constitutional forms enshrining the principles under which taxes could be extracted and wars undertaken. Paradoxically, every time they struggled over this, and whether or not the outcome of the struggle was despotism or constitutionalism, they cemented the universal, monopolistic, territorial and national character of the state. This can be seen clearly in the changing nature of economic expansion itself. What had started out in the twelfth century as a highly transnational economy, in which long-distance trade travelled virtually regardless of state boundaries, became increasingly *inter-national*, bounded and regulated by states. By the early nineteenth century the emerging economy of industrial capitalism was largely a segmented series of national economies, each one largely confined to the territory, the colonial dependencies and the client-states of the major powers.

Capitalism was not encouraging transnationalism – quite the reverse, for it was *hardening* state boundaries.

This meant that neither capitalism nor industrialism was inherently pacific. They adapted to, and reinforced, a multi-state system in which international economic advantage was assisted, as it always had been, by a mixture of diplomacy and war. In any particular period the probability was that one power would be rationally attracted to war. For as yet the *costs* of war were not particularly severe.

The industrial phase of capitalism brought those massive and familiar changes referred to already. First it mobilized the people and brought them into this international society. The rise of the masses or the classes (according to one's perspective) is the most familiar story of modern and political science. But it is not so often recognized that it is virtually the *same* story as the rise of the nation. Class consciousness and national consciousness rose up together. The economy and polity that the bourgeoisie, proletariat and peasantry became integrated into had already been established as a national one by the interplay of monarchs, lords and merchants over several centuries. Their participation converted it into a nation-state. Militarism became popularly mobilized.

We can easily exaggerate the force of this new militarism, however. It did not become more ferocious. Rather, relatively rational diplomatic decisions percolated downwards to the people as a whole. The balance of advantage to be gained from war rather than peace is rarely tipped decisively. Thus in the late nineteenth century the British masses probably began to gain somewhat from the successful imperialism of their state. At the same time the German masses would gain somewhat if Germany could acquire access to the British sphere of interest. Life and death did not depend on either, however. In fact, the balance of advantage was probably not dissimilar to that of English and Dutch merchants and commercial farmers in the late seventeenth century (or English, Flemish and Burgundians in the fourteenth).

The decisive tipping factor is really whether the war could be won at relatively little cost. Here we must always remember that in most of history, and in the medieval and early modern history of Europe, the costs of war were relatively low. That is why it was a relatively rational policy. But now came the second contribution from industrialization: the increase in kill ratios and in economic mobilization. Wars became so costly that they became, finally and wholly, irrational. However, the devastation increased so rapidly that each successive escalation was unexpected. It is characteristic of the nineteenth and twentieth centuries that the actual calculations of costs made before wars have been proved later to be severe underestimates. But it is also characteristic that once the masses have realized this, they have recalculated and either rejected militarism (as in 1870 in France, 1905 in Russia, 1917–18 in several countries) or demanded reform as a price for it. The relatively rational 'diplomatic game' concerned the peoples as well as the state elites and it now took novel, radical paths.

Finally, however, all these novel contributions, though pioneered by capitalism, became the common property of industrialism. Capitalism did make the late twentieth century a uniquely dangerous place. There is no hiding place from nuclear devastation and we must thank the tremendous vitality and dynamism of capitalism for the predicament we find ourselves in. But the danger would be maintained by *any* form of society which did not abandon the level of technology bequeathed to it by capitalism and which remained militaristic. The Soviet Union is one such case; China is another. A revolution in the United States, or Britain, or France, which established 'socialism in one country', or Fascism, or a democratic empire, or whatever – would also maintain the danger. Whatever we do about capitalism, the danger would remain. The *techniques* of danger are the common property of industrial society. The forms of organization of these techniques will obviously differ. In the West large-scale capitalistic industries have emerged with a close relationship to the military arm of the state: 'the military-industrial complex'. In the Soviet Union, the economic-military coordination is wholly within state organizations. These particular organizations obviously have a vested interest in war (unless they can quickly diversify their activities) and are specific, highly militaristic interest groups. But as E. P. Thompson has argued – against writers like Sir Solly Zuckerman – these are not the *sources* of 'the logic of exterminism'. That source is the more general militarism of societies involved in a multi-state system in which warfare has been historically relatively rational. It is the common legacy of industrial society. The techniques have ended that rationality – but some elites and mobilized peoples still need convincing!

Conclusion

I anticipated these conclusions in the six points listed near the end of my introductory section. There is really very little that is peculiarly militaristic *or* pacific about capitalism. The only necessary connection has lain in the peripheral expansion of capitalism which has always required a high level of expropriation of non-capitalist property rights. This expropriation still occurs in the Third World today, but it is not easy to evaluate its significance. For it has become closely entwined with the conflict of the super powers. This, I argued, has very little to do with the nature of capitalism (or socialism). By far the greatest contributor to militarism is the multi-state system in which warfare has been a normal, and often rational, element throughout recorded history. If it is no longer rational (and hopefully not normal either) that is because of capitalism's unique and historic technical contributions to the methods of warfare. But even these contributions have become part of the general property of industrial societies.

Politically speaking, neither the capitalism of the West, nor the state socialism of the Soviet Union, are the key enemies of those who desire peace and survival today. The enemies are rather the common geo-political pretensions of the super-powers – the *same* pretensions as Greece and Persia, Rome and Carthage, possessed, now rendered more technically alarming to the world. More particularly, the weapons of war are now so lacking in political discrimination that they render inappropriate any political strategy based on class or modes of production. Nuclear weapons cannot distinguish between classes or modes of production. Indeed, they can barely distinguish any more between individual states. In Europe, for example, geo-political solutions on a continental scale are required. Capitalism may be worth fighting on other grounds. But on the agenda concerning our survival it should barely figure.

References

Anderson P. 1974: *Lineages of the Absolutist State.* London: New Left Books.

Andreski S. 1971: *Military Organization and Society,* Berkeley, Ca: University of California Press.

Brock T. and Galtung J. 1966: 'Belligerence among the primitives: a reanalysis of Quincy Wright's data', *Journal of Peace Research*, vol. 3.
Collins R. 1974: 'Three faces of cruelty: towards a comparative sociology of violence', *Theory and Society*, vol. 1.
Divale W. T. and Harris M. 1976: 'Population, warfare and the male supremacist complex', *American Anthropologist*, vol. 78.
Hall J. 1984: 'Raymond Aron's sociology of states, or the non-relative autonomy of inter-state behaviour', in M. Shaw (ed), *War, State and Society*. London: Macmillan.
Jessop R. 1977: 'Recent theories of the capitalist state', *Cambridge Journal of Economics*, vol. 1.
Kissinger H. 1964: *A World Restored*. New York: Grosset and Dunlop.
Moore B. 1972: *Reflections on the Causes of Human Misery*. Boston: Beacon Press.
Otterbein K. F. 1970: *The Evolution of War: a Cross-Cultural Study*. New Haven, Conn.: Human Relations Area Files Press.
Richardson L. F. 1960: *Statistics of Deadly Quarrels*. London: Stevens.
Robinson J. P. 1977: 'The neutron bomb and mass-destruction conventional weapons', *Bulletin of Peace Proposals*, no. 4.
Shaw M. 1974: 'The theory of the state and politics: a central paradox of Marxism', *Economy and Society*, vol. 3.
—— 1984, 'War, imperialism and the state system: a critique of orthodox Marxism for the 1980s', in Shaw (ed), *War, State and Society*. London: Macmillan.
Singer J. D. and Small M. 1972: *The Wages of War 1816–1965*. New York: Wiley.
Sorokin P. A. 1962 ed: *Social and Cultural Dynamics*, vol. 3. New York: Bedminster Press.
Spanier J. W. 1972: *Games Nations Play*. London: Nelson.
Thompson E. P. 1980a: 'Notes on exterminism, the last stage of civilization', *New Left Review*, no. 121.
—— 1980b: 'Protest and survive', in Thompson and D. Smith, *Protest and Survive*. Harmondsworth: Penguin Books.
Tilly C. 1975: *The Formation of National States in Western Europe*. Princeton, NJ: Princeton University Press.
Wallerstein I. 1974: *The Modern World System*. New York: Academic Press.
—— 1979: *The Capitalist World Economy*. Cambridge: Cambridge University Press.
Wright Q. 1942: *A Study of War*. Chicago: University of Chicago Press.

5
War and Social Theory: into Battle with Classes, Nations and States

It would be easy to polemicize against 'orthodox sociology's' shameful neglect of war; to lament the paucity of sociology's contribution to the most urgent social problem of our time – peace; and to deride the naive, pacific optimism of the 'classic theorists' whose writings form the theoretical core of our own education and that of our students. But the neglect may now be over. Recently sociology has been paying more attention to war and peace; while the surrounding political and cultural climate has changed more radically. In the 'Star Wars' programmes – I do not mean the fantasy version by Ronald Reagan, but the real one by George Lucas – whole planets can be destroyed by a single weapons system. Today both adults and children recognize that as contemporary reality. This is paralleled by the more surreptitious growth of chemical weapons, persuading many commentators that the world may soon end, not with a bang but with a blister. If sociology has anything useful to say, it will have a large and receptive audience.

Thus I will not polemicize, but attempt to be constructive. First, I distinguish two relevant schools of nineteenth-century sociological theory: the liberal/Marxian and the militarist. Second, I draw out from each a core concept – respectively 'class' and 'nation' – and one shared concept – 'the state' – and revise them in the light of the twentieth century. Third, I chronicle the interrelations between these three major social actors in the recent

This chapter was first published in M. Shaw and C. Creighton (eds), *The Sociology of War and Peace* (1986). London: Macmillan. We are grateful for permission to reproduce it here.

history of war. I argue that much of our present danger stems from the way in which classes, nations and states have become closely entwined in the nineteenth and twentieth centuries. Finally, I conclude that the world might be a safer place if we could take class out of geo-politics.

Two schools of theory: liberal/Marxian and militarist

From the Enlightenment to Durkheim most major sociologists omitted war from their central problematic. This was not neglect; it was quite deliberate. They believed the future society would be pacific and transnational. Industrial, or capitalist, or 'modern' society would be unlike the preceding feudal, or theocratic, or militant societies. Power could now operate pacifically, without physical force. In their various theories rational, technocratic 'industrials' might now rule; 'profit' might replace 'plunder'; the surplus might be extractable by purely 'economic means'; or the market or the division of labour, once under way, might be self-regulating. Power would also operate transnationally. The state would remain puny, or even wither away, in the face of the massive global impact of industrialism, capitalism and science. Social classes would also become transnational. Whether classes were defined according to property, the market, or occupation, they could be found interchangeably at both the global level and the level of the individual national state. These notions dominate the theories of Smith, St-Simon, Comte, Spencer, Marx and Durkheim – our liberal and Marxian founding fathers.

This was an understandable view of the nineteenth century, as seen from an Anglo-French perspective. It is often said that there was a century of peace from 1815 to 1914. This is approximately true for the experience of Great Britain, and up to 1870 of France. It is not so true of the other Great Powers, Russia, Austria, Germany and the United States. But pacific transnationalism suited the interests of the two greatest powers of the early nineteenth century. Global penetration by industrialism, capitalism and science would enhance British, and to a lesser extent French, hegemony.

The view from central Europe, and for a time from the United States, differed. Friedrich List, supported by American economists, challenged the *laissez-faire* theories of Manchester. Germany and the United States overthrew British economic hegemony from the 1880s. Germany and Austria also harnessed economic growth more explicitly to military might from mid-century. Theorists there drew upon Social Darwinism to develop a more militarist approach. Gumplowicz, like Marx, was a materialist: society was driven forward by desires for economic gain and possibilities for the exploitation of labour. But militarism was the way to achieve both. Class structure resulted from wars between 'peoples' and from the expropriation by the victors of the vanquished. Rustow transformed this into a theory of 'superstratification'. 'Peoples' became ethnically homogeneous units, nations and even *races*, struggling for survival, in the work of Ratzenhofer (an Austrian general) and others. The political climate affected liberals like Hintze and Weber, and some Marxists wavered, developing theories of imperialism in which national classes perpetrated wars. In the United States, writers like Sumner explored 'folkways', 'in-groups' and 'outgroups' and ethnocentrism. Few of these sociologists believed the future lay securely with transnational pacifism – unless the world was first conquered by a single nation.

Who won this struggle over sociological theory? The result was deeply ironic. The appalling slaughter of 1914–18 and 1939–45, together with Fascism, would seem to support militarist theory. Peoples solidified under slogans of extreme, often racist, nationalism. Class struggle withered away at the onset of war, was often institutionalized faster as a result of victories, and intensified most in defeat. Geo-politically, Europe exhausted itself and suffered 'superstratification' imposed by US and Russian imperialism.

But unfortunately for the militarists, *their* armies lost. The Austrian Empire disintegrated; Russia was conquered by Marxism; Germany lost two wars and its militarist theories were outlawed from civilization. Finally, the United States became a super-power and re-discovered the usefulness of British transnational *laissez-faire* for its own global hegemony. As liberalism and Marxism divide up the geo-political and geo-economic world, they naturally dominate its sociology. Since 1945 the militarists have been forgotten, the waverers purged of their more violent side (e.g. Weber's *Herrschaft* became not 'domination' but 'authority' in English translation), and the 'classic tradition' of liberal/Marxist pacific transnational sociology has been enshrined in pedagogy.

In fact neither school's theories can be accepted today. Liberals and Marxists exaggerated the peaceful transnational powers of industrial capitalism, militarists exaggerated the power and cohesion of the nation and the race. We can appreciate the contemporary circumstances which led them to their conclusions, but place them in a broader historical perspective. We have to start this from scratch, however, because the liberal/Marxist conspiracy has suppressed much of the history of the relationship between war, classes, nations and states.

Amending the master-concepts: class, nation and state

Class

The liberal/Marxian school stressed the power of classes in modern society. In agrarian societies classes had been particularistic aggregations of households and lineages; now, however, classes would act as universal collectivities over the whole space of a society. In particular, they would have a profound collective impact upon the state. I will not quarrel with this. In the rest of what I say, collectivities like 'the capitalist class', 'the working class' etc. will stride about modern history. I hope I can be allowed this crudity without having to either define or qualify these classes at length.

But the liberal/Marxian school also saw classes as transnational. This I wish to question. In fact, we can hypothesize three possible types of class structure: transnational, international and national.

1 *Transnational:* class organization and struggle proceeds right across state boundaries, without significant reference to them, occurring throughout the global reach of industrial or capitalist (or whatever) society. States and nations are irrelevant to class struggle, and are weakened as power actors by the global reach of classes. The material 'praxis' of classes can thus supervise and correct the state's conduct of geopolitics. There can be no autonomy of the state here. This was the liberal/Marxian view.
2 *International:* all or some of the inhabitants of one state form a 'class' in relation to all or some of the inhabitants of another. Nations can struggle with one another, exploit one

another, and so become classes with their own distinctive class praxis. This was the 'superstratification' theory of the militarist school, and it has also influenced Marxism in the shape of theories of imperialism and dependency. International class relations will often turn warlike because such classes control armies.

3 *National*: class organization and struggle occurs within the confines of state boundaries, without significant reference to the world outside or to class struggles occurring in other states. In this case class praxis is not 'anchored' in international space. Though classes might get caught up in domestic struggles over the identity of 'the nation', they are inward-looking, divorced from, and incompetent in geopolitics. This possibility was neglected by both schools.

From the perspective of the late twentieth century we can see the role of all three in recent historical reality. I will stress *national* classes, which will support neither school of theory but lead to a more complex view of modern war.

Nations

Here we must amend militarist theory. We cannot define nations ethnically or racially. Nations do not derive from the same 'blood' or 'ethnic stock'; their genealogical histories are myths; they have no 'natural' existence or rights to their own states; warfare, no matter how ferocious, is not conducted between gene groups. The closest real approximation to the nationalist myth is when societies differ by physical phenotype, but their conflict still needs further explanation (and this type of warfare has not dominated Western history). The furthest away is the present super-power confrontation, for the United States is a nation-state created recently out of polyglot immigrants from several continents; while in the Soviet Union nationality provides only a regional and not a state-wide identity. Indeed, before the nineteenth century, there were very few 'nations'. Community identities were far more often provided by locality, class and religion, than by ethnicity or state membership. Yet in the nineteenth and twentieth centuries nations were indeed created, and almost all states came to legitimize themselves as 'nation-states'. Wars were fought between these states, often with the enthusiastic support of the 'nation'.

So what are nation-states, if they are not ethnic groups? They are *citizen* states, states of mass political membership, the first states in history in which all adult inhabitants have been active participants. At first citizenship was restricted by class and to men. But the meaning of 'nation' became clear right at the start. In the French Revolution, as Hans Kohn (1967) has noted, 'nation' changed its meaning – from the inhabitants of a territory or an aristocracy linked to their monarch by blood, to a political community of free, participating citizens. It kept this predominantly political meaning for almost 100 years, until Social Darwinism pushed blood and territory back into the definition. Thus the forward surge of nationalism and the continued relevance of war and militarism was connected to mass citizenship. The connection was made obvious with the emergence of mass mobilization warfare. Citizens did more than wave banners. Men fought in the front-line, and men and women accepted additional labour burdens in the 'rear'.

States

The two schools had different views of the modern state. The liberal/Marxian school saw it in domestic and primarily economic terms; the militarist school in geo-political and military terms. Nevertheless, both saw the state as a single cohesive institution, reducible to the dominant groups in its civil society. Thus the state elite represented the interests of the dominant class(es) – the Marxian view; or it mediated systematically between classes – the liberal view; or it represented the interests of the dominant military caste or of the nation or race – the militarist view. In these theories the state has little autonomy or 'privacy': the praxis of classes or nations supervises its activities.

I shall challenge this. The modern (Western) state is not single but dual, its domestic separable from its geo-political life. Moreover, the state elite has retained, even increased, its autonomy in the sphere of geo-politics. Geo-political privacy, even extending in war-making, has been much greater than in the domestic sphere. This is for two reasons.

The first reason concerns the general nature of geo-politics. Diplomacy is far less regulated, routinized and predictable than are major domestic politics. Diplomacy involves a number of autonomous states among whom there are few normative ties, yet continuous re-calculation of the main chance. The actions of one set up ripple reactions among the others, amounting to an unpredictable whole. Thus all states find, from time to time, that they are suddenly boxed into a corner, faced with unwelcome enemies or allies, or with a Hobson's choice between 'backing down' or actions that will be defined as highly aggressive. The *crisis* is essential to geo-politics, and, if serious, may suddenly confront nations or dominant classes with wholly unexpected, potentially devastating, but restricted policy choices. Secret diplomacy is set up to counteract some of the 'ripple effects' of geo-politics, and this further increases the privacy of the state. Indeed the state rulers may find that their diplomats and soldiers have developed their own secret procedures.

There were some spectacular examples of all these processes in the run-up to 1914: the Agadir crisis, the exposure of the secret Anglo-Russian naval treaty, the Russian choice in July 1914 between backing down before Austrian aggression in Serbia or having to mobilize aganinst both Austria and Germany (the Russian High Command suddenly assured the Tsar that mobilization only against Austria was technically impossible). Thus states, and even state departments, in all historical periods have dragged even the most powerful of domestic classes into geo-political strategies and even into wars that were not of their choosing.

Second, the state's autonomy and privacy varies according to the dominant type of class organization. *Transnational* classes are anchored in geo-political space. They can supervise their state's diplomacy. *International* classes have a clear geo-political strategy of their own. They can supervise the state's diplomacy and steer it against their enemies abroad. But *national* classes have no geo-political anchorage or strategy; they are inward-looking and lack expertise or interest to supervise their state. I will argue that the importance of *national* classes in the modern world has increased the autonomy and privacy of the state, even to war-making.

For these two reasons, modern *states*, as well as classes and nations, have made war – as my title suggests.

So classes may be transnational, national or international. Nations must be defined by political citizenship, not ethnicity.

War and Social Theory 153

States have an autonomy and a privacy in geo-politics. Let us now consider these actors in three phases of Western history.

Historical phase 1: pre-1780

Making war and peace was formally the private prerogative of the medieval prince. However, in reality war also required the feudal levies of the nobility or their consent to taxation. The nobility was additionally a *transnational* class, linked by genealogy and culture across Europe as a whole. So geo-politics and war were anchored in its rivalry for land, heiresses and honour. Moreover, wars were not devastating, did not involve the mass of the population, and were profitable to most surviving states.

However, the expansion and commercialization of agriculture then created quasi-national markets at home; while abroad it thrust merchants into a closer relationship with their own state. The nobility lost much of its transnational solidarity, and its military levies lost effectiveness. Nobles became military and civil office-holders of the state. Mercantilism increased the *international* class rivalry of merchants and nobilities. Stronger national markets and states also turned them inwards into *national* class organization. The prince retained his formal geo-political prerogatives. The masses were still uninvolved in geo-politics and war (except in religious wars). War remained profitable because of spectacular European expansion, and because it was not particularly devastating. Between 1500 and 1780 there was also a massive reduction in the number of states, from about 500 to just under 100 (Tilly, 1984), largely as a result of war. In a strict sense there were more losers than winners. But history is written by winners. Progress was seen as coming, among other things, from war.

Three legacies were thus handed down to industrial society. First, states' geo-politics and war-making was formally private. That remained their prerogative even in countries where their domestic prerogatives had been severely curtailed. Second, though they usually pursued foreign policies that were in the broad interests of the dominant domestic classes, the transnational anchorage of these classes had declined. Thus the state's geo-political privacy increased. Third, war was a normal and rational part of geo-political strategy for the relatively advanced state: it brought territories, markets and geo-political dominance, and it did not cost much in social resources.

I have a quotation that will illustrate the legacies. In 1740 Frederick II of Prussia invaded Silesia and eventually wrested it from Austria. Silesia became central to the Prussian economy, and so to Germany's rise as a Great Power. This is how Frederick himself described what turned out to be a world-historical act:

At my father's death, I found all Europe at peace ... The minority of the youthful Tsar Ivan made me hope Russia would be more concerned with her internal affairs than with guaranteeing the Pragmatic Sanction [the treaty allowing a woman, Maria Theresa, to succeed as Austrian Empress]. Besides, I found myself with highly trained forces at my disposal, together with a well-filled exchequer, and I myself was possessed of a lively temperament. These were the reasons that prevailed upon me to wage war against Theresa of Austria ... Ambition, advantage, my desire to make a name for myself – these swayed me, and war was resolved upon. (Quoted by Ritter, 1969, I, p. 19)

Note also how the rival states are personally named – another indication of the geo-political privacy of these dynasts.

I will now pursue these legacies – the privacy of geo-politics, the decline of class supervision and the rationality of war – into modern times.

Historical phase 2: 1780–1945

The Industrial Revolution had contradictory implications for class organization. On the one hand it converted the territories of the major states into fully fledged 'civil societies' in which universal, extensive classes cooperated and conflicted with one another. Regulating their relationships involved politics, focusing class organization inward, on to the national terrain, away from both local and transnational arenas. On the other hand, industrial capitalism became global, involving classes in transnational and international praxis. The situation of classes became more complex, and we must distinguish carefully between the organization of different classes in different periods and different states.

First, I discuss the capitalist class up to about the First World War. After 1815 industrialization went through a transnational phase. Capital and commodities flowed straight through state boundaries. In continental Europe most of the first industrializing areas were cross-border regions, like northern France and the Low Countries, the Saar and Rhineland, and Silesia and Bohemia. Capital was organized transnationally and it favoured conciliatory geo-politics. This was the breeding ground of liberal and Marxian theory.

But after mid-century the rise of Germany, of protectionism, and of greater state participation in the economy created national and sectoral divergencies among capital. In Germany heavy industry became more closely enmeshed with the state, and favoured more aggressive geo-politics than light industry or finance capital. In France the opposite was true: the closest geopolitical connection was between finance capital and the Quai d'Orsay. In Britain no major section of capital favoured aggression – the hope was that Germany would either go away or learn proper geo-political behaviour. But as international competition intensified, industries like steel and metal manufacture could grow by building warships and heavy guns. The growth of mass consumption markets within each country also expanded inward-looking national organization among many other capitalists. Capital became divided.

There were different resolutions in different countries. In Britain capital's divisions were partly responsible for the weakness of British foreign policy, especially its inability after 1900 to give unambiguous signals to Germany as to how far British treaty commitments would be backed up by force. German capital became more united behind the aggressive geo-politics of the Alliance of Rye and Iron – the Junker class and heavy industrial capital. This was the breeding-ground of militarist theory. But the unevenness of capital's influence – ambiguous in Britain, more militarist in Germany – made diplomacy more difficult and Europe more dangerous. It lessened the chances for the transnational predictions of liberalism and Marxism.

Thus no single form of capitalist class organization predominated. Capital's disunity consequently prevented this 'ruling class' from supervising state diplomacy to anything like the same extent as had the medieval nobility. The capitalist class might rule domestically – but not geo-politically.

Other classes were even less anchored transnationally. The

middle class was mainly concerned with obtaining citizenship – the franchise, legal and religious equality and educational opportunity. It demanded meritocratic reforms of institutions, a fair taxation system and protection from the 'dangerous classes' below. All these demands were addressed to the national state. When they were granted, political success 'naturalized' the middle class (leaving on one side the special situation of multi-national states like Austria). Without transnational anchorage, and without direct experience of international competition, the middle class became overwhelmingly *nationally* organized.

But the middle class went further. It correctly identified its own economic, political and cultural progress with the achievement of national citizenship. It became intensely proud of being 'British', 'French', 'German' etc. Its nationalism is often portrayed as paranoid, the projection of personal anxiety and repression on to the world. But its nationalism was joyous, celebratory, the expression of its sense of participatory citizenship. In Germany, Britain and France, the middle class dominated jingoist, chauvinist, militarist and even racist pressure groups. In the last decades before 1914 states found themselves confronted by a new problem. When boxed into geo-political crises, they were urged on to further aggression by this middle class 'public opinion'. Middle class supervision of geo-politics was unstable, however, because it was not anchored in international praxis.

The working class was not so chauvinist. It had not achieved full citizenship by 1914, so the state was not 'its' state. Nevertheless, its most organized class struggles – for Factory Acts, legalization of trade unions, the franchise, reform of Poor Laws, etc. – were directed at the state. Despite the transnational rhetoric of socialism, workers were not transnationally anchored. Their praxis and their organization was becoming steadily more *national*, leaving them without great interest or expertise in geopolitics. Radical workers followed the leadership of pacific, transnational liberals who were their allies in their domestic class struggles. On occasion the mass of workers could be rallied round the flag, and in 1914 they went loyally to war, though with far less enthusiasm than the middle class.

So the rise of extensive, universal classes had made states more accountable for their domestic actions, but not for their geopolitics. Before 1914 capital pushed in contradictory directions, the middle class shoved erratically towards an uninformed militarism, the working class had other priorities.

Thus the second historical legacy, the conduct of geo-politics, changed little in the nineteenth century. In semi-parliamentary regimes like Austria or Germany, the constitution reserved foreign policy – sometimes excluding trade treaties, but including military budgets – as the monarch's preorgative, not to be scrutinized by parliament. Even in Britain scrutiny was limited. Foreign policy was supposedly initiated by Parliament, but discussion of policy was kept private. The Foreign Secretary normally sat in the Lords, not the Commons. He brought policy matters not to full Cabinet but to informal meetings of a few senior statesmen. Parliamentary requests for information were regularly repulsed with the phrase 'not in the public interest' (Cromwell and Steiner, 1972). The British state kept its geo-political privacy even while miners' MPs were crowding into the House of Commons.

But would geo-politics still routinely involve war? Was not the third historic legacy, the rationality and cheapness of war, now ended? With hindsight, obviously yes. In the twentieth century it became rational only to enter wars towards the end, as the early combatants exhausted themselves, and on terms, as the United States did. The costs of 'success' also rose phenomenally. Perceptive observers could see the escalation of the costs and casualties of war, from the Napoleonic Wars, through the American Civil War, to the arms race around 1900.

But the states, the diplomats and the General Staffs did not pay much attention to the American Civil War. The General Staffs believed that the Prussian victories in 1867 and 1870 over Austria and France had demonstrated that speed of mobilization, advance and reinforcement could bring a decisive result. That is why in the run-up to 1914, when the geo-political situation became really dangerous, the generals stopped restraining the militarists and added their weight to them. 'Get your retaliation in first' was the advice of the Austrian generals over Serbia, of the Russians in mobilizing, and of the Germans in their pre-emptive strike into Belgium and France. The escalation of the horrors of war only happened in Europe because the French armies held their ground in 1914 and 1915 despite enormous losses. Until then the place of war in geo-political strategy was unchanged.

So was everything changed in the mud of the Somme and the

Marne? Did the full devastation of war between equally matched opponents now bring a more pacific tone to geo-politics? With hindsight we know this did not happen, and for a variety of reasons. But one reason is germane to my theme. The war became a 'people's war' and the people wanted victory even at the cost of slaughter. The people were somewhat isolated from the front (except in France) and did not appreciate its full devastation. But also, the experience of the middle class before the war — progress through the nation — now became more generalized to the people as a whole. The people sacrificed but not for nothing. A bargain was struck, fairly explicitly: at the end of the war there would be extension of the franchise (probably including women) and welfare reforms. The downpayment was made already: full employment and greater trade union rights. The entry of the working class, and of women, into citizenship was accelerated by mass mobilization warfare. This had occurred already in the North during the American Civil War; it was to happen again in Europe in the Second World War.[1]

So in the first half of the twentieth century the middle and working classes became national citizens, and were prepared to fight and toil to defend the symbols of their citizenship — monarch, flag, homeland and kith and kin. As modern classes emerged, they became predominantly *nationally* organized. As class struggles were regulated and institutionalized, nations emerged and classes developed a certain loyalty to the nation. But, contrary to militarist theory, this was not anchored in international praxis. Nations were not interested or competent in geo-politics. Peoples were still plunged into wars through the private machinations of state elites. True, when tensions were high and policy options began closing down, or when war was actually under way, 'public opinion' could become bellicose and make it difficult for the diplomats to back down. But mass militarism was not anchored in praxis and so was volatile. If the leaders of the nation could not deliver victory, then the cry of 'treason' went up against them. Sections of the middle, and especially the working class escalated citizen demands, supported revolutionaries and appeared sudden converts to transnationalism. This happened in all the defeated

---

1 These generalizations apply best to Britain; they apply largely to Austria-Hungary and Germany in the First World War, and partially to the United States in both wars and to Italy in the First World War; they apply least to Russia in both wars and France in the First World War.

powers (Russia, Austria, Germany and Hungary) in the years following 1917.

We can draw three conclusions about this phase. First, war remained a rational, accepted part of a geo-political strategy that in turn remained largely the private responsibility of the state. Second, class organization took a largely *national* form, and not either the transnational form predicted by liberalism and Marxism or the international form predicted by militarist theory. This meant that class praxis could not supervise geo-politics. Third, when the rationality of war weakened, in the twentieth century, a shallow, volatile chauvinism emerged to disguise this, at first among the middle class, then among the working class (and probably among women) too. Our present predicament stems from this 'negative reinforcement' which classes have added to the willingness of state elites to use war as a rational instrument of geo-politics. The way that class struggle was resolved in citizenship had made the world a more dangerous place.

Historical phase 3: post-1945

Since 1945 the most obvious change has been in the devastation of war. The 'kill ratio' of weapons has been estimated to have increased half-a-million times from the V-2 warhead of the Second World War to even a 25-megaton nuclear warhead today (Robinson, 1977). If the two super-powers went to war against each other, Armageddon would result. One of the historic legacies, war as profitable and rational, has ended. This may not yet be true of the confrontation of minor states, but militarism between the super-powers has changed fundamentally.

It might seem, therefore, that geo-politics is now too important to be left to the state. But it still is. Despite looming Armageddon, the combination of private geo-politics and volatile, shallow popular chauvinism continues. In chapter 6 I identify those two types of contemporary militarism in Western and Soviet societies as 'deterrence science militarism' and 'spectator sport militarism'. The former is shared by diplomatic, military and political elites of both super-powers and their allies. Regarding deterrence as workable, they have evolved a complicated set of geo-political strategies, rules of behaviour and signals to each other, in which public opinion has little knowledge or interest. In recent years the public has only become aware of these geo-political complexities at exactly the same point as in the previous historical phase: when the rules falter, usually because of the independent action of supposed clients, and the super-powers become boxed into crises, with options narrowed to 'backing down' or aggression. That is where mass public opinion begins to show an interest. Its 'spectator-sport militarism', which shouts xenophobic encouragement from the sidelines to 'our boys', the professional soldiers, then becomes dangerously destabilizing.

So why has so little changed? If my model is correct, the answer lies in the stability of the historic relations between transnational, international and national class organization. Yet there has been one major change in the relationship between class praxis and geo-political struggle. The latter is not now between capitalist states, but between them and a self-styled socialist bloc of states. Moreover, since 1945 the economies of both blocs have become internally integrated. Within the West capital has enormously increased organizations of a kind we normally call *transnational*. These co-exist with peaceful *international* rivalry between capitalist nation-states. Various global institutions embody this duality of class praxis: the International Monetary Fund, the World Bank, the General Agreement on Tariffs and Trade (GATT), multi-national corporations, Euro-dollars etc. Yet in relation to the super-power confrontation, this class praxis is really *national* – confined within the sphere of interest of the United States, the capitalist super-power state. No capitalist organizations significantly penetrate across the Iron Curtain, though there are state-supervised trading links between the two blocs. Thus class struggles in the West do not directly affect the economic interests of Soviet or East European citizens. Nor do class struggles in the Soviet bloc greatly affect the economic interests of Western citizens. Thus social classes have neither transnational nor international praxis which would give them genuine interest or competence in geo-political rivalry between the super-powers. This is in marked contrast to their interest and competence in geo-politics internal to world capitalism, where classes lobby constantly on issues such as free trade versus protectionism. The geo-politics of economic and military power have become largely separated.

But there is another, novel linkage between class struggles and super-power conflict. The external geo-political enemy can be plausibly associated with an internal class enemy, and the combined struggle is then presented as a struggle for world civilization itself. This is not unique to the contemporary world — for example, classical Greece and Persia struggled in this way — but it means that geo-politics becomes peculiarly ideological. In its official ideology the Soviet Union represents the vanguard of the global proletarian revolution, while the West and internal opposition both represent the capitalist enemy. Western hawkish ideology argues the converse: Western socialism is a covert agent for state dictatorship on the Soviet model. Both super-powers assert that their struggle is rooted in class praxis, of a novel, mixed transnational/international type.

Indeed, this was plausible in the years after 1917. A large part of the Western working class movement looked to Moscow for inspiration; the Bolsheviks led the Comintern against global capitalism; and Western capital sought to snuff out Bolshevism in its homeland. But ever since its plausibility has declined. The Comintern was wound up in 1942 in the interests of the geo-political alliance against Fascism. Since 1945 the super-powers have learned the rules of 'deterrence-science militarism' (see chapter 6) refraining from encouraging 'class allies' in each other's territories. In any case, Western socialists now distance themselves from Soviet-style 'socialism'. Eurocommunism and the decline of Communist parties still loyal to Moscow have been the last, decisive nails in the Comintern's coffin. There is an additional conspiracy theory that ruling classes in both West and East deliberately use the threat of the enemy to keep down their subordinate classes. Maybe they do in the East; but in the West, outside of the paranoid Right, capital does not feel itself in imminent danger of class revolution even if the Soviet bogy was withdrawn. Capitalists are not sufficiently threatened by the working class movement in any advanced country rationally to continue risking nuclear war. So there has been a historical lag between reality and ideology. Today no genuine, deeply rooted transnational/international class praxis directly divides the super-powers.

However, we must also consider more indirect links between class praxis and the super-powers. The first is routed through developing countries, whose reformers sometimes turn to the Soviets for help against Western capital. The West often also pre-empts this possibility by precipitously repressing the reformers. There is an element of international class rivalry in this, both blocs seeking economic as well as military dominance over developing countries. For these reasons the capitalist class has maintained its aggressive geo-politics against 'world-wide communism'. This also applies, for slightly different reasons, to the Soviet ruling class.

But the economic part of this rivalry is asymmetric. Western capitalism offers developing countries far greater investment capital and markets than can the Soviets. Countries have turned to the Soviets primarily for arms, and because they have been spurned first by the West. Only the terms of interdependence with the West have raised stumbling-blocks, but these have been either geo-political or Western opposition to local reform, not local preference for economic and political interdependence with the Soviets. For example, Western support for Israel has been the key factor in the pro-Soviet phases of Egypt, Syria and Iraq; local geo-political complexities brought the Soviets into the Horn of Africa; while Western resistance to local reform was decisive in Cuba and Vietnam and has changed the outcomes of class struggles throughout central and Latin America. Again the genuine linkages of class praxis are weaker than the ideology of geo-politics suggests — a point to which I return in my conclusion.

The second indirect link between class praxis and geo-politics is provided by the historic legacy of nationalist citizenship. Are Western middle and working classes still trapped within pre-dominantly *national* organizations, spouting superficial chauvinism? The answer is yes, but perhaps in Europe (and Japan), if not in the United States or the Soviet Union, we are coming to the end of an era. The popular equation of citizenship with war mobilization ended around 1950. It is not likely to be revived, given the nature of war today. The equation of prosperity with economic-military hegemony is still real in the United States, but it has faded in Europe and Japan. A sense of social progress and citizenship may still be associated in the United States and the Soviet Union with national military greatness; but it is becoming anachronistic in Europe and Japan.

So in this third phase two historic legacies have remained unscathed: the state's geo-political privacy and its willingness to use the threat of war as a rational instrument of diplomacy. Classes have still not emerged fully from the second historical phase, in which citizenship in the nation-state turned them inward into *national* rather than outward to *transnational* organization, yet also encouraged them to embrace the politics of *international* aggression. The latter received a peculiarly dangerous twist when the Bolshevik Revolution gave geo-politics an ideology of direct *transnational* class struggle. Thus all three of my collective actors – classes, nations and states – share responsibility for our present danger. Indeed it is their interconnections that make us fear the end of the world. The mass enthusiasm of class struggle and national citizenship has been added to the private geo-political strategies of state elites, now armed with nuclear and chemical weapons.

Hope for the future: taking class out of geo-politics

So to see how the situation might improve we must centre on whether class and geo-politics can be further separated. Perhaps mild optimism might be in order. In the late twentieth century the destabilizing role of class in geo-politics is declining, and its decline can be further assisted.

First, the Western working class movement might finally sever the last link with the vision of 'socialism' as represented by the Soviet Union. A few intellectuals and trade unionists still retain the sentimental attachments of their youth. What especially lingers is an anachronistic appraisal of Soviet foreign policy, based on events in the Soviet civil war period (Soviet realistic fear of encirclement, purely defensive mentality etc.), supposedly still dominating Soviet geo-politics. Yet Soviet *realpolitik* is not greatly influenced by the nature of its domestic regime (whether we see that as socialist or as totalitarian). It is the *realpolitik* of a Great Power, little different from those of any Great Power in history, including Great Britain in the nineteenth century. Socialists could perhaps send an even clearer message to capitalists: yes, we are engaged in class struggle against you, but this is not remotely connected with the super-power confrontation. Similarly, Western capital might perhaps be encouraged toward greater realism: Western socialist movements have nothing in common with the interests of the Soviet Union; the Soviet Union is neither particularly socialist nor particularly evil in its geo-political intent but just a foreign Great Power; and nuclear brinkmanship is not in anyone's class interests. The recent alliance in the West between capitalism and militarism is obsolete. Class politics and geo-politics are separable.

Thus could be rendered obsolete some of the historic linkage between *national* and *transnational* class struggles, and *international* geo-political confrontation. The only remaining linkage would be Western capital's fear of Third World reform movements backed by the Soviet Union. But on this point my analysis renders pertinent a strategy long advocated by Western liberals. President Carter's Angolan policy provides the model. Angola needed the West; it could get little objective benefit from the Soviet Union; therefore the West could negotiate amicably with whatever regime arose there, no matter what it called itself. The Western oil companies might receive lower profits from a self-styled 'Marxist' regime than from a South African-backed one. But this was worth sacrificing for (a) keeping Western influence and profits for other companies in Angola (the Carter argument) and (b) defusing the last remaining linkage between Western class politics and the super-power confrontation (my argument). The geo-political benefits for the West, and the boost to world peace, would be considerable. Such a strategy might increase tension by isolating the Soviet Union in her own bloc. But if the Soviet Union wishes to compete with a more enlightened West over the developing countries, then it could do so, with butter rather than guns, and by encouraging real socialist democracy there. And if propaganda of all hues were confined to geo-political issues, then it would at least be dealing more with the reality of the situation.

To take class out of geo-politics would not in itself bring peace. But it would concentrate our minds on a simpler, less emotionally laden choice: is the game of geo-political rivalry alone worth the risk of Armageddon?

References

Cromwell V. and Steiner Z. 1972: 'The Foreign Office before 1914: a study in resistance', in G. Sutherland (ed.), *Studies in the Growth of Nineteenth-Century Government*. London: Routlege.

Kohn H. 1967: *Prelude to Nation-States: the French and German Experience 1789–1815*. Princeton, NJ: van Nostrand.
Ritter G. 1969: *The Sword and the Sceptre*, vol. 1: *The Prussian Tradition, 1740–1890*. Coral Gables, Fa: University of Miami Press.
Robinson J. P. 1977: 'The neutron bomb and mass destruction conventional weapons', *Bulletin of Peace Proposals*, vol. 4.
Tilly C. 1984: 'The geography of European statemaking and capitalism since 1500', Center for Studies of Social Change, New School for Social Research, New York, Working Papers, no. 4.

6
The Roots and Contradictions of Modern Militarism

I define militarism as a set of attitudes and social practices which regards war and the preparation for war as a normal and desirable social activity. This is a broader definition than is common among scholars. It qualifies people other than John Wayne as militarists. But in an age when war threatens our survival, it is as well to understand any behaviour, however mild in appearance, which makes war seem either natural or desirable.

In many societies militarism has been 'up-front'. Young men have been educated in violent pursuits to teach them the techniques of riding, shooting and close combat and their accompanying forms of morale. Notions of skill, bravery, honour, leadership and cunning acquired military coloration among males. We have examples from many societies – from ancient Persia to Republican Rome to medieval Europe to early modern Prussia. But modern society is not like that. Education and the socialization of the young are largely pacific. Our sports do not relate well to modern warfare, even violent ones like boxing. True, the play of young boys is often militaristic, and male notions of honour retain some of the coloration of traditional militarism, but these are elements in a diverse modern culture, not its core. Nor could they be reasonable preparation for the highest nuclear level of warfare.

So contemporary militarism is not up-front. It is subtle and diverse. I want to tease out three types of contemporary militarism. First, *deterrence-science militarism* is shared by elites of East and West. Second, *militarized socialism* predominates among the Soviet people. Third, *spectator-sport militarism* pre-

This chapter was first published in New Left Review, (March/April 1987), no. 162. We are grateful for permission to reproduce it here.

dominates among Western citizens. Each may be dangerous to our survival: but other dangers emerge from the essential instability of the relationship between the two Western forms. The instability has been largely contributed by the rapidity of revolutions in military and geo-political relations over the past century or so. Thus I analyse the problem historically, distinguishing three main phases of the highest level of warfare, labelled *limited, citizen* and *nuclear* war. Elements from each co-mingle in the contemporary world, and their uneasy co-existence is our problem. I concentrate on the experience of Europe, Russia and the United States. I make no claim that the patterns I identify apply to other areas of modern militarism.

Phase 1: limited war, 1648–1914[1]

I start with two examples.

Example A: the Austro-Prussian War, 1866–1867 When Bismarck saw the performance of a small, mobile Prussian army in Denmark in 1865, he thought that a war against Austria would be one of rapid movement, would be short and would probably result in Prussian victory. The Austrian leaders shared the first two assumptions because after initial defeats in 1866–7, they negotiated. Imperfect knowledge helped the rationality of this war since European strategies were based on recent European examples, not on the American Civil War, a war of attrition. Had Prussian staff colleges studied that, they may not have gone to war in 1866, or again in 1870 against France. Nor, perhaps, would their opponents have sued for peace after initial defeats. These were relatively rational wars on the part of Bismarck and Wilhelm because (a) war was believed to be short, low in casualties and in damage to the economy; (b) on balance it could result in victory; (c) victory would acquire territories and German hegemony; and (d) it would unite the Prussian nation, and it would unite the German nation behind Prussia, thus deflecting internal class antagonisms and restoring military morale to the more 'citizen-oriented pattern of 1813–14, and so in turn increase the likelihood of further victories. For their part, the Austrians made not

---

1 An excellent recent analysis of the organization of war in this whole period can be found in McNeill, 1983. An older, classic review is Vagts, 1959.

dissimilar calculations: (a) they believed the war would be short and low in damage; (b) they did not believe they would be defeated – since they had the greater overall resources and the greater recent experience of wars; (c) victory would bring territory and hegemony; and (d) it could divert the multi-ethnic and class tensions of the Empire (apparently they had no thought of a more popular, mobilized militarism). The Austrian reactions after defeat were congruent with this. They blamed the Prussian needle gun and their own commanders; but they also believed that wars were many and varied and that they might win the next one, as they had always bounced back in the past. They were wrong for the first time, because of the second of the reasons given under (d) Prussia above. 'Citizen armies' were arriving – far more powerful than their predecessors.

So this war is not difficult to explain rationally. The reasoning of both sides was good in terms of their prior knowledge. The more acute and better organized, the Prussians, were also the aggressors.

Example B: the Seven Years War, 1756–1763 This was a war of many aspects and motives, but British motivation gradually emerged as straightforward – to take over French colonies in North America, the West Indies and India. British strategy was to use the numerical superiority of British settlers in America, and to pay the Prussians and recruit mercenaries for Ferdinand of Brunswick to open a 'second front' against the French in central Europe. French military resources were stretched; the British Navy had the edge at sea: but as Pitt said, 'Canada will be won in Silesia'. It was. So was North America, the West Indies, Senegal and India. As soon as they were ceded, Prussia was abandoned by the British (and nearly destroyed). The colonies were not really won for the British state, as were the Prussian victories of Example A, because the state did not exist as a force 'above society'. Rather, the colonies were won for the private companies who ruled them for profit. They saw huge future profits in an extension of monopolies. For the Prussians the war was not limited, for their state was almost destroyed. But for the British, using relatively few troops, it was limited and likely to be profitable given Britain's unique geo-political advantages.

French activity is also explicable, but in different terms. Unlike the Austrian losers in my other example, their conduct 'didn't make sense'. We are tempted to call it irrational, because the reasons for their defeat seem almost inevitable to us. True, Prussia's resilience and Clive's brilliance in India were unexpected. But beyond lay a century of French failure (a) to decide whether to be a European land power or a world colonial one (the same dilemma had earlier destroyed Spain), and (b) to develop a fully fledged fiscal–military system based either on universal despotism or on taxation with representation. But this is not really irrationality, because states are not persons. States are composed of various families, classes, elites and interest groups, sometimes relatively united, as in the other states considered, sometimes disunited, as in the French case. France's motives in the colonial war were the same as Britain's. Her failure to achieve them does not indicate lack of rationality but lack of political unity to allocate enough priority to them.

I have chosen these wars as representative of most European and North American wars between about 1648 and 1914, that is, between the ferocity of the Wars of Religion, and the weaponry devastation and tactical attrition of twentieth-century wars. In this period there were wars that do not fit the pattern I now identify. I will return later to one of them, the French Revolutionary and Napoleonic Wars. Such exceptions apart, early modern European war and planning for war involved six elements. They were:

1 Relatively short set-piece battles or mobile campaigns in which
2 manpower and material losses, though sometimes high, would not need continual replacing and which, therefore,
3 had relativly little impact on society as a whole (unless fought over its territory – recognized by the Prussians as an argument for fighting just over their borders!);
4 where war planning was relatively 'private' to the state elite and its clients, not being of great concern to the mass of the population (I discussed this further in chapter 5) and
5 where it was relatively rational from the point of view of both ends and means.

The ends were highly desirable, worth the sacrifices involved; and Europe as a whole gained as it expanded through wars into the globe. All the foregoing also enabled war risks and means to be calculated more precisely, and the calculations could be inserted into a rational geo-political diplomacy. This was the age of the theorist-generals and diplomats, especially in central Europe – of Clausewitz and von Moltke, and Metternich and Bismarck. Through the staff college system militarism became military science, harnessed to the logic of geo-political strategy, partaking in the scientific and technological developments of industrial capitalism. So finally (a sixth point to add to the list above) both sides shared common understandings of the 'rules' and 'signals' of military and diplomatic science.

The formal rationality of 'limited war' is the first root of modern militarism. As a form of warfare it was superseded by another, but it is still relevant today in three ways.

1 In most European countries and to a lesser extent in the United States and the Soviet Union, a military tradition was laid down in that period which still dominates. Through regimental structures, flags, parades, national anthems and martial music much of the public display and private *éspirt de corps* of militarism has been relatively unchanged since. It arose to provide *some* public legitimation for what was essentially a private militarism; as we shall see, it still fulfils that role.

2 The formal rationality of limited war planning has endured and its central procedures are still those of military science embodied in staff colleges. Clausewitz enabled that rationality to be transferred to the warfare of industrial societies. He argued that the essence of military success is the mobilization of the resources of the state and their concentration upon the armies of the enemy. The mobilization powers of the industrial state and its ability to deliver them into battle increased exponentially through the nineteenth century, but no qualitative shift of strategy occurred until the Second World War. Then the principle of 'concentration' was weakened: not just armies, but global communications routes and civilian populations, were now aimed at. Nuclear strategy has added shifts of emphasis. But overall military science has had an unbroken history – what Michael Howard (1970, pp. 154–83) has called the 'classic tradition' of

strategic thinking, from Jomini and Clausewitz to Pentagon war-gamers.
3 As we see later, military science has been strengthened by nuclear deterrence theory.

So the legacy of Phase 1 is the continuity of traditions which view war and the planning of war as a normal part of the repertoire of geo-politics, relatively rational in means and ends, an essential part of modern scientific mentality. So, though liberals or Marxists or pacifists often regard professional military men and their attendant politicians as 'throwbacks' to more bestial ages, it is important to recognize that this is the opposite of how they see themselves, as an essential part of modern, progressive, positive science.

Phase 2: citizen warfare, 1914–1945

The origins of this phase are usually traced to 1792, to the cannonade at Valmy and to the consequent *levée en masse* of the French Revolutionary Armies (see Best, 1982, for this paragraph). At Valmy, the Prussian army was beaten off from an attack on Paris by the effectiveness of French artillery, whose officers were predominantly bourgeois and loyal to the Revolution. Then mobilization *en masse* produced large, enthusiastic but relatively untrained citizen-soldiers. War was public and national. Napoleon developed recent tactical innovations towards greater flexibility (divisions, columns, skirmishes etc.) and such soldiers became unusually effective. This also meant that war was more devastating and long-drawn-out. After 1815, the victors acted consciously in concert to suppress citizen-soldiers and resurrect the military science of limited war.

A second origin can be found in the American Civil War. The northern commanders realized they would win a war of attrition. They devastated the terrain, mobilized the economy and accepted very high troop losses. Limited war was in effect over. But only one of two lessons was drawn by many Europeans; they realized that Clausewitz had to be developed further, that mobilization of the nation's whole resources on battlefield brought victory; but they still viewed wars as limited in time. They believed that the nation would not tolerate a long war.

Nevertheless, from 1880 onwards, obvious changes were occurring everywhere. An arms race, especially in the building of ships and their guns, escalated state military budgets and mobilized industrial resources. As these states were by now quasi-democratic, public opinion was mobilized. Imperialism and militarism became popular currents of opinion, though mostly confined to the middle class before 1914. In August 1914, however, most classes were caught up in war-fever and mass voluntary enlistment.

By 1916, almost all the characteristics of limited war seemed obsolete. War was long-drawn-out; it was appallingly destructive of men and material; it drained the resources of societies; its conduct was public and publically supported; and it was difficult to regard it as a rational means towards a valued end. But violence was still confined to the battlefield – the main surviving characteristic. The generals continued to plan in a military-science manner, but the more acute realized that the game they were playing was no longer chess but mass hara-kiri.

The First World War inaugurated a period of war fare which seemed to reverse the characteristics of the previous period. War between Great Powers was appalling, yet it was public and even popular. This characterization is not wholly secure. Anti-war riots and mutinies occurred from 1916 onwards. Inter-war militarism was very unevenly spread. The causes of the Second World War were much more specific than those of the First. The German High Command made determined efforts in the late 1930s to avoid another war of attrition, and they were partly successful. Militarism after the Second World War has been rather different. Nevertheless, a paradox has existed in twentieth-century militarism which had not earlier been present: *war is appalling, but it is popular.*

Intellectuals have had difficulty in dealing with this paradox, especially liberals and Marxists. They have reacted with three types of theory. First, Freudian theories of the unconscious, of man's (not woman's!) innate aggression, of displaced aggression, of collective unconscious which emphasize the irrationality of militarism. Second, Marxists and others have advanced a kind of perverted, cataclysmic economic interest theory, in which war represents the death-throes of capitalism, or the wrong choice between 'socialism and barbarism'. Third, liberals have stuck grimly to classical, nineteenth-century theory: somehow militarism must represent the last gasp of 'traditional' society, soon to be rendered obsolete. Respectable academic versions of these general theories seek to explain many of the deatils of twentieth-century militarism, purporting to show, for example, that the lower middle class was status-insecure or paranoid; that big business supported Hitler's militarism; or that the First World War represented the triumph of the 'old order'. All these claims are essentially incorrect – though this can hardly be demonstrated here.

The problem is still relevant today. We plan for a war that would be utterly devastating, and yet that planning has broad popular support. So it is important for us to understand this paradox, the second root of modern militarism. My explanation builds upon orthodox accounts of the development of class relations and citizenship, merely taking this further than liberal or Marxist accounts (with their horror of war) are willing to do. But we must distinguish between the two World Wars.

The causes of the First World War include the growth of bourgeois nationalism. Studies of nationalist, militarist and imperialist pressure groups in the late nineteenth century reveal consistently their middle class basis. Studies of the political process reveal the successful pressure exercised electorally by the middle class on political parties. In the end, in 1914, this pressure helped push reluctant statesmen over the brink into war. Though analysis of peace and war parties must obviously be detailed and complex, studies tend to show that the most pro-war faction was the middle class, and that its pressure was effective. But, in contrast to the views of most of the authors of these studies, its nationalism was not primarily a response to frustrations, anxieties, uprootedness, economic decline and the like (see Mayer, 1975 for a typical view). This cannot explain why, first, nationalism was joyous and expanded with economic growth, not decline; why, second, it was celebratory in spirit; and third, why its doctrine was so bound up with a confident view of progress. Nationalism was a typically evolutionary theory of society: it constructed historical stages of the nation's evolution and pointed, through contemporary social mobilization, to the 'destiny' of the nation, 'its place in the sun', often, of course, through 'duty', 'sacrifice' and a Darwinian struggle with others. There is a ghastly optimism about a series of nations each convinced that sacrifice and struggle will ultimately favour it. This is an important part of what has always been seen as the 'irrationality' of nationalism.

But the optimism had a real social base. From about the 1860s to 1914, middle class experience was one of progress – not just of material progress, though this was marked, but political and cultural too. The middle class became house-owners, servant-employers, voters, jurors, literate participators in national culture and commerical markets– these were all solid achievements, summing up to the first mass-participatory societies seen anywhere since the Roman Republic. There were two variant forms. In continental Europe, nationalism from 1789 onwards had first been a domestic ideology of citizen rights for male householders. In countries like Britain and the United States, where these rights were achieved relatively early, nationalism was less an overt ideology than an implicit sense of identity, stake and community in the nation. In both, the aggressive and militarist nationalism which began to appear in the last decade of the nineteenth century was built on top of the notion of a progressive, prosperous bourgeois nation in control of its own destiny.

With hindsight we can call this new aggressive nationalism 'irrational'. In 1914, not many knew of the extent of the sacrifices to come. The German Chancellor, Bethmann Hollweg, said he was expecting 'a war lasting three, or at the most, four months . . . a violent, but short storm'. Furthermore, employing the traditional rationality of limited war of a Metternich or a Bismark, he expected the war to lead to a friendly relationship with England and France against the 'Russian colossus' (Fisher, 1967, pp. 87–92). Two years later, stuck in the mud of the Somme and of Verdun, this world of short, instrumental, privately negotiated wars had come to an end. The nations were fighting a terrible war of attrition and they hated one another so much that diplomats who tried to end the war could not do so. It is at this point that the new nationalist militarism might seem irrational.

But by 1916 we have to widen our focus. The nationalists were no longer centred on just the middle class and sections of the upper classes. The war was one of mass mobilization of both soldiers and civilians. The rulers needed the masses. So the war escalated tendencies already under way in peace-time to bring representation and reform to workers and peasants. This had happened already to the North in the American Civil War. In Britain, Austria-

Roots and Contradictions of Modern Militarism 175

Hungary and Germany the bargain became explicit: war participation must mean civic participation. This was the demand of the working class movement, and it was in varying and grudging degrees conceded both formally and informally. In Britain the replacement of Asquith by Lloyd-George symbolized the new 'People's War'. Thus the working class was involved in a speeded-up and explicitly military version of the bourgeois dialetic: progress through the nation. So there was a 'rationality' even in the slaughter: popular rule could be the better advanced through militarism. In France the dialectic was weaker. Citizen militarism was more defensive – defending the citizen Republic against foreign despotism. The same ideology of citizen defence, though far milder, was also found in the United States after American entry into the war. As we shall see, defensive forms of citizen militarism have come to predominate in the modern world.

On the Western front the dialectic was prolonged through distinctive features of the fighting – the lack of class divisions in the experience of officers and men, the insulation of the British and German troops (under military discipline) from their civilian populations and the illusion that defeat was unlikely because no territory was being ceded. Morale was thus higher and longer-lasting than we might have expected. On the Eastern Front it was different: a war of movement could lead to massive experience of defeat during the war, the sphere of operations was not so easily isolated from the civilian population, and distinctions of rank were more clearly experienced. Moreover, the Russian regime was not prepared to concede demands for civic participation. Morale there proved more brittle.

In 1917 and 1918, we must add a new variable: victory or defeat. Popular sacrifice was less easily sustainable in defeat. First in Russia, then in Germany and Austria-Hungary, came revolution after defeat. Correspondingly, in Britain and to a lesser extent in France and the United States came reformist demands for payment to the working class of the fruits of victory. But amid all the diverse outcomes of these struggles, there was one surprisingly constant thread: the nation was not abandoned. In Britain, France and the United States, the nation-state was strengthened; in Germany and Italy there was intense struggle between two alternative conceptions of 'the people' and two alternative sets of unpatriotic scapegoats for defeat (or for poor performance in a victory attained by its allies in the case of Italy); in Russia the Bolsheviks managed to equate the people with the working class and its party; while in the old territories of Austria-Hungary, the legitimacy of the new regimes was located in nations. The people/nation emerged vastly strengthened and with pretensions to democracy almost everywhere.

I do not claim that what happened next fits into any general pattern. Closely contested events in Germany resulted in Nazism. The Second World War resulted, for Germany and Japan, in a pattern of post-1945 military–civil relations that is peculiar, and which I will not attempt to explain.

Elsewhere the Second World War tended to accentuate earlier tendencies. Other combatants witnessed a revival of the dialectic of development of civic and military participation. In Europe, welfare state democracy was intensified. In the Soviet Union, the success of the war effort may well have saved Stalin's regime, and revived the equation of party, working class and nation. This remained relatively militaristic as we see later. In the Soviet Union and the United States the dialectic was weaker than in Western Europe and the ideology of citizenship more defensive: 'socialism' or 'democracy' had been successfully defended by popular effort.

So our conclusion in relation to the second phase of militarism, lasting and existing from just before 1900 to about 1950, must be that mass notions of progress and democracy – so important to twentieth-century culture – have been closely associated with, and boosted by, mass mobilization warfare. Militarism has been relatively rational – more so than liberalism or Marxism admit – not intrinsically, as it was in Phase 1, but because it served broader, desirable goals. I am not asserting that either world war was intrinsically rational. Both were too destructive. Rather they can be glossed by contemporary ideologies as being regrettably necessary for the achievement and preservation of a more important and desired social state, citizenship and democracy either of the Western, liberal type or the Soviet (or Chinese) version of socialism. Phase 2, like Phase 1, has been part of the forward thrust of society, and so popular citizen militarism is an important part of the way in which modern masses feel good about themselves and their achievements. These feelings carry forward into the contemporary world as the principal legacy of Phase 2.

Phase 3: the nuclear age, 1945–

In the contemporary world nuclear weapons have introduced revolutionary consequences; but geo-politics have also changed – no longer a balance of power between several Great Powers but a Cold War between two super-powers plus allies. Just as the internal social structure of the two differs considerably, so too does the form of militarism diffused among their peoples. Their elites share a common militarism, which I shall term 'deterrence science'. But among the Soviet people we find 'militarized socialism'; while in the West we find 'spectator-sport militarism'. I now explore these three types of militarism and the contradictions existing between them.

Nuclear weapons, once fully developed and dominant in the 1960s, rendered the highest level of warfare – mobilizing all one's resources against the enemy's armies and population – absolutely irrational in terms of ends. No human goals (except combined murder and suicide) would be served by letting off the nuclear arsenals of the super-powers. Surely, militarism has been rendered obsolete?

But the possession of nuclear weapons has had a curious opposite effect: to increase the rationality-as-means of militarism, and so to revive the military science of the limited war phase. This depends on the theory of deterrence. If political and military leaders accept that their weapons are too terrible to use as an instrument of policy, and if they believe that the enemy thinks likewise, then they will keep well short of using them. Parameters can be laid down within which military activity can be used as a rational instrument of policy. In fact, a set of 'conventions' have developed between the super-powers parallel to the general conventions of diplomacy in the nineteenth-century Balance of Power. There are six main ones:

1. Nuclear weapons may be continuously developed and deployed, but weapons actually used by self and clients will stop short of the nuclear (or, indeed, the biological) arsenal. This was recognized by the United States in Vietnam when the intrinsic conduct of the war might have been served by their use.

2 Each super-power has its own sphere of influence – an understanding established in the wake of the Cuban missile crisis and not altered by the level of rhetoric occasioned by Afghanistan, Grenada or central America.
3 Partly as a consequence, there will not be direct clashes between NATO and Warsaw Pact combat troops – 'advisors', for example, will behave and be treated as civilians if encountered in the field.
4 Client states not part of NATO or the Warsaw Pact may fight against each other to the limits of their capabilities either on their own initiative or prompted.
5 The conventions may be continuously tested and amended by actions consistent with (1) – (4), e.g. Cuba may challenge the US sphere of influence, and may be encouraged to do so by the Soviet Union, but if the United States challenges, Cuba will be left to sweat it out.

Finally comes a contested convention which the West seeks to establish and the Soviet Union claims to resist.

6 Among the nuclear arsenal one may distinguish between levels of confrontation: inter-continental, theatre and battle-field weapons. None will be used in the activities listed above. But in the event of first-line deterrence failing, precise low-level nuclear signals can still be sent to the enemy as a rational instrument of policy, i.e. the use of battlefield nuclear weapons by NATO will merely 'balance' Soviet conventional superiority. Though the Soviets denounce this, they must presumably have planned balancing retaliatory signals, as well as any possible all-out retaliation, in case it actually happened. And their recent weapon deployments – especially the SS9 and SS20 – accept covertly the reality of this convention.

'Deterrence-science militarism'

This deterrence system has many points of instability. That is not my problem here, though it is the most important problem of all. But it has led to the re-emergence of war as, to quote Clausewitz, 'the continuation of politics by other means'. Clausewitz has been modified by nuclear weapons into 'deterrence-science militarism'.

This has two levels. The first is new to the history of militarism – a global confrontation between super-powers, and continuous revolutionizing of nuclear arsenals and of tactical deployment of mass armed forces. The rational purpose is to achieve parity or even a slight (though not often usable) advantage over the rival, and a huge disparity and hegemony over all other powers. The rational means involve more and more use of high science, computers and mathematical theory to build the weapons and simulate the decision-making implied by their deployment. The second level returns us with full force to Phase 1: intrinsically rational and privately planned limited wars as an instrument of policy. The wars are relatively short and costless for the super-powers – though often not for client states, if used; there is a degree of mutual understanding between super-power elites; their civilian populations are insulated from them; and planning is privatized within the state and its various elites.

There are differences from the early nineteenth century. The technology of global confrontation actually increases the privacy of the planning in three ways. First, the technology is probably less central to modern economies than was that of the industries involved in nineteenth-century war, railways, iron and steel and coal. This is marked in the Soviet Union where war-related industry is often quite separate from the rest of the economy. The United States has also seen something of the emergence of a distinct 'military-industrial complex', whose interests are not those of the economy as a whole, and whose *modus operandi*, the cost-plus contract, is not that of competitive capitalism.

Second, rational planning procedures have become more abstruse and scientific. Officers, especially higher commands, are introduced to complex techniques of the behavioural and natural sciences. They play war-games in which computer simulation of complex chains of interaction between levels of decision-making and weapon capacity require clear, logical thought. As this is 'to think the unthinkable' it develops a distinctive form of *ésprit de corps*: 'tough-mindedness', the clear-sighted 'hawk', with a capacity to keep logic going while the bombs fall. This seems also characteristic of civilian/diplomatic advisers like Kissinger or Brzezinski – exuding a certain contempt for the 'civilians', the liberals, the doves who would substitute hope and faith for *realpolitik*. Third, the states attempt and generally attain a level of secrecy about weapon development above that of nineteenth-century states, whose weapons were often bought from the same independent armaments manufacturers.

Much of the knowledge contained within this private state/military sphere is necessarily held secret. But much else is held secret because it conflicts fundamentally with any principle of legitimation that could be safely shared with the public. This is true of chemical weapons and of many diplomatic activities. It is more problematic for Western states, and especially for the United States with open traditions of government. It has been partially solved by the proliferation of private agencies, of which the CIA is the most notorious. The activities of the CIA and the extent to which they are submitted to public approval indicate the continuing tensions between private and public militarism in the West.

Such then is deterrence-science militarism, instrumentally rational, modernistic, private and shared between the superpowers. I have emphasized that this is largely a private, even a secret militarism, of which even in the West the public has little knowledge and virtually no participatory role. Nevertheless, it is broadly supported by much of public opinion. But this support takes different forms.

'Militarized socialism'

Mass militarism in the Soviet bloc differs from that in the West because of both geo-politics and domestic politics (see Holloway, 1983, for much of this section). The geo-political centre of the confrontation, and the likely sphere of military operations in the event of major war, is Central Europe, adjacent to Soviet territory but a continent away from the United States. As in the world wars, the US army is less visible to its people than is the Soviet army, and the possibility of mass conventional war is far more remote from its territory. Though nuclear deployment is far removed from social life in both countries, conventional, mass deployment is more visible in the Soviet Union than the United States. Also, the Warsaw Pact forces are necessary to maintain Soviet geo-political hegemony in Eastern Europe, as NATO troops are not in Western Europe. Thus armed forces are central to the political life of the East, but are isolated enclaves throughout the West (though the NATO forces in West Germany are probably too numerous to be described in quite this way). In the West European states (as in Japan) the centrality of their own military power to their internal politics and social structure has declined in the post-war period. It has been in non-mainstream NATO countries like Turkey or Francoist Spain that military forces have had the greatest penetration of social structure as a whole. Though conscription is still general outside of the UK, and though Northern Ireland constitutes an exception, the military is far less public in Europe than it was in Phase 2.

The centrality of militarism in the Soviet Union is heightened by its domestic politics. Though scholars nowadays shy away from the label 'totalitarian', none the less the Soviet regime is authoritarian, dependent on top-downward command structure throughout its institutions. At the height of Stalin's purges, plain repression played the major role. But in the Second World War the Soviet leadership discovered a more subtle authoritarianism, which it has subsequently blended with its geo-political needs into what I term 'militarized socialism'. Its own label is the 'military-patriotic' society. Various war-time tools of social control have been refined. These range across the whole of social life from labour brigades, factories, kolkhozes and solkhozes with military discipline, training in mass sports with defence applications, the activities of Komsomol, Party, trades unions, schools and the whole of the media. The lessons of what is universally referred to as the 'Great Patriotic War' are continuously re-affirmed through all the propaganda organs of the state. As Marshall Grechko said in 1973, and has said on many other occasions: 'The Communist Party regards military-patriotic work as an integral part of the communist education of the Soviet people.'

Militarized socialism has emerged unscathed through the period of domination by nuclear weapons. I quote Marshall Grechko again:

military-patriotic work in this country is conducted along two avenues. The first and more important . . . is moral-political and psychological training intended to rear Soviet people, in the spirit of revolutionary vigilance, as staunch fighters for the communist cause and as convinced patriots capable of withstanding any war-time ordeals and worthily fulfilling the duties of the Soviet citizen under the most difficult conditions at the front and in the rear. It is very important to instill psychological stability in the future defenders of the Motherland – the ability to display self-possession, courage, valor and selflessness in difficult situations. The *sina qua non* here is a high degree of mental staunchness, political awareness and devotion to the Motherland, the party and the people. The second avenue is military training for the population. The range of tasks here has also broadened immeasurably. Particular significance is attached to instructing the population in defence against weapons of mass destruction, and in the ability rapidly to neutralize the consequences of enemy nuclear strikes ... Both these avenues are closely interlinked, complement each other, and are subordinated to the single objective of rearing worthy defenders of the Soviet Motherland. (US Air Force, 1976, pp. 20–1)

This is quite explicit: Soviet citizenship and socialism require military discipline. But note also that the dialectic between mass military mobilization and social progress has ended. Mobilization is defensive and conservative – Grechko's speech is peppered with words like 'vigilance', 'withstanding', 'psychological stability', 'staunchness', 'defence' and 'defenders'. This is more than the customary geo-political claim that the Soviet Union eschews aggression; it reflects the historic confinement of the USSR to an (admittedly very large) regional rather than a global sphere of interest; and it is also a domestic claim that socialism has been achieved and now merely requires defending.

This is, of course, propaganda and does not describe present or potential future reality. For example, the possibilities of the Komsomol 'rapidly neutralizing the consequences of enemy nuclear strikes' may seem absurd. But a strategy of social control is revealed which makes Soviet militarism relatively consistent and controllable by the state. The first global level of deterrence-science – the nuclear and mass conventional confrontation – is reinforced by the pervasive presence of the Soviet armed forces and by the institutions of militarized socialism. In other words, militarized socialism *institutionalizes* global militarism in the lives of the people, which is not so in the West. One consequence of its defensive character is that Soviet leaders do not have to deal with dissidents urging them to greater aggressiveness, unlike US leaders (as we shall see). Indeed, the hope for peace in militarized socialism is that it does not legitimate aggression. If a Soviet leadership ever did strike out massively against the West, it would have a negligible reservoir of public support to fall back on should the war prove difficult – which would not be the case if the West were the aggressor.

The Soviet leaders may have more difficulty legitimating the second level, limited wars and conspiratorial geo-politics involving client states. There are not historic precedents for a global role, and no resonance in militarized socialism for one now. However, the leaders are far more in control of the dissemination of information about areas remote from popular experience. They can play down Soviet global involvement, and preserve a level of secrecy over Afghanistan and other activities which the United States could not equal.

Thus, Soviet militarism, though perhaps stronger because more deeply rooted in its historical experience of war and in its present social structure, is more of a piece, more stable and predictable, more in the control of its leaders than is Western militarism. If we fear it, we fear a known danger, directly represented at the conference table.

'Spectator-sport militarism'

Unlike the Soviet Union, the United States has a global presence, leading capitalism throughout three-quarters of the globe, inheriting this position directly from the European powers, especially Great Britain. Thus, there is far more knowledge and material interest at stake in debates about global issues in the United States and the rest of the West than there is in the Soviet Union. Western corporations, trade unions, professional and cultural associations and political parties all have global reach. Because the leading Western powers are liberal democracies, these interest groups express divergent geo-political strategies. However, all are committed to defending Western democracy, most seek to preserve Western hegemony over the globe (especially if the alternative is Soviet control), while conservative and capitalist interest groups seek to conserve a great deal more from 'socialism', whether coming from the Soviet Union or not. Thus the equation of citizenship with militarism has also turned defensive in the West: not further social progress, but preservation of what we have, requires military force. But unlike the Soviet Union, defence is expected to be global rather than regional.

Yet, as we saw earlier, militarism is not central to Western social structure. Its major armed forces are relatively marginal to society; there is no equivalent to militarized socialism (such as in the past at least two capitalist powers, Germany and Japan, provided). And the United States is, perhaps, the country where militarism is least evident. Thus, though perhaps much of Western public opinion supports in the abstract both levels of 'deterrence-science militarism', they are less directly implicated in them than are Soviet citizens.

My metaphor of 'spectator-sport militarism' conveys this sense of indirect participation. Part of it is the simple residue of Phase 2. The nation has become the main symbolic identity of the modern world, the community, the 'we' of social life. In our secular part of the world, larger or smaller religious identities are weaker, while class identities have been institutionalized within the nation, thus strengthening it. The nation is not primordial; it only has a short history. But for about a century the nation has been the way in which the mass of the population participated for almost the first time in history in the life and power of a whole society. The nation became real because democracy, the welfare state, mass mobilization warfare – in short *citizenship* – became real. The nation is no longer being extended, but it needs defending.

The nation is still real but with one significant change. It can no longer be tested, and so re-affirmed or disintegrated, through warfare of the highest level. Nuclear war would destroy all nations involved in it. But, given deterrence, the abstract nuclear confrontation and limited wars have been encouraged. The latter, limited conventional wars involving client-states aided by 'our' professional advisers and small expeditionary forces in 'our backyards', do not mobilize the nation as players but as *spectators*. This is also true, though in a more abstract fashion, about the nuclear confrontation. The spectators are quite well informed about conventional wars. Knowledge through actual participation in two world wars among the older age-groups is transmitted to the young through comics, books, magazines, movies and televsion documentaries. Conscription provides experience at the 'amateur playing' level in most countries. The media are also experienced at quickly relaying abstruse military technique and performance to a mass public. We see diagrammatic representations of missile and tank strength, and public relations documentaries on the latest hardware. A major weapons system – the Strategic Defense

Initiative – has even been named 'Star Wars' after a Hollywood saga. During the Falklands War all Britain was regaled with technical data on the performance of the Exocet missile and the supposed 'Vector Flight' of the Harrier jet. In all these respects, wars like the Falklands or the Grenadan invasion are not qualitatively different from the Olympic Games. Because life-and-death are involved, the emotions stirred up are deeper and stronger. But they are not emotions backed up by committing personal resources. They do not involve real or potential sacrifice, except by professional troops. The nuclear and mass conventional confrontation involves at most 10 per cent of GNP – a tithe paid to our modern 'church', the nation. The symbolic strength of the nation can sustain popular support for adventures and arms spending.

However, popular support is shallow and volatile. The people will not willingly countenance much sacrifice, either real or symbolic. If the nation is called to real sacrifice, we see that its militarism is not rooted deep. Americans in Vietnam and French in Algeria and Indo-China found that conscript armies would not consent to suffer heavy losses merely in pursuit of a global geopolitical strategy, that is of deterrence-science militarism. But, whether fortunately or unfortunately, nuclear weapons and deterrence prevent this discovery from having its full political force. If the salience of national militarism is only tested through major wars and they are not allowed to occur (or if one did it would devastate everything), then the test is not made. Spectator sport militarism, despite probably being only skin-deep, may still rule.

The second restraint is on the nation's level of symbolic sacrifice. If military spending appears to damage the whole economy, jeopardizing existing living standards, it is contested. And professional soldiers are still 'our boys' – they must not be 'pointlessly sacrificed' in limited wars. This means that they must win, or fight honourably in a not-hopeless venture. President Carter's disastrous attempt to rescue the American Embassy hostages in Iran or President Reagan's aborted Lebanon venture, were afterwards unpopular. But such failures need not lead to an anti-militarist policy in general, but to calls for a more rational diplomatic/military limited way strategy.

Militarism also serves powerful political interests. Like many

Great Power confrontations, this one has its ideological aspects; and like a few of them, this one has the characteristic that the opponent's ideology can be plausibly associated with a faction internal to one's own state. Conservative rulers in East and West use the enemy without to prevent internal change; and most do this quite consciously. The survival of capitalism/freedom and socialism/freedom are bolstered by militarism. This is a comparatively safe tactic if a major war, the great tester of the reality of modern political ideologies, is considered unlikely.

This draws attention to the fact that political/military elites in both East and West, unlike the general public, actually participate in both forms of militarism and in two foreign policies. One is the *realpolitik* of deterrence-science, the other for domestic consumption is geared to ideology, militarized socialism and spectator militarism. Thus the Soviet Union's media for several weeks in October/November 1983 were dominated by outrage at the US invasion of Grenada, but the Soviet government did nothing whatever in real terms to oppose it, recognizing realistically that this was a US sphere of influence and, perhaps also, that its attempt, or that of Cuba its client, to alter the 'rules' in the Caribbean has failed. Similarly, but in reverse, with the Soviet invasion of Afghanistan: this provoked Western outrage and symbolic sanctions – including, and very much to the point given my analogies, the Olympic Games boycott – but there was no geopolitical or military response, beyond pressures on regional client-states and, perhaps, CIA activity. The point about what Lord Carrington termed the 'megaphone diplomacy' of the Reagan–Brezhnev period is that the closer you stand to the megaphone, the louder the message. It is primarily for domestic consumption.

There are two possible stances from which we can assess the relationship between these two foreign policies. If deterrence works, if the tacit mutual understandings between East and West elites are good, and if they can control their public opinion, then the result is a gigantic conspiracy perpetrated jointly upon their peoples. Militarized socialism and spectator-sport militarism is used consciously, rationally to bolster their mutual power positions internally, pending the outcome of their private, rational, geopolitical struggle. If, on the other hand, deterrence is unstable, mutual understandings shaky and elite and popular levels of militarism cannot be kept properly insulated from one another, then the existence of two foreign policies, two militarisms, is destabilizing. Full insulation requires that leaders are immune to public opinion. Unfortunately, this requires a degree of insincerity among Western politicians of which they may be incapable. Soviet leaders do not have to contest elections or even tell direct lies – manipulation of opinion is institutionalized there. President Reagan seems to believe that the Russians *are* evil – for him belief and election strategy seem to coincide, as it does for many Western politicians. But the sincerity of President Reagan is not good news. If we are back to 1914 where mass, part-manipualted electorates can then push their diplomats over the brink, then we may end up dead. 'Better misled than dead' is the motto of Soviet militarism – not ideal, but not likely to start a war by mistake. But in the West the present unstable combination of the two militarisms may mean that future generations are first mislead and then dead.

References

Best G. 1982: *War and Society in Revolutionary Europe: 1770–1870*. Leicester: Leicester University Press.
Fisher F. 1967: *Germany's Aims in the First World War*. London: Chatto and Windus.
Holloway D. 1983: *The Soviet Union and the Arms Race*. New Haven, Conn.: Yale University Press.
Howard M. 1970: 'The classical strategists', in *Studies in War and Peace*. London: Temple Smith.
McNeill W. 1983: *The Pursuit of Power*. Oxford: Blackwell.
Mayer A. 1975: 'The lower middle class as a historical problem', *Journal of Modern History*, vol. 47.
US Air Force 1976: *Selected Soviet Military Writings, 1970–1975*. Washington, DC: US Government Printing Office.
Vagts A. 1959: *A History of Militarism*. New York: Free Press.

7
Ruling Class Strategies and Citizenship

Novel, important and true ideas are rare. Such ideas which are then developed into a coherent theory are even scarcer. T. H. Marshall is one of very few to have had at least one such idea, and to develop it. That is why it is important to understand and to improve upon his theory of citizenship.

Marshall believed that citizenship has rendered class struggle innocuous; yet citizenship is also in continuous tension, even war, with the class inequalities that capitalism generates. He identified three stages of the struggle for, and attainment of, citizenship: *civil, political* and *social*. Civil citizenship emerged in the eighteenth century. It comprised 'rights necessary for individual freedom – liberty of the person, freedom of speech, thought and faith, the right to own property and to conclude valid contracts, and the right to justice'. Political citizenship emerged in the nineteenth century: 'the right to participate in the exercise of political power, as a member of a body invested with political authority or as an elector of the members of such a body'. The third stage, social citizenship, developed through the twentieth century: 'the whole range from the right to a modicum of economic welfare and security to the right to share to the full in the social heritage and to live the life of a civilized being according to the standards prevailing in the society'. It is what we mean now by the Welfare State and social democracy.

Through these stages the major classes of modern capitalism,

This chapter was first published in the journal of the British Sociological Association, *Sociology* (August 1987). We are grateful for permission to reproduce it here. An earlier version of this article was given as the 1986 T. H. Marshall Memorial Lecture at the University of Southampton. My thanks go to the University's Department of Sociology for its invitation and hospitality and to John Hall and David Lockwood for their helpful criticisms of that version.

bourgeoisie and proletariat institutionalized their struggles with the *ancien régime* and with each other. Citizenship and capitalism were still at war, Marshall declared, but it was institutionalized, rule-governed warfare. Such was the model developed in his famous 1949 lecture, *Citizenship and Social Class* (1963 edition). It has continued to seem true and important. Major sociologists like Reinhard Bendix, Ralf Dahrendorf, Ronald Dore, A. H. Halsey, S. M. Lipset, David Lockwood and Peter Townsend have acknowledged his influence (e.g. Halsey, 1984; Lipset, 1973; Lockwood, 1974). It remains strong today (see, for example, the recent admiring work by Turner, 1986). This is for a good reason: Marshall's view of citizenship is essentially true — at least as a description of what has actually happened in Britain.

There is one rather remarkable feature of *Citizenship and Social Class*. It is entirely about Great Britain. There is not a single mention of any other country.[1] Did Marshall regard Britain as typical of the capitalist West as a whole? He does not explicitly say so. Yet the most general level of the argument explores the tension between economic inequalities and demands for popular participation, both generated everywhere by the rise of capitalism. This certainly implies a general evolutionary approach, and indeed he does intermittently use the term 'evolution'. In his book *Social Policy* (1975 edition), evidence from other countries is only introduced to illustrate variations on a common, British theme. Finally, others have used his model in explicitly evolutionary theories of the development of modern class relations (e.g. Dahrendorf, 1959, pp. 61–4). Flora and Heidenheimer (1981, pp. 20–1) have observed that general theories of the modern welfare state have been dominated by British experience, chronicled especially by Marshall and Richard Titmuss.

Six counter-theses

I wish to deviate from this Anglophile and evolutionary model in six ways.

1 The British strategy of citizenship described by Marshall has been only one among five pursued by advanced industrial

---

1 I write 'Great Britain' rather than 'the United Kingdom' because there is also no reference to Northern Ireland, which, of course, would not fit well into his theory.

countries. I call these the *liberal, reformist, authoritarian monarchist, Fascist* and *authoritarian socialist* strategies.

2 All five strategies proved themselves reasonably adept at handling modern class struggle. They all converted the head-on collision of massive, antagonistic social classes into conflicts that were less class-defined, more limited and complex, sometimes more orderly, sometimes more erratic. Thus evolutionary tales are wrong. There has been no single best way of institutionalizing class conflict in industrial society, but at least five potentially durable forms of institutionalized conflict and mixes of citizen rights.

3 In explaining how such different strategies arise, I will stress the role of ruling classes. By 'ruling class' I mean a combination of the dominant economic class and the political and military rulers. I do not mean to imply that such groups were unchanging or even united – indeed the degree of their cohesion will figure importantly in my narrative. But I do imply the pair of general explanatory precepts expressed in (4) and (5) below.

4 Influence on social structure varies according to power. As a ruling class possesses most power, its strategies matter most. In fact, many *anciens régimes* could survive the onslaught of emergent classes with a few concessions here and there. Neither the bourgeoisie nor the proletariat has been as powerful as has been argued by the dominant schools of sociology, liberal, reformist (like Marshall) and Marxist. Indeed, ruling class strategies tended to determine the nature of the social movements generated by bourgeoisie and proletariat, especially whether they were liberal, reformist or revolutionary. This argument has also been made by Lipset (1985, chapter 6).

5 Tradition matters. We generally exaggerate the transformative powers of the Industrial Revolution. That Revolution was preceded by centuries of structural change – the commercialization of agriculture, the globalization of trade, the consolidation of the modern state, the mechanization of war, the secularization of ideology. *If anciens régimes* had learned to cope with these changes, they could master the problems of an industrial society with traditional strategies, up-dated. If not, they were usually already vulnerable and internally divided before the actual bourgeois or proletarian onslaught. Others have also stressed the survival of tradition through the Industrial Revolution – classically

Moore (1969) and Rokkan (1970), more recently Mayer (1981) and Corrigan and Sayer (1985).

6 The durability of regime strategies has been due less to their superior internal efficiency than to geo-politics – and specifically to victory in world wars. The geo-political and military influences on society have been considerable but neglected in sociological theory. However, they have recently been receiving the attention they deserve (e.g. Giddens, 1985; Hall, 1985; Shaw, 1987; Skocpol, 1979).

Let us approach the historical record with these six theses in mind. What were the traditional regime strategies used to cope with the initial rise of the bourgeoisie?

Absolute and constitutional regimes

We can divide the regimes of pre-industrial Europe into approximations to two ideal-types, absolute monarchies and constitutional regimes.[2]

By 1800 the principal absolutists were Russia, Prussia and Austria. Their monarch's formal *despotic* powers were largely unlimited. Citizenship was unknown. The rule of law supposedly operated, but personal liberties, and freedom of the press and association could be suspended arbitrarily. Indeed, any conception of universal rights was restrained by the proliferation of particularistic statuses, possessed by corporate groups – estates of the realm, corporations of burghers, lawyers, merchants and artisan guilds. Yet the real, *infrastructural* powers of the monarchs were far from absolute. They required the cooperation of the regionally and locally powerful. Repression was cumbersome and costly, and far more effective if used together with 'divide-and-rule' negotiations with corporate groups. The monarch's crucial power was tactical freedom: the capacity to act arbitrarily both in conducting negotiation and in using force. It is important to realize that these three characteristics – arbitrary divide-and-rule, selective tactical repression, and corporate negotiations – survived intact into the twentieth century.

Britain and the United States were the main constitutional regimes. There civil citizenship was well-developed. Individual life

---

2 For the distinction between despotic and infrastructural power, see chapter 1 above.

and property were legally guaranteed, and freedom of the press and of association were partially recognized – they were 'licensed' under discernible rules. Political citizenship also existed, though it was confined to the propertied classes who 'virtually represented' the rest. Social citizenship was as absent here as in absolutist regimes. All this was well understood by Marshall.

Not all regimes were either predominantly absolutist or constitutional. Some formerly absolutist regimes had experienced revolution or serious disorder, and were now bitterly contested between constitutionalists and reactionaires: France after 1789, Spain and several Italian states. In others absolutism and constitutionalism merged through less violent, more orderly conflict: principally the Scandinavian countries.

Capitalist industrialization changed much, but we can none the less see the initial imprint of these four types of regime: absolutist, constitutional, contested and merged. Let us follow this in more detail, concentrating in turn on the United States, Britain and Germany.

From constitutionalism to liberalism – the United States and Britain

In Britain and the United States the rise of liberalism strengthened civil and political citizenship. The rule of law over life, property, freedom of speech, assembly and press was extended, as was the political franchise. But any social citizenship remained equivocal. The regime provided basic subsistence to the poor out of charity and a desire to avoid sedition. But provision came from local worthies and private insurance; and legislation encouraged rather than enforced. Subsistence was not a right of all, but the result of a mixture of market forces, the duty to work and save, and private and public charity. The state was not interventionist or 'corporatist': interest group conflict was predominantly left to the economic and political marketplaces, its limits defined by law. However, collectivities could legitimately exploit their market powers, and the regime devised rules of the ensuing game. Under liberalism individuals and interest groups, but not classes, could be accommodated within the regime. Repression, now fully institutionalized, was reserved only for those who went outside the rules of the game.

Such was one basic strategy of dealing with the rise of the bourgeoisie. But could it cope with the working class? The two main cases, the United States and Britain, coped differently.

In the United States labour was eventually absorbed into the liberal regime. A broad coalition, from landowners and merchants down to small farmers and artisans, had made the Revolution. White, adult males could not be easily excluded from civil and political citizenship. By the early 1840s all of them, in all states, possessed the vote – 50 years earlier than anywhere else, 50 years before the emergence of a powerful labour movement. Thus the political demands of labour could be gradually expressed as an interest group *within* an existing federal political constitution and competitive party system. As Katznelson (1981) has shown, workers' political life became organized more by locality, ethnicity and patronage than by work, unions or class. In the sphere of work there was severe and violent conflict, between unions and employers aided by government and the law courts. But here too the ruling class eventually came to accept the legitimacy of unions in essentially liberal terms; while the Wagner Act allowed unions to negotiate freely, Taft-Hartley compelled them to act only as the balloted representative of their individual members.

The United States give us the truest picture of what would have happened to class conflict without the politics of citizenship. If class struggle had only concerned the Marxist agenda, of relations of production, labour processes, and direct conflict between capitalists and workers, then liberal regimes would have dominated industrial society. As the (white) working class was civilly and politically *inside* the regime, it had little need for the great ideologies of the proletariat excluded from citizenship – socialism and anarchism. American trade unions became like other collective interest groups exploiting their market power. If workers did not possess effective market powers, they would be outside this liberal regime and tempted by soicalism and anarchism. But they could be repressed – with the consent of labour organizations accepting the rules of the game. Consequently, neither class nor socialism has ever appeared as a fundamental organizing principle of power in the United States. Those groups who in other countries constituted the core of the labour and socialist movement – male artisans, heavy industrial, mining and transport workers – became predominantly interest groups inside the liberal regime, while the unskilled, those in other sectors, females and ethnic minorities were left outside.

Liberalism was thus the first viable regime strategy of an advanced industrial society. It still dominates the United States, and is also found in Switzerland. In these countries social citizenship is still marginal. Economic subsistence and participation is provided overwhelmingly out of the economic buoyancy of their national capitalisms, from which the large majority can insure themselves against adversity. Below that, there are welfare provisions against actual starvation, though they vary between states and cantons, are often denied to immigrant workers, and are sometimes provided only if the poor show their 'worth'. It is closer to the eighteenth century Poor Law than to what Marshall meant by social citizenship. Its social struggles remained defined by liberalism. If civil and political citizenship could be attained early, before the class struggles of industrialism, then social citizenship need not follow. The most powerful capitalist state has not followed Marshall's road. It shows no signs of doing so.

But Britain strayed from liberalism towards reformism, as Marshall depicted. Britain's initial struggle for liberal political citizenship was more of a class struggle, waged predominantly by the rising bourgeoisie and independent artisans. However, the British constitution has not excluded classes or status groups as systematically as have most constitutions of continental Europe. The franchise before 1832 was extraordinarily uneven; then, until 1867, it passed through the middle of the artisan group; between 1867 and 1884 it grew to include 65 per cent of the adult male population. In 1918 all adult males and many females were included, and in 1929 all females. Hence at any particular point in time emerging dissidents – petty bourgeois radicals, artisan and skilled factory worker socialists, feminists – have been partially inside, partially outside the state. Thus liberalism and socialism have both remained attractive ideologies. Indeed, perhaps only the splits in the Liberal Party consequent on the First World War may have ensured that a joint liberal/reformist ideology would be carried principally by an independent Labour Party, rather than through Lib-Lab politics. Britain has enshrined the rule of both interest groups and classes, jointly. The labour movement is part sectional interest group, part class movement, irremediably reformist, virtually unsullied by Marxist or anarchist revolutionary tendencies.

Britain is thus a mixed liberal/reformist case. The state remains liberal, unwilling to intervene actively in interest-group bargaining – it has incorporated the lower classes into the rules of the game, not into the institutions of 'corporatism'. Yet social citizenship has advanced somewhat beyond the American level. The state guarantees subsistence through the welfare state, but this meshes into, rather than replaces, private market and insurance schemes. Thus its major social struggles are fought out in terms of an ideological debate, and a real political pendulum, between liberalism and social democracy. In reaction to the Thatcher government's liberal strategy, the reformist strategy is now becoming more popular again.

Contested and merged regimes – France, Spain, Italy, Scandinavia

In France, Spain and Italy, reactionaries (usually monarchist and clerical) and secular liberals struggled over political citizenship for most of the nineteenth and twentieth centuries, with many violent changes of regime. Citizenship remained bitterly disputed, though there was undoubtedly some secular progress in the Marshallian direction. As radical bourgeoisie, peasantry and labour were erratically but persistently denied political citizenship, these developed competing excluded ideologies. Sometimes they rejected the state, as in anarchism and syndicalism; sometimes they embraced it, as in Marxist socialism. The fierce competition between anarcho-syndicalism, revolutionary socialism and reformist socialism was not solved until after the Second World War, for reasons I mention later.

In several other countries the absolutist/constitutional struggle proceeded to more peaceful victory for a broad alliance between bourgeoisie, labour and small farmers. Over the first four decades of this century they achieved civil and political citizenship, and proceeded furthest along the road to social citizenship. The absolutist inheritance, never violently repudiated (unlike in France), provided a more corporatist tinge to regime negotiations which still endures. The Scandinavian countries are the paradigm cases of this route, less affected by the dislocations of war than any other. This second road, a corporatist style of reformism, corresponds closely to Marshall's vision (more so than the British case does). Its social struggles are avowedly class ones, but they are managed by joint negotiations, and constrained more by pragmatic than ideological limits. Continuing reform, it is agreed, will be limited primarily by the growth record of each national economy.

But to investigate properly the absolutist legacy suggests a methodology of examining the 'purer' and longer-lasting cases of absolutism, in Russia, Austria, Japan and especially in Prussia/Germany.

From absolutism to authoritarian monarchy – Germany, Austria, Russia, Japan

The absolutist regimes entered the nineteenth century with two conflicting predispositions. First, monarch, nobility and Church were unwilling to grant *universal* citizen rights to either bourgeoisie or proletariat, since that would threaten the particularistic, private and arbitrary nature of their power. Second, despite their despotic appearance, they were pessimistic about their infrastructural capacity to overcome determined resistance with systematic repression. When it became obvious that neither the bourgeoisie nor the proletariat would go away, the regimes not only cast around for other solutions to maintain their power – they also realized that to incorporate these rising groups would 'modernize' the regime and increase its Great Power status. The most successful regime in Europe was Wilhelmine Germany, on which I will therefore concentrate.[3]

German absolutists were willing to concede on civil citizenship. Often this did not seem like 'concession' at all. *Ancien régime* members were major property-holders, gradually using their property more capitalistically. They were not opposed to the spread of universal contract law and guarantees of property rights – including the liberal conception of freedom of labour. Recent Marxists have observed that classical liberalism, combining capitalism with democracy, has not often appeared subsequently: much civil can exist with little political citizenship (e.g. Jessop, 1978). Blackbourne and Eley (1984) have demonstrated this case with respect to nineteenth century Germany: liberal legal rights

---

3 The literature on Wilhelmine Germany is enormous and often controversial. Apart from works cited later, good concise general accounts are provided by Calleo, 1978, pp. 57–84, and by various essays in Sheehan, 1976.

(civil citizenship) were achieved through a consensus between the Prussian regime and the bourgeoisie over what was needed to modernize society.

Absolutist regimes also favoured a minimal social citizenship. Their ideology and particularistic practices were already paternalist. Particular groups like artisans or miners often had their basic wages, hours and working practices guaranteed by the state. When state infrastructural powers expanded, after about 1860, so could a minimal social citizenship. As is generally recognized today, Bismarck and Kaiser Wilhelm, and not liberals or reformists, were the founders of the Welfare State, though it is true that they did not take it very far (Flora and Alber, 1981).

The sticking-point was over political citizenship. Real parliaments could not be conceded; democrats could not be allowed absolute freedoms of the press, speech or assembly. Gradually, however, the more astute monarchists institutionalized a workable political strategy. The regime conceded a parliamentary shell but weighted the franchise, rigged ballots, and only allowed elected representatives limited powers alongside an executive branch responsible to the monarch alone. Thus the bourgeoisie, even the proletariat, could be brought within the state but could not control it. By this sham political citizenship they were 'negatively incorporated', to use Roth's (1963) term.

The tactics were divide-and-rule: negotiate with the more moderate sections of excluded groups, then repress the rest; play off incorporated interest groups and classes against each other; and preserve a vital element of arbitrary regime discretion. In the hands of a Bismarck the discretion could be used quite cynically: Catholics, regionalists, National Liberals, classical liberals, even the working class, would be taken up, discarded, and repressed according to current tactical exigencies (see the brilliant biography of Bismarck by Taylor, 1961). Divide-and-rule was corporatist and arbitrary – both qualities inherited from absolutism. Groups and classes were integrated as organizations into the state, rather than into rule-governed marketplaces. The state could alter the rules by dissolving parliament, restricting civil liberties and selecting new targets for repression. By these means authoritarian monarchism emasculated the German bourgeoisie, dividing it among Conservative, National Liberal, Catholic and regionalist factions, all vying for influence within the regime. By 1914 the

German bourgeoisie was finished as an independent political force (as Max Weber so often lamented). Only a small radical rump was prepared to ally with the excluded socialists against the regime.

The proletariat was treated more severely. Though the regime became somewhat internally divided, and though different *Länder* also varied (with liberals arguing that concessions to labour unions would detach them from socialism), in the end the authoritarians proved to be the heart of the regime. Apart from a brief period (1890–4) under the Chancellorshop of Caprivi, a liberal Prussian general, the politics of conciliation never carried the court – and the Kaiser dismissed Caprivi rather than make concessions to labour. The regime was essentially united and so could respond with a clear strategy. The German working class could elect representatives to the Reichstag, but these were excluded from office or influence on the regime. Unions were permitted, but – even after the anti-Socialist Laws were repealed in 1889 – their legal rights were unclear. The state could exploit legal uncertainties or invoke martial law to repress strikes, meetings, marches, organizations and publications. It did so arbitrarily, according to its traditions.

Faced with a strategy largely of civil and political exclusion, labour responded predictably. It followed the Marxist Social Democrats, ostensibly revolutionary but geared up in practice to fight the elections. Most activist workers joined the socialist unions, committed to SPD rhetoric, but able to make reformist gains in some industries and localities. But to be a reformist brought frustration, because of regime intransigence. By 1914 Karl Legien, the crypto-reformist leader of the socialist unions, had carefully built up a measure of autonomy from the SPD. But he was forced to confess that reform was impossible without a fundamental change in the state. The working class was largely outside political citizenship. It responded with a flawed revolutionary Marxism – extreme rhetoric, practical caution and a leadership, conscious of the isolation of the movement, concentrating on electoral politics.

How frightened was the regime of the socialist threat? In the 1912 election the SPD achieved its greatest success, capturing a third of the votes, and becoming the largest single party in the Reichstag. The regime was taken aback but quickly recovered. The

Chancellor, Bethmann-Hollweg, used the Red Scare against his major enemy at the time, which was the Right, not the Left. He exploited the fears of the propertied classes finally to push through an income tax, long desired by the regime, long resisted by the agrarian landlords.[4] Authoritarian monarchy was still successfully dividing-and-ruling and modernizing at the onset of the First World War.

Each of the authoritarian monarchies provided its variation on this German theme. I discuss them briefly in order of their success, beginning with Japan, the most successful.

The Japanese monarchy itself had less freedom of action. Instead a tightly knit Meiji elite, modernizing but drawn from the traditional dominant classes, used the monarchy as its legitimating principle. The Meiji Revolution represented an unusually self-conscious regime strategy of conservative modernization. After a careful search around Western constitutions, the German constitution was adopted and modified according to local need.[5] It is worth adding that forms of organization from liberal-reformist countries were also borrowed where they could fit into an authoritarian mould – notably French army and British navy organization.[6] Authoritarian monarchy became rather more corporate, less dependent on the personal qualities of the monarch, than in Europe – an apparent strengthening of the strategy.

Less successful was Russia, whose regime generally favoured more repression and exclusion, yet vacillated before modern liberal and authoritarian influences from the West. Two periods of regime conciliation (1906–7 and 1912–14) enabled the emergence of bourgeois parties of compromise and labour unions run by reformists. But each time the subsequent return to repression cut the ground from under liberals and reformists. They could promise their followers little. Many became embittered and moved leftward. Socialist revolutionaries took over the labour and peasant movements and even some of the bourgeois factions (see, e.g., on the workers' movement, Bonnell, 1983, and Swain, 1983). Divisions and vacillation at court prevented successful emulation

---

4 Kaiser, 1983, pp. 458–62, makes this argument, against the more traditional view of writers like Berghahn, 1973, that the regime feared the Left and militarized society to counter its threat.
5 Bendix, 1978, pp. 476–90, gives a succinct summary of the Meiji strategy.
6 I am grateful to Professor Michio Morishima for this observation.

of the German model. The *ancien régime* still possessed the loyalty of the nobility and propertied classes in general, but its modernization programme began to disintegrate from within (as Haimson, 1964 and 1965, classically argued). The regime lacked a corporate core of either liberal or conservative modernizers. Stolypin, the architect of the agrarian reforms designed to recruit rich and middling peasant support, was the potential conservative saviour of the regime, yet his influence at court was always precarious. The divided regime became buffeted by the personal irresoluteness of Nicholas and the reactionary folly of Alexandra. When monarchy begins to depend on the personal qualities of its monarchs, it is an endangered species. Russia represented the opposite pole to Japan within the spectrum of authoritarian monarchy – no corporate regime strategy, much depending on the monarch himself. On the other hand, economic and military modernization was proving remarkably successful in pre-war Russia. Could the regime find a comparably coherent political strategy? In 1914 the answer was not yet clear. Though regime weaknesses had begun to create what later proved to be its revolutionary grave-diggers, their influence was still negligible in 1914.

The least successful case was Austria (become the Dual Monarchy of Austria-Hungary in 1867), uniquely beset by nationality conflicts as well as class struggle across its variegated lands.[7] The monarchy attempted divide-and-rule on both fronts at once, but was faced by defections among *ancien régime* groups (Hungarian and Czech nobilities) as well as the hostility of bourgeois liberal nationalism. As the monarchy faltered, some peculiar alliances developed. After 1867 the most loyal and dominant groups in the two halves of the Dual Monarchy were the German nobility and bourgeoisie and the Hungarian nobility. But the monarchy found their support unwelcome because it alienated all the other nationalities these two exploited. After 1899 the Marxist SPD rejected nationalism as a bourgeois creed, thereby becoming to its surprise the major de facto supporter of the transnational monarchy. The monarchy belatedly converted to parliamentary institutions similar to Germany's (universal suffrage

---

[7] Historical sociologists have tended to ignore Austria, except in relation to nationalism. For a narrative that enables us to piece together most of the complex relations between regime, classes and nations, see Kann, 1964.

to parliaments whose rights were subordinate to the monarchy's), and tried to reach out to exploited nationalities and even classes.

But noble and bourgeois nationalists, not the proletariat, made the parliaments unworkable, and they were dissolved. This authoritarian monarchy could not even retain the loyalty of the whole *ancien régime*, let alone incorporate the bourgeoisie. By 1914 the regime consisted of the monarchy, the army and the largely tactical support of various national and class groupings. Its corporate solidarity was probably the weakest of the four cases.

The four cases reveal considerable variation in regime strategy and success. The crucial criteria of success were to maintain the corporate coherence of the *ancien régime*, and to modernize by incorporating sections of the bourgeoisie. It is outside the scope of this article to attempt to explain why some regimes did much better than others at these tasks. However, regimes seem not to have prospered or faltered because of the strength in general class and numerical terms of bourgeoisie and proletariat. In these terms the rising classes in Germany were initially the most threatening, those of Japan the least threatening, with Austria and Russia somewhere in between. This is not the same ordering as for regime success. The bulk of the explanation of success would seem to lie among the traditional regimes and classes, not among the rising classes.

At its most coherent, authoritarian monarchy provided a distinctive mixture of citizen rights – a fair degree of civil citizenship, minimal social citizenship, limited political citizenship, the whole varying by class and tactically undercut by an arbitrary monarchy and court-centered elite. Its social struggles were part ideological class struggle, part incorporated interest-group jostling, erratically violent yet institutionalized none the less. Was this the third viable strategy for advanced industrial societies? Could it have survived the working class pressure indefinitely? But for the fortunes of war, would it still survive today in three of the four greatest industrial powers in the world, a united Germany, a Tsarist Russia and an Imperial Japan? We cannot be sure because these regimes collapsed in war. But let us consider four supports for this counter-factual possibility.

First, in its own time Wilhelmine Germany was not idiosyncratic. Its emerging institutions were better-organized versions of the European mainstream. As Goldstein (1983) has shown, the combination of selective repression and sham parliaments was the late nineteenth century norm, not well-developed liberalism, still less reformism. For this reason German institutions were much copied, especially by Austria and Japan.

Second, by the time of their entry into the decisive war, 1914 (or 1941 in the case of Japan), the authoritarian monarchies were already becoming great industrial powers. Germany had overtaken Britain and France and was matched only by the United States. Japan and Russia were industrializing rapidly and successfully; and Russian economic resources, then as now, made up in quantity what they lacked in quality (quantitative indices of the economic strength of the Great Powers can be found in Bairoch, 1982). Authoritarian monarchy *was* surviving into advanced industrial societies in Germany and Japan, still had a reasonable chance in Russia, and was obviously failing only in Austria, where nations, not classes, provided the main threat.

Third, we must beware a too-homogeneous view of industrial society and its class struggles. The main reason the working class was not so threatening was its limited size. National censuses conducted between 1907 and 1911 show Britain to be exceptional. Only 9 per cent of its working population was still in agriculture, compared to 32 per cent in the United States, 37 per cent in Germany and more than 55 per cent in Russia. Among the major powers only in Britain were more working in manufacturing than in agriculture (Bairoch, 1968: table A2 has assembled the census data). Outside Britain, labour needed the support of peasants and small farmers to achieve either reform or revolution. It achieved this partially in the 'contested' cases of France, Italy and Spain, and more sustainedly in the 'mixed' cases of Scandinavia. But in Germany, Japan and Austria it failed dismally. Socialism was trapped in its urban-industrial enclaves, outvoted by the bourgeois-agrarian classes, and repressed by peasant soldiers and aristocratic officers. Authoritarian monarchy could continue to divide and rule and selectively repress provided it could manipulate divisions between agrarian and bourgeois classes, and motivate them both with fear of the proletariat. Few twentieth-century socialists have broken this strategy – Lenin being the obvious exception.

Fourth, the numerical weakness of labour has continued, though in changed form. The rise of the 'new middle class' and of the 'service class', the re-emergence of labour market dualism, and the increasing size and variety of service industries soon introduced new differentiations among the employed population, just as agriculture declined. Successful labour movements in the post-war period, like those of Scandinavia, have managed to repeat their earlier populist strategy (Esping-Anderson, 1985). They have recruited white-collar workers and new economic sectors into the Social Democratic movement, just as they earlier recruited bourgeois radicals and small farmers. But could labour movements which had already failed to attract the bourgeoisie or farmers, as in Germany or Japan, now do better among newer groups? It is surely more plausible to conceive of divide-and-rule, selective repression strategies, wielded by arbitrary authoritarian monarchies, surviving successfully today in Germany and Japan, and possibly also in Russia and constituent parts of Austria-Hungary.

I conclude that the third strategy, authoritarian monarchy, could probably have survived into advanced, post-industrial society, providing a distinctive, corporately organized, abitrary combination of partial civil, political and social citizenship. This was not envisaged by Marshall, or indeed by any modern sociologist.

Fascism and authoritarian socialism

The First World War resulted in two further strategies, fascism and authoritarian socialism. Nazi Germany and the Soviet Union are their exemplars. Both used more repression, using the infrastructural capacities of the twentieth century state, and proclaiming violent legitimating ideologies. In practice, as in all regimes, repression had to be combined with negotiation. Both regimes delineated out-groups with whom they would not negotiate; for both, anyone providing principle opposition – for the Nazis labour leaders, socialists, Jews and other non-Aryan groups, for the Soviets, major property-owners. But other interest groups – never acknowledged as antagonistic classes – could join the regime, establish cliques within and clients without, and bargain and jostle in time-honoured absolutist style. Now social struggles were not openly acknowledged at all. But within the regime they would continue, flaring into intermittent life with purges, riots and even armed factional struggle.

Neither regime provided civil rights; neither provided real

political citizenship (though they provided the institutions of sham corporatism and socialism). Yet they moved furthest toward social citizenship. Fascism's move was hesitant: full employment and public works programmes were not greatly in advance of others of the time (and were partially an outcome of a more important policy goal, rearmament). But had the regime survived the war, its encroachments on capitalism would surely have extended the state's role in guaranteeing subsistence. The Soviet regime has gone much further, proud of its programme of social citizenship. The state formally provides the subsistence of all (though the reality, with private peasant plots and black markets, is less clear-cut).

Of course, German Fascism was deeply unstable. But this was due to the restless militarism of its leaders in geo-politics, not to its class strategy. Indeed, *this* was remarkably successful in a short space of time. The proletariat was suppressed more completely than any of the regimes discussed so far would have believed possible. Its leaders were killed or exiled; its organizations disbanded or staffed by the regime's para-military forces; its masses silenced, seemingly with the approval of other social classes. The bourgeoisie was emasculated even more effectively than the Wilhelmine regime had managed. The liberals were killed or silenced, the rest kept quiet or loudly voiced their support. Ruthlessness was no longer hidden by scruple. Thus Fascism might have offered a fourth, chilling resolution to class struggle in advanced societies. Its main test would have been the next one: could it take on capital too? It was already beginning to do this by subordinating economic profit to militarism. This proved its downfall – but not at the hands of domestic social classes, who fought loyally for the Nazi regime down to its last days.

The stability of the fifth solution, authoritarian socialism, cannot be in doubt. The Bolsheviks and their ruling successors soon cowed the bourgeoisie, and gradually domesticated the labour movement. The trade unions were converted into apolitical welfare state organizations (sometimes headed by ex-KGB men). It took almost 50 years for the institutionalization to be complete. But once in place, it appears no less stable than other enduring types of regime.

The impact of war and geo-politics

I have described five viable regime strategies and mixtures of citizenship: liberalism, reformism, authoritarian monarchy, Fascism and authoritarian socialism. Yet industrial society today has lost some of this variety. Authoritarian monarchy and Fascism no longer exist. Why? Is it because of their inherent defects or instability? I have already suggested not.

There is an alternative explanation. To paraphrase a famous epitaph on the Roman Empire — these regimes did not die of natural causes, they were assassinated. Of course, Fascism and authoritarian socialism were also born out of assassination. But for the fortunes of the First World War, authoritarian monarchy might be alive today, while Fascism and authoritarian socialism might never have been born. But for the fortunes of the Second World War Fascism might dominate the world today. True, it is difficult to see American liberalism being overthrown by the German, Austrian and Japanese alliances. But Europe and Russia might well have had viable futures under very different regimes.

Of course, proof of this argument would require disposing of the reverse causality: regime type might have determined the role of war. This could have happened in two stages. Certain regimes — obviously the more authoritarian ones — may have been more militaristic and provoked the world wars; yet they may have been less effective at fighting them. The first stage has validity. The Nazis and Japanese were aggressors in the Second World War; and, in a more confused, stumbling way, the authoritarian monarchies did start the First World War. But is the second stage of the argument valid? Were liberalism, reformism and authoritarian socialism better suited to mass mobilization warfare? The ideologies of the victors suggest the answer 'yes'. I have only time here to give fragmentary evidence, but my answer is 'no'.

In both wars the German army fought better than its enemies, who continuously needed numerical superiority to survive. German civilians also loyally supported their regimes to the end. Both points hold also for the Japanese in the second war. The Eastern Front in the first war offers further shocks to the liberal/reformist perspective. Authoritarian monarchy Russia outfought the by now semi-authoritarian monarchy of Austria-Hungary, whose troops in turn outfought the by now largely liberal regime of Italy.

Indeed, when in 1917 the Austro-Hungarian armies against Russia collapsed, they were stiffened by Prussian officers and NCOs and then began to get the upper hand (Stone, 1975). The Central and Axis powers were correct in their view that the fortunes of war turned less upon citizenship than on efficient military organization. Unfortunately for them, military efficiency became over-weighted by numbers. Numbers resulted principally from the alliance system – how many powerful states were on each side? Authoritarian monarchy and Fascism were defeated by superior geopolitical alliances, not by their domestic socio-political structure.

After 1945 this result was deliberately rammed home by the victors, careful not to repeat the mistakes of the peace treaties of 1918 (see Mayer, 1981). Eastern Europe was made safe for authoritarian socialism by the Red Army. Western Europe and Japan were more subtly made safe for liberal/reformist regimes (though Japan's regime does not fit happily into this categorization, because of the survival of many authoritarian traditions). In Western Europe the authoritarian Right was eliminated by force, the revolutionary Left had the ground cut from under it by reforms and economic growth offered to governments and industrial relations systems of the Centre and Centre-Left. By 1950 the contest was over. A cross between Marshallian citizenship and American liberalism dominated the West, less through its internal evolution than through the fortunes of war. It still dominates today.

Marshall's general argument was that industrial society institutionalized class struggle through mass citizenship. This seems true. All regimes have guaranteed *some* citizen rights. But they have done so in very different degrees and combinations. It is a more complex and less optimistic overall picture than he envisaged. But for the logic of geo-politics and war – including the sacrifices of his own generation – it might have been a very different and infinitely more depressing picture in Europe.

Sociologists are prone to forget that 'evolution' is usually geo-politically assisted. Dominant powers may impose their strategies on lesser powers; or the lesser may freely choose the dominator's strategy because it is an obviously successful modernization strategy. This means that what 'evolves' depends on changing geo-political configurations.

Let me quote Ito Hirobumi, the principal author of the Meiji constitution of 1889:

> We were just then in the age of transition. The opinions prevailing in the country were extremely heterogeneous, and often diametrically opposed to each other ... there was a large and powerful body of the younger generation educated at the time when the Manchester theory was in vogue, and who in consequence were ultra-radical in their ideas of freedom. Members of the bureaucracy were prone to lend willing ears to the German doctrinaires of the reactionary period, while, on the other hand, the educated politicians among the people having not yet tasted the bitter significance of administrative responsibility, were liable to be more influenced by the dazzling words and lucid theories of Montesquieu, Rousseau and similar French writers.

I have taken this quotation from Bendix (1978, p. 485) who uses it in support of a general evolutionist model of how Western ideals of popular representation supplanted monarchy everywhere. He rightly notes the importance of 'reference societies', more advanced societies to which modernizers could point with approval. But the quotation reveals that at the end of the nineteenth century there were at least three – Britain, France and Germany – and this reflected a real balance of power among several great powers. No single power could impose its will on others (outside its colonial or regional sphere of influence). Modernizers could choose from among several regime strategies. That is far less the case today. The Soviet and Anglo-American strategies were imposed – in the East by force, in the West by assisting certain political factions and subverting others. The two strategies have worked in their different ways for 40 years, and are now backed by the economic, ideological, military and political resources of two hegemonic super-powers. Eastern Europe is still held down by force. In the Western European periphery, deviant regimes in Portugal, Spain and Greece have succumbed to the Anglo-American vision of modernization desired increasingly by their domestic elites. In the Third World there is more variety of choice, because most countries are more insulated from both Western and Eastern blocs, but the choices tend to be around the two models provided by the super-powers.

Geo-politics has also provided a second recent change: the emergence of nuclear weapons. Warfare at the highest level would now destroy society. Therefore, the war-assisted pattern of change dominant in the first half of the century cannot be repeated. The emergence of the super-powers and of nuclear weapons both indicate that the future of citizenship will be different from its past. Our assessment of its prospects must combine domestic with geo-political analysis.

References

Bairoch P. 1968: *The Working Population and its Structure.* Brussels: Université Libre de Bruxelles.

—— 1982: 'International industrialization levels from 1750 to 1980', *Journal of European Economic History*, vol. II.

Bendix R. 1978: *Kings or People. Power and the Mandate to Rule.* Berkeley, Ca: University of California Press.

Berghahn V. 1973: *Germany and the Approach of War in 1914.* London: St Martins Press.

Blackbourne D. & Eley G. 1984: *The Peculiarities of German History.* Oxford: Oxford University Press.

Bonnell V. E. 1983: *Roots of Rebellion: Workers' Politics and Organizations in St Petersburg and Moscow, 1900–1914.* Berkeley, Ca: University of California Press.

Calleo D. 1978: *The German Problem Reconsidered. Germany and the World Order, 1870 to the Present.* Cambridge: Cambridge University Press.

Corrigan P. and Sayer D. 1985: *The Great Arch: English State Formation as Cultural Revolution.* Oxford: Blackwell.

Dahrendorf R. 1959: *Class and Class Conflict in an Industrial Society.* London: Routledge and Kegan Paul.

Esping-Anderson G. 1985: *Politics against Markets: The Social Democratic Road to Power.* Princeton, NJ: Princeton University Press.

Flora P. and Alber J. 1981: 'Modernization, democratization, and the development of welfare states in Western Europe', in Flora and A. J. Heidenheimer (eds), *The Development of Welfare States in Europe and America.* New Brunswick, NJ: Transaction Books.

Flora P. and Heidenheimer A. J. 1981: 'Introduction' in their *The Development of Welfare States in Europe and America*, New Brunswick, NJ: Transaction Books.

Giddens A. 1985: *The Nation State and Violence.* Oxford: Polity Press.

Goldstein R. J. 1983: *Political Repression in 19th Century Europe.* Beckenham: Croom Helm.

Haimson L. H. 1964 and 1965: 'The problem of social stability in urban Russia, 1905–1917', Part 1 and 2, *Slavic Review*, vols 23 and 24.

Hall J. 1985: *Powers and Liberties.* Oxford: Blackwell.
Halsey A. H. 1984: 'T. H. Marshall: Past and Present, 1893–1981', *Sociology*, vol. 18.
Jessop B. 1978: 'Capitalism and democracy: the best possible political shell?', in G. Littlejohn et al. (eds), *Power and the State.* London: Croom Helm.
Kaiser D. E. 1983: 'Germany and the origins of the First World War', *Journal of Modern History*, vol. 55.
Kann R. E. 1964, *The Multinational Empire*, 2 vols. New York: Octagon Books.
Katznelson I. 1981. *City Trenches: Urban Politics and the Patterning of Class in the United States.* New York: Pantheon Books.
Lipset S. M. 1973: 'Tom Marshall – Man of Wisdom', *British Journal of Sociology*, vol. 24.
—— 1985: *Consensus and Conflict: Essays in Political Sociology* New Brunswick, NJ: Transaction Books.
Lockwood D. 1974: 'For T. H. Marshall', *Sociology*, vol. 8.
Maier C. S. 1981: 'The two postwar eras and the conditions for stability in 20th century Western Europe', *American Historical Review*, vol. 86.
Marshall T. H. 1963: 'Citizenship and social class', in his *Sociology at the Crossroads.* London: Heinemann.
—— 1975: *Social Policy*, 4th rev. edn. London: Hutchinson.
Mayer A. J. 1981: *The Persistence of the Old Regime.* London: Croom Helm.
Moore B. 1969: *The Social Origins of Dictatorship and Democracy.* Harmondsworth: Penguin.
Rokkan S. 1970: *Citizens, Elections, Parties: Approaches to the Comparative Study of the processes of Development.* Oslo: Universitetsforlaget.
Roth G. 1963: *The Social Democrats in Imperial Germany.* Totowa, NJ: Bedminster Press.
Shaw M. 1987: *The Dialectics of Total War.* London: Pluto Press.
Sheehan J. J. 1976: *Imperial Germany.* New York: Franklin Watts.
Skocpol T. 1979: *States and Social Revolutions.* Cambridge: Cambridge University Press.
Stone N. 1975: *The Eastern Front, 1914–1917.* New York: Charles Scribner's Sons.
Swain G. 1983: *Russian Social Democracy and the Legal Labour Movement, 1906–1914.* London: Macmillan.
Taylor A. J. P. 1961: *Bismarck: the Man and the Statesman.* London: Arrow Books.
Turner B. S. 1986: *Citizenship and Capitalism: the Debate over Reformism.* London: Allen and Unwin.

8

The Decline of Great Britain

In the perspective of world history it is not unusual for civilizations and Great Powers to decline and fall. None remains pre-eminent for more than a few centuries. Moreover, in a competitive multi-state civilization like Europe – where no power has ever managed to make the whole continent its empire – they have risen and fallen rather more quickly. Over a thousand years, numerous powers/civilizations have acquired a certain pre-eminence in Europe. The main cases over the last millenium have been:

- The ninth-century Carolingian Empire, occupying northern France and south-west Germany.
- The eleventh-century Norman states – Normandy, England, south Italy and the central Mediterranean.
- The thirteenth/fourteenth-century city-state civilization of Italy.
- The sixteenth-century Spanish Empire (including the Low Countries and Austria).
- Mid-seventeenth-century Holland.
- Late seventeenth/early eighteenth-century France (with a near-miss at recreation by Napoleon).
- Nineteenth-century Great Britain.
- Post-1945 United States (hegemonic over the West, though kept out of Eastern Europe).

All these rose to dominate the Continent, but then all declined (US decline has probably just begun). None remained dominant for more than 100 years. Moreover they usually declined greatly, not merely to the level of the principal competitors. Only France might be said to deviate, maintaining a Great Power presence until 1940, and reviving again since then. Let us perhaps hope that Britain can

The Decline of Great Britain 211

emulate France rather than the others, where decline was usually catastrophic. In my list the early ones leave no trace of a state over their areas today, while the later leave only enfeebled ones. It is easy to forget their former glories when we look at Spain or The Netherlands today. But they nearly prevented Britain from ever being Great. The Spanish Armada may have only failed because of bad weather; while Admiral van Tromp sailed his fleet up to London with a broomstick tied to his flagship's mast, an arrogant symbol of power, 'sweeping the Thames free of the English' he called it.

So the problem of the decline of Britain can be fitted into broader patterns provided by historical and comparative sociology. If we examine the reasons for decline in these historical cases we find three.

Three general causes of decline in multi-state civilizations

First, the competitors learn fast whatever power techniques were pioneered by the dominant power, and they add local variants that often improve them. The dominant power's vital edge then disappears. Spanish infantry techniques were imitated, then improved, first by Sweden, then by almost everyone. Dutch naval and commercial techniques were mastered and extended by Britain. In a multi-state civilization it is virtually inevitable that this will happen. The dominant power will be caught up by several others and then be merely one among equals.

Secondly, the other powers gang up on the dominant one and deliberately finish it off. This can be done either by a concert of powers (as defeated Louis XIV and Napoleon) or by one or two rivals rising to dominance. Thus Britain ruthlessly eliminated Holland at sea, while Spain was attacking on land. Again this is more or less inevitable in a multi-state civilization. No one has yet been able to conquer the whole of Europe, and the overmighty have been deposed.

Thirdly, there are internal fetters to further development within the social structure of the dominant power. These have taken a particular and interesting form. The conditions that first led to success are institutionalized, but then those very institutions hold the power back from further development if the environment changes. Spain's greatness was based on dynastic acquisitions of huge and sometimes wealthy territories across Europe, backed up by an efficient land army and the windfall profits of gold and silver from the New World. Its rulers then bled the country in a succession of costly dynastic land wars in Europe, in which the New World was used for loot rather than as a productive resource. Though these wars helped eliminate Holland, they also assisted the rise of Britain and France, who used the New World, and trade generally, more productively. Spain was thus trapped in the conditions that had led to her success.

So my argument will be that the decline of Britain can be explained with reference to the same three causes: imitation and extension of British techniques by others, murder by other powers and the internal social fetters provided by past British success. The first two are relatively obvious, though social scientists tend to downplay the importance of the second because most are uncomfortable at handling geo-political and military power. Most of the literature concentrates on the first and third causes. I will take them in turn.

British greatness

First, however, we should remember just how 'Great' Britain was. Britain was hegemonic in the period 1815–80. The British Navy patrolled the world's seas, at first with a massive dominance, then kept deliberately at the 'Two Power Standard' (maintained at a strength greater than that of the next two powers combined). Britain invented the Industrial Revolution and kept its early lead for about 100 years. Around 1860 British manufactures constituted almost half of the world's, and the proportion was over half for some of the most advanced products (like iron and steel). Its merchant marine carried a third of total world trade. Her exports were a quarter of those of the world. All these proportions are significantly higher than those of today's greatest power, the United States (Bairoch, 1976, pp. 169). Sterling was the reserve currency of the world (as the dollar was undisputedly between 1945 and 1971, and more precariously since). The City of London traded over half the world's stocks and shares (a proportion which Wall Street has never remotely approached). British ideas and culture – from liberalism and *laissez-faire* to the sports the world still plays – became global.

British decline

1 The imitation and extension of techniques

Shortly after 1880 that pre-eminence no longer existed. This is a conventional date for two main reasons, both connected with my first cause: the imitation and extension of technique by other countries. First, the 'Second Industrial Revolution' began, centred on further developments in the steel, metal manufacturing and chemical industries. This revolution, unlike the first one, involved high science and massive capital investment in industry. In turn this developed large corporations, investment banks and greater state assistance to industry in the form of both capital and scientific training. For reasons I explore later, Britain lagged in these respects, its institutions geared to the conditions that had brought earlier success. Second, British *laissez-faire* lost its international dominance. Britain's rivals raised tariffs and emphasized selective protection for their manufactured and agricultural products. Again Britain lagged, wedded to the free-market principles that had served its interests in the past (though in practice retreating into the protection of the British Empire). Two particular countries led the way in these transformations, Germany and the United States. By 1910 their level of economic development had just overtaken that of Britain, though the three of them were well ahead of any other power (Bairoch, 1982, esp. tables 5 and 6). Sterling remained the premier world currency, and the City continued pre-eminent in financial markets, but in all other respects there was no longer a single leader.

This story could be continued right up to the early 1950s, showing the way in which Britain gradually became just one among five or six advanced industrial countries, as the conditions of technical progress became more equally distributed among them. In other words, Britain's decline to being one among several was more or less inevitable and obvious. But, of course, Britain has declined further than that.

Britain's standard of living is now among the lowest in Europe, as is its output per worker. Investment (i.e. gross capital formation per capita) has actually been the lowest among the OECD countries over the past decade. Manufacturing output has declined. In 1984 Britain became a net importer of manufactured goods for the first time since the Industrial Revolution (indeed, probably for the first time ever). True, there are two other processes involved in 'de-industrialization', besides British decline. They are (1) a switch in all advanced capitalist countries from manufacturing to services; and (2) the recent economic faltering of the West in general. But on top of these global processes, Britain is also de-industrializing because of continued decline. So we must introduce other causes.

2   Murder and world wars

We must introduce the second cause, murder by other powers. It may not seem particularly obvious that this has occurred. In twentieth-century geo-politics the murder of Great Britain has been merely an incidental part of the century's major catastrophe, the suicide of Germany. Without defeat in two world wars there is every reason to expect that Germany would now be the dominant world power, using the resources of most of Europe and the European colonies, faced by an alliance between the two Great Powers on its borders, Russia (perhaps still Tsarist) and the United States. But in two wars the German leaders suicidally embarked on a two-front campaign against all their rivals and were overwhelmed. Those wars also finished off the global pretensions of the other European powers, especially Britain, and secured the joint pre-eminence of the United States and Soviet Russia.

The wars had both geo-political and geo-economic effects. Against the expectations of the German leaders, in the end these were not professional soldiers' wars, with victory going to the best organized. They were mass mobilization wars and victory went simply to the big battalions. In the end two factors decided the issue: the sheer size of the American and Russian economies, and the ability of the mass of their middle managements and skilled workers to build and drive tanks and airplanes. The super-powers are now continental powers, unlike their predecessors. I doubt if this was purely a logic of development internal to industrialism. It seems also to have depended upon the fortunes of war.

The wars changed fundamentally the development of industrial

The Decline of Great Britain

societies by ensuring that the United States and Soviet Russia would be their leading powers rather than Germany. They also furthered British decline at the hands of collapsing Germany. Amid these events we can find a few murderous acts committed by the rising power, the United States, against Britain. The terms of US entry into the Second World War and the terms of the settlement of 1945–6 were both designed to weaken British postwar power. Thus US goods now had equal access to the Empire; thus the crippling burden of dollar debt in 1945 was to be paid for by the import of US goods; thus the US insistence on the convertibility of sterling. In 1946 a rush to convert sterling holdings into dollars depleted Britain's gold and dollar reserves and caused a crisis. Convertibility was suspended in 1947 after a demonstration, satisfactory to American eyes, of sterling's vulnerability. This was calculated to finish off Britain's remaining global rivalry to the United States. It was not nice behaviour, even if it was typical of a Great Power on the make (as Britain itself had earlier been).

But these mildly murderous acts proved less important to the continuing decline of Britian than the combination of nominal victory but real exhaustion in both wars. Thus apparently all was well, and all could be restored, but in reality the geo-economic means to Great Power status had gone. In any case American (and Russian) murder was concentrated on Germany and Japan, with different results. Their military might has been destroyed, their regimes carefully controlled (at least for the first ten years), but their economies have been allowed to grow again, to the point where they actually rival the United States. Here attempted murder seems to have proved beneficial to the victim.

So again, though geo-political rivalry does help explain the rise and fall of Great Powers, including Britain's relative decline, it still leaves much unexplained. We can see why Britain is no longer an imperial power, no longer holds the world's reserve currency, no longer enjoys the economic benefits that spin off from a military lead. But this cannot explain why Britain is not a Germany, a Japan, or even a France in terms of contemporary economic trends.

3 British internal fetters: institutionalizing success

If my general model is correct, we should expect to find that Britain's present problems lies with the very institutions that arose with her original rise to greatness. We will find exactly that.

Britain's rise was based on a number of causes, some accidental, others more structural. Over the long term, power in Europe had shifted to the north-west of the continent, towards wetter, heavier soils and open sea navigation. The discovery of the New World privileged navigation; the agricultural revolution of the seventeenth and eighteenth centuries privileged wetter soils. Power had obviously passed to the Atlantic coastline of Europe by 1700.

Britain's unique advantage lay in two principal aspects of its social structure. First, being a westerly island, Britain could concentrate economic and military strategy single-mindedly on sea-borne trade and commerce, without being distracted by European territorial disputes and land warfare. Whereas France and Spain always split their resources between the two, and Holland was reluctantly forced to do so to defend itself, Britain concentrated on naval and commercial enterprises from the 1650s onwards. That meant that British foreign policy was consistent, popular with the dominant classes and backed with adequate financial resources because it was principally aimed at commerical, naval goals. These financial resources came partly from taxation by consent, and partly (especially at times of war) by the floating of government bonds. State and wealthy classes became closely entwined. As we will see, their cooperation centred on the nexus of City/Treasury/Bank of England. It was necessary to reduce French power on land, too, but this would be done by subsidizing Hanoverians, Prussians and others to do the fighting. 'Canada will be won in Silesia', as Pitt correctly predicted. The success of this strategy was to have two enduring legacies. External commerce, rather than production, was the aim of state policy; and militarism was pushed to the margins of British life. *Laissez-faire* could appear natural, even though it rested on naval and geo-political force.

The second British advantage lay in its agriculture. Farming was dominated by neither large estates nor an independent peasantry, but by medium-sized farmers, some tenants, some proprietors, but all with real control of their farms and of farm labour. There was something in this that led to a peculiarly prosperous and *competitive* agrarian structure. Most historians now believe that the principal immediate cause of the Industrial Revolution in England was the market effects of the demand of these farming households. Markets for products such as pots and pans, horsehoes and clothing, led to an interaction btween small-scale enterprises in iron, textiles and mining that led towards the steam engine and the Revolution (Eversley, 1967; Pawson, 1979; Lee, 1986; but see McCloskey, 1985, for the traditional view emphasizing technological innovation and external commerce). But this also left a legacy: success was the result of free market forces, competition between free, autonomous property owners. The Industrial Revolution did not change this. It was pioneered by small jobbing artisans, engineers and entrepreneurs (Pollard, 1965). It did not involve complex science or technology or large capital expenditure until, first, the railway revolution of the 1840s, and then more massively the 'second' revolution of the 1880s (Crafts, 1985).

Classical political economy arose to generalize these real characteristics of the British economy into natural laws. The Invisible Hand, perfect competition, equal net advantages, the laws of supply and demand − all were not inaccurate descriptions of the economy that made Britain great. From Adam Smith to Mrs Thatcher the connection has been made between national greatness and free competition, and it is correct − or at least it *was* correct. That is how Great Britain rose up. Unfortunately, however, these conditions of success were then institutionalized to become the core of the British ruling class. When global economic realities changed, the British ruling class tightened up the institutions which had made them Great, leaving Britain trapped into a downward spiral of inappropriate institutional response to change.

As Britain rose to global dominance, four institutions solidified:

1 A global militarism, based on naval power, carried the *pax britannica* to the world. Because naval and global, this militarism did not intrude much on British social life (unlike, for example, the European-centred and land-based militarism of Germany). Nevertheless, attachment to Great Military Power status has remained deep among British rulers.
2 Britain became committed to a *laissez-faire*, free trade world

economy. By free trade Britain could exploit its early industrial lead and export its manufactured goods, dominating the world until about the 1880s. Britain has remained attached to such a global economic order, which has left Britain as an 'open' economy ever since.

3 Britain's industrial lead was based on the inventiveness and competitiveness of small entrepreneurs using simple, imitable techniques, small organizations and low capital resources. It required little external financing. Thus big capital was put to predominantly commercial rather than industrial uses.

4 Financial-commercial institutions became unusually well developed. Their main roles were to lend the savings of the wealthy to the British government, and to use naval hegemony to monopolize trade and shipping. The City of London was the power base of this essentially *commercial* capitalism, but its political links to government were strong, much stronger than those of industry.

These institutions have been responsible for three specific economic failures.

1 A failure to invest in industry.
2 A commitment to an open, free-trade economy, giving priority in economic policy to the protection of sterling and the balance of payments rather than to domestic production.
3 A commitment to military spending and research and development.

Investment failure British domestic productive investment has been the lowest among the OECD countries for many years. Investment goes elsewhere. Why?

One answer, given by Wiener (1981), seems plausible and has been reportedly influential among the Thatcher government. His evidence is from literary and philosophical sources about the social life of the upper classes since the mid-nineteenth century. He argues that 'the entrepreneurial spirit' of industrialists declined as they were seduced into the institutions of the Victorian upper class. Their sons went to public schools and the elite universities. They learned to be gentlemen and to despise trade and industry. They aspired to be either cultured men of leisure or to work in more refined professions, in the armed forces, the civil services, the colonial administration, or the City. The pinnacle of achievement was a title and access to court, not mere vulgar wealth. That is why Britain declined, and that is why it is still declining, says Wiener. It is the fault of the ruling class, for they have pursued status not profit.

But there are three serious flaws which vitiate Wiener's argument. First, taking the views of literary and philosophical figures as reflecting social reality is dangerous. Suppose we did the same exercise for Germany, and took its philosophers. Since Hegel they have been long on metaphyscis and obscure profundity, short on pragmatism and empiricism – in contrast to British philosophy. Clearly on this basis Britain is more likely to house the entrepreneurial spirit!

Nevertheless, some of the views of Wiener's men of letters have had a real basis (see Mann, 1975, for evidence to support the argument of this paragraph). There has long been a net outflow through the universities from industry to the professions, the City and the civil service. That is, more sons of industrial entrepreneurs and managers take that route, than there are sons of professional families going through university into industry. And clearly trade and industry have often been regarded as low status by the upper class, while industrialists have often searched desperately for culture and titles. But – and this is the second flaw – these same patterns tend to be found in all advanced capitalist countries. The occupational outflow from industry is found in the United States and probably elsewhere. The status striving is general – for example, German industrialists at the turn of the century were famous for wanting their sons to acquire duelling scars and become Prussian reserve officers. It has been characteristic of Western cultured circles as a whole to regard business as slightly immoral. And the essence of Wiener's argument is sometimes described as the 'Buddenbrooks Syndrome' after the German novel by Thomas Mann in which the burgher vigour of the Buddenbrooks family is sapped away by its pursuit of culture and gentility.

Nevertheless, there is probably a residual difference between Britain and most other countries. The City in Britain – financial and commercial capital – does command more status and power than industry. But – and here is the third flaw – this is emphatically not because of the argument put forward by Wiener.

He argues that industrialists' families choose status rather than profit. Yet the evidence is the reverse: that choosing to go into the City rather than industry brings more, not less personal wealth. Rubinstein (1974, 1977) shows that in the course of the nineteenth century finance capital joined the great landowners (and often merged with them) as the richest men in the country. Scott (1982) shows that the tendency has continued in the twentieth century. The problem – if problem it is – is that the entrepreneurial spirit in Britain leads to the City not industry. It has been economically rational not to keep one's resources in industry.

Investors are not idiots. If they do not invest in industry, it is because they can probably get a higher rate of return elsewhere. Classical and neo-classical economists and pundits believe this to be the end of the matter. The market must rule: interference with the laws of supply and demand can only be detrimental. It is impossible to persuade capitalists to invest in British industry if they can reply 'but our previous investments in British industry have not brought as good returns as other types of investment'. It would be irrational to force investors to divert from the most profitable to less profitable ventures.

But the sociologist can reply to this that economic markets have institutional preconditions. There is nothing 'natural' about them. The world of Adam Smith's Invisible Hand was created precisely because of the British power institutions described above. British investments have subsequently taken particular channels, different from those of other countries, because of the distinctive institutions of British capitalism. They have created a particular form of economic rationality. If those institutions changed, either because of government policy or as part of social change, so too would economic rationality. It would then become more profitable to invest differently. What economists and sociologists together must consider is whether present rationality is self-destructive, leading to a downward spiral of adjustment to competition resulting in lower profits. And what economists must also consider is whether an alternative set of institutions, and their accompanying form of rationality, would bring better results.

So where does British investment go? The conventional view, especially of the critics, is that it goes abroad in investment in foreign industries. This is partially true. But as Ingham (1984) points out, it is only part of the story. There are actually four main types of investment outlet. My brief account of them depends heavily on his excellent analysis.

The first is in government stocks. The City rose to power because it lent to government and because it discounted commercial transactions. Government lending predominated in the eighteenth century, though it then declined somewhat and is now the least important. However, its significance has endured because it led to close interconnections between three institutions: the Bank of England, the Treasury and the City. Ever since, the three have cooperated very closely to dominate British government economic policy as a whole (Longstreth 1983). In the eighteenth and early nineteenth centuries, because the dominant classes were essentially agreed about the commercial aims of British foreign policy, they were willing to lend money to the government. Those three institutions arose because of this, not the Industrial Revolution. Industrialization was fitted into existing economic planning arrangements and has indeed barely changed them. The City/Treasury/Bank of England power nexus has ensured that current economic planning is dominated by commercial rather than industrial considerations.

Let us also notice the form of this type of investment. Government stocks do not involve taking risks of an unknown magnitude in productive investment, but investing savings for a fixed return. Thus the City was also well organized later to channel savings into other similar types of secure, supposedly low-risk investment. In the post-war period this has been most notably landed property. Hence the property boom since the 1960s has revitalized this type of City role.

The second type of investment is in commerce, or 'money itself', the second original function of the City. From 1830 to the present day, with the exception of the period about 1890–1914, the City's earnings from insurance, the foreign exchange and money markets, the financing of trade, freight and commodity broking has exceeded income and dividends from overseas investment. This has become spectacularly so since the 1960s, as the City has become the primary place for organizing the flow of petrodollars and Eurdollars.

The essential practice involved here is discounting. Merchants had long accepted bills-of-exchange from each other. Once beyond direct barter, unless everyone carries massive amounts of international currency (it would have had to have been gold or silver then), they must sell goods on credit, often without knowing much about the creditworthiness of the other merchant. They must also pay for future deliveries from the other merchant, taking a bill-of-exchange, due to mature on a certain date. As they attained commercial pre-eminence, first Holland, then England, took over a specialized role of guaranteeing creditworthiness – of course, for profit. London merchants used surplus cash to buy merchants' credit notes before they matured – at a rate slightly less than their face value.

Discounting involves bankers as middlemen between different productive sectors. They are not involved at all in productive investment, but in commerce. They buy and sell, not ownership of productive resources, but money. These commercial activities exist in all countries, but the City of London has kept most of its early international lead. The 'bills-on-London' issued by London merchants became international short-term credit as Britain became hegemonic. These men and institutions are thoroughly international in their orientation, having no particular expertise in British industry, or indeed industry anywhere. Their sole interest in Britain is that it remains an open economy, committed to the free flow of money through its territories.

The third type of investment is foreign investment, that is in productive enterprises abroad. In the early nineteenth century Britain led in two relevant characteristics: the wealth of its upper and middle classes and the international expertise of its financiers. In the period 1880–1914 there was a massive outflow of savings in the form of 'portfolio investment', principally in foreign government stocks and railway companies. Portfolio investment means investing one block of wealth in a diversity of stocks and shares, rather than in a single company, which is termed 'direct foreign investment'. The most common form of direct foreign investment in the twentieth century has been by a single company, generally termed a 'multinational company'. Foreign investment has declined relative to the other three types of investment, but remains a higher proportion of GDP than in any other country. As in other countries, foreign investment since 1945 has become more direct, led by multinationals. Both portfolio and direct foreign investment have an interest in a relatively open international economy, rather than protectionism – as has commercial investment.

The Decline of Great Britain

The predominance of these three types of investment leaves little capital spare for the fourth, investment in British industry. Industry is largely self-financing out of its own profits and out of merger activity. In particular (1) the banks lend less than half the proportion of new investment that they do in Germany and Japan (and two-thirds of the American proportion); and (2) the new issue share market is underdeveloped here – as opposed to the trading of existing stocks (the 'secondary stock market').

In recent years there has been a spectacular growth of pension and insurance funds and unit trusts. These now hold over half the securities in Britain – far higher than in any other country. This has brought the people into capitalism. Almost all the middle class, and about the half the working class, now have a small part of their income invested through these outlets. But this has not changed the overall direction of investment. Most of these funds go either abroad, or into government stock or property development, or into the secondary share market.

Thus British industry cannot easily raise large sums of money for new investment on the scale of its foreign competitors. Yet this does not result in massive discontent among industrialists. True, small business does often express discontent (and has received considerable help from the present government). But big business, represented by the Confederation of British Industry (CBI), does not. In 1976 the CBI did a survey of its members for the Wilson Committee inquiring into the City. It found that 89 per cent of member companies had not been prevented in recent years from carrying out a potentially profitable investment programme by the difficulties of getting external finance.

The reason is that they have had long experience of British banks, know that they have difficulty satisfying their lending requirements, and have learned to adapt and live by other methods. The banks lend short, as they have traditionally done, rather than for long-term capital investment. According to Williams et al. (1983), they also lend according to a 'liquidation approach'. Does the firm have assets which could be sold off to repay the loan after liquidation? Most foreign banks in the United States, France, Germany and Japan adopt a 'going concern approach'. Will the firm generate a sufficient flow of funds to make the repayments (Hu, 1975)? This favours the big conservative firm, not the thrusting, dynamic one. As Williams et al. put it, had

Soichiro Honda turned up in a Barclays branch in West Bromwich in the 1950s, the manager would have interpreted the progress of Honda Motor Co. as a cautionary tale of overtrading, and would have suggested, not a bank loan but the appointment of a receiver.

Are the banks irrational? Not from their own perspective, because they have rarely lent long to industry. Their expertise is bound up in the short term, and in that sphere there is a lot of competition. Thus repayments are less of a problem for them than the security for a long-term loan.

The point is that these practices have endured for more than 100 years. British industry has *never* relied on external finance. After 1880, faced with German and US competition in high science and capital-intensity, it defended itself with cooperative mergers. Industry became big by combining resources, not finding external capital. In post-1945 conditions of intense competition from many countries it also reacted with a merger boom, this time contested takeovers.

Let us examine mergers (with the aid of Williams et al., 1983). A high price–earnings shares ratio in the secondary market is the key to predatory merger success. But that is only imperfectly related to long-term productivity. To stay in business companies have to concentrate on the secondary market, not new issues, which will reduce the price–earnings valuation in the short term. Williams concludes that the form of the massive merger boom of the 1960s and 1970s resulted from the nature of the stock market in Britain, not from the requirements of industrial productivity. True, mergers may serve the same purpose as capital investment. After mergers, managements can raise money by selling off taken-over assets; and takeovers are normally financed not with real money but with the paper resources of their own shares. But the evidence shows that after the merger companies have on balance been slightly less profitable than before. The now massive British firms (the most concentrated in the world) are in reality only loose federations. For they have been united not by productive logic, but by the logic of price–earnings ratios. In other words, the rationality of the banks and of the stock market dominate over productive rationality *in industry itself*. It is not that industry and the financial institutions are at loggerheads, but that the practices of the financiers are also internalized as economic rationality by industry.

This is a perfect example of the downward spiral. Trapped into certain dominant institutions – the primacy of the banks and stock market over industry – adjustment to competition actually worsens the record of productive investment by encouraging non-productive takeovers. This is despite the fact that everyone concerned is behaving with impeccable economic rationality. They are making the best possible decisions within the institutions available. If we wish, like Wiener, to attack the ruling class, it is their institutions that are at fault, not their abilities and entrepreneurial spirit as individuals.

Overcommitment to Laissez-faire *and sterling* I have already indicated the two fundamental roots of *laissez-faire* in Britain. British greatness was based upon it in the nineteenth century; and most of British finance and commercial capitalism has always derived its profits from *laissez-faire*. This is necessary to its commercial role – acting as middleman in world trade and credit – and to its foreign investing role. And in the very period when commercialism declined (1890–1914) its place was filled by an increase in foreign investment. Since 1830 the two have constituted well over half of City activity. Thus the City is truly 'an offshore island'. It has been more oriented toward the international than the British economy. But it does have one strong domestic attachment – a vital interest in the strength and stability of the British medium of exchange, the pound sterling.

The City's lending to government has given crucial economic decision-making powers to the City/Bank of England/Treasury nexus (Longstreth, 1979). British governments have not favoured even the mild degree of protectionism which other countries have engaged in from time to time. And British governments have given high priority to the world role of sterling. In the inter-War period this involved keeping on the gold standard even while crippling currency reserves and reducing domestic investments.

In recent years it has also had more subtle consequences on policy. The pound sterling is itself a valuable economic resource. The viability of the City depends on it, as in turn do the savings of most of us, because of the rise of the pension and insurance funds. But the currency is no longer strong enough to be backed by gold. Speculation on the pound is a part of the normal practice of world financial markets, but it potentially destabilizes the whole British economy. If there is a run on the pound, then there is an immediate balance of payments deficit. In the 1950s and 1960s this led to the stop–go economic cycle. The deflationary 'stop' cut domestic demand to curb imports (it also raised interest rates to encourage foreigners to move back into sterling). Cutting demand also discouraged productive investment. When the balance of payments recovered the 'go' then stimulated domestic consumption rather than investment, encouraging imports rather than domestic production of more capital-intensive goods. Steadily throughout this process productive capacity fell behind competitors.

None of this policy is foolish. While British capitalism plays this global economic role, it needs help. But protecting sterling contradicts the protection of domestic industry. Supposing a massive programme of industrial investment was embarked upon. This could only be done by diverting resources perhaps from personal consumption, perhaps from the City's preferred forms of investment. If the latter, then the City's international role would be threatened. Choices must be made, and something is sacrificed by each choice.

The choice could be made according to the best technical economic arguments. Or it could be made according to economic power. There is no doubt, as Longstreth shows, that power decides. Industry is quite effectively organized when it lobbies against unions, or for particular self-interested policies. But it rarely questions the received commercial orthodoxy. It is very striking that in the history of British political economy we do not find a specifically *industrial* lobby of a quasi-corporatist kind, in which industrialists and unions alike jointly press for protection, investment and corporatist arrangements. Conservative and Labour governments alike have put as their first priorities the role of sterling and the balance of payments. Nothing is more revealing than Harold Wilson's diaries (1971): all economic planning is revealed to be at the mercy of day-to-day events on the money markets. Wilson does not denounce that, though he does grumble – he treats it as a fact of life, as economic rationality itself.

What policy would ensue if the issue were decided not by power but by a proper cost–benefit analysis? I am not sufficiently expert to say. Manufacturing industry still generates more jobs and wealth than do financial services, and it generates them more equally through the regions and the social classes. A simple choice of one or the other would seem to favour industry, as does the political economy of most other countries. However, it is possible that British industrial decline has gone so far, and City revival has been so successful, that such a policy would be to kill the only golden goose of the British economy. I return to such consequences in a moment.

Overcommitment to militarism Britain devotes more of its GDP to military spending than does any other advanced capitalist nation except for the United States (it is closely followed by France). Only the United States rivals Britain in the proportion of total research and development expenditure going into military products. Up to a third of R&D expenditure went into aircraft manufacture alone until the 1970s. More than the other issues and choices I have discussed so far, this has been straightforwardly irrational, the result of delusions of imperial grandeur. However, it is not easy to change because militarism has never been very up-front or conspicuous in British society. This stems from our naval past. Britain is the only European country without conscription. Until the Falklands War the defence burden lay rather hidden – and, unfortunately from this perspective, the Falklands War was a great success.

We may object to the extent of British militarism because it endangers peace, but there are also two grave economic disadvantages of such an unbalanced research allocation. First, the main competitor in military hardware has been the United States. Military demand in the United States is large and it is protected from foreign competition. Thus British airplanes, missiles, radar systems etc. can rarely compete effectively in the United States or equally on world markets. Now and again a British (or French) product like the Harrier jet (or Exocet missile) may be good enough to overcome US competition, or a few foreign governments may want to keep their distance from the Pentagon. But that is insufficient to keep major industries going.

Second, there have been few civilian technological spin-offs from military products in the post-war period, especially in more recent years. Many economists today believe that Germany and Japan's technologically advanced industries have boomed precisely because they do not have to service substantial defence programmes. American economists now look askance at Reagan's Strategic Defense Initiative (Star Wars) programme. This threatens to absorb virtually the whole of the US R&D budget over the next decades. They suggest that militarism will bleed dry the US economy. Britain's experience seems to confirm this expectation.

Partly because of the failure of this military-led R&D effort, Britain's whole commitment to high technology has been jeopardized. From being second only to the United States in per capita R&D expenditure in the 1950s and early 1960s, Britain has fallen below the level of Germany, Japan, Sweden and Switzerland – and France has had similar problems (Freeman, 1978).

A further problem has resulted from the connection and mutual reinforcement of *laissez-faire* and militarism. Britain's commitments in the late nineteenth century were global, just as are US commitments today. The notion of Britain's global role survives through the contemporary strength of the City and through imperial military delusions. Of course, in reality a retreat had to occur. First, this was to the Empire, renamed as the Commonwealth. At the same time geo-political realism urged retreat to Europe. What has resulted is an uneasy relationship between three different notions of the British sphere of interest and influence: is it global, Commonwealth or European? Thus, for example, membership or non-membership of the EEC has probably proved less damaging to Britain than the uncertainties through the 1960s and 1970s of whether Britain was in or out.

This seems to have had special effects on British marketing of products. Various authors have pinned considerable blame on Britain's export salesmen. As Williams et al. (1983, pp. 217–81) note in their case study of British Leyland, the problem may be that export drives depend on targeting particular markets and then hitting them hard. British uncertainties about where our fundamental interests lay, coupled with a general interest in the whole world as a sphere of operations, may have prevented a consistent strategy of market concentration from occurring.

An explanation of failure: blaming the ruling class

This empirical analysis can buttress a general explanation of decline. Britain became Great partly because of accidents of its soil and maritime position. But its social structure also helped in two decisive ways. First, unity among its ruling class over commercial and naval interests created a geo-political and commercial strategy aimed single-mindedly at naval, commercial hegemony over the world, backed by an efficient taxation and government loan system involving close cooperation between government and the wealthy. Second, both an agrarian and an industrial revolution arose directly as a result of competition on relatively free markets between a large number of farming and industrial entrepreneurs.

As these two social structures had worked such wonders, understandably enough they became institutionalized as the very centre of the British ruling class. For a time free trade was institutionalized globally by force, but this could not survive the end of British hegemony. Domestically its ruling class also institutionalized three main forms of its own rise: (i) a slightly hidden (because initially naval-based) militarism; (ii) a free, autonomous, self-financing industry, into which it was considered undesirable, even 'unnatural' to intervene; and (iii) an essentially *commercial* capitalist class with strong controls over the formulation of government policy through the City/Treasury/Bank of England nexus.

When German and American competition hit hard, from the 1880s, the response came from an essentially commercial political economy. Industry hit back through its own resources, largely unaided by government. Mergers, at first cooperative, then often contested, attempted to find investment funds through concentration. Though British firms became proportionately the biggest in the world, this was not a very efficient route to greater productivity, as we saw. But industry's efforts were further harmed by government economic policy, dominated by commercial reasoning and actually implemented by the City/Treasury/Bank of England nexus. Industry has been left unprotected from either foreign competition or the vagaries of international currency movements. The positive side of the balance is that British capitalism's essential commercialism enabled the City to retain considerable power as the main money middlemen of the whole world. With the rise of Europe relative to the United States from the 1960s the offshore island in the Thames has been well placed and organized to bring great prosperity to its members. Commerce prospers while industry decays. I hope I have shown that this is the fault of the ruling class: but as I have repeatedly argued, the fault lies with its institutions, not with its personal or collective drives or abilities.

Other classes, other explanations

I have given a particular account of Britain's decline. It is not idiosyncratic. It is highly congruent with the arguments of sociologists like Ingham, Longstreth and Scott, and economists such as Pollard (1982) and Williams. But the literature does contain a coherent, alternative view to the one I have expressed. British decline, it is argued, is the result of class struggle. Interestingly, this view is common to the extreme Right and Marxist Left. The Right argues that decline is largely due to the obduracy and conservativism of unions and workers, and the feebleness of management and government in combating them. Marxists (e.g. Glyn and Harrison, 1980; Gamble, 1981) argue that British class struggle has imposed a 'profits squeeze' on capital, leaving insufficient surplus for investment. The Marxists, and a few on the Right, would also accept many of my arguments. But they pin fundamental blame on class struggle. The Right say 'suppress class struggle and let markets rule'; the Marxists say 'increase class struggle beyond mere defence of workers' living standards to the overthrow of capitalism'. But *all* these views have the defect of overstating the power – for good or ill – of workers and trade unions, both in capitalism in general and in British capitalism in particular. I have only time to argue this briefly here. First I consider the industrial record, then the political one.

In almost all countries workers and trade unions have no role in the fundamental decisions within either industry or commerce about investment or general strategy. German co-determination formally gives union representatives such a role, though they are generally content to react to the initiatives of management. The boards of large corporations rarely discuss industrial relations problems – as the research of Pahl and Winkler (1974) revealed. It is rare for companies to have industrial relations directors with seats on the board. Leadership positions are dominated by accountants, salesmen and engineers. This is a reasonable reflection of their real problems, as we can see from accounts such as that of Williams and his collaborators (1983) of GEC, the shipbuilding industry and British Leyland. The discussion of British Leyland is especially revealing. Despite all the publicity given to strikes, they figure only as a minor irritant. British Leyland declined because

The Decline of Great Britain

the company did not produce the right models for the right markets — deficiencies in engineering, styling, investment and marketing dominate its post-war history. These are all deficiencies of top management.

Blaming strikes also raises two general problems. First, British strike rates are not especially high. They are about average among the advanced capitalist countries. Second, there is no relationship between strike rate and economic growth, either internationally or nationally. Internationally, the high growth economies have low strike rates (Germany and Japan), sometimes high ones (the United States in the 1950s, Italy today). Nationally, periods of high strike rates are not generally those of low growth (as both Britain and Italy demonstrate in the post-war period).

Of course, there are aspects of British industrial relations practices which are harmful. Union structure is somewhat chaotic, being a jumble of different inheritances from the past. Craft and industrial unions exist alongside each other, in the same industries and firms. As the Donovan Royal Commission of Inquiry into Trade Unions reported 20 years ago, formal and informal (shop steward dominated) union hierarchies compete with one another. Similarly, it cannot be helpful for major companies to be dominated by men educated at private schools who have never encountered the working class until they are thrust into conflict with it on the shop-floor. But these problems do not concern the commanding heights of power in a capitalist economy. It is rather absurd to blame those who do not have power, rather than who do (a point made in a broader comparative context in the previous chapter).

In politics we can make similar points, though they apply more strongly to the case of Britain than to several other European countries. Over the first half of the twentieth century the struggle between reform and revolution in Western socialist parties was decisively settled in favour of reform. It was not the result of the inevitable logic of capitalism, for both World Wars and Adolf Hitler also played their role in the suppression of the Left. But by 1950 labour movements everywhere aimed, not at the overthrow of capitalism but at getting the best possible deal from within it. That included largely abandoning the notion that socialism was the way to *create* wealth. Capitalists would create wealth, socialists would then drag as much of it from them as they could.

Capital initiates, labour reacts. That is roughly what labour parties and trade unions do.

But in the early 1930s one labour party, the SPD of Sweden, discovered a modification. With hindsight and British chauvinism it is often called 'social Keynesianism', though it owed little to Keynes. Sweden discovered a path out of depression through state investment in industry and a reflationary expansion of public works and the welfare state. Reflation was also tried mildly in Roosevelt's New Deal, and massively in Hitler's re-armament. The Second World War made it a general strategy, though by now it had lost most of its socialist tinge. So a more aggressive, though still reformist, socialist political economy has emerged in various countries. Labour parties in Scandinavia, Austria and to some extent Germany have an economic strategy aimed deliberately at creating more wealth, with the cooperation of unions and workers in incomes policies and productivity deals, in return for economic expansion and welfare redistribution at the end.

The British labour movement has not shared in this strategy, or has tried to and failed. Why? Basically because the British labour movement was not involved at all in the rise of British power or prosperity. This was done by the ruling class I described earlier. When the labour movement emerged as a major organized force around 1900, it was reacting against an already institutionalized capitalism and national 'Greatness'. Thus the labour movement, parties and unions have consistently *reacted*, concentrating on the politics of redistribution of existing resources.

It was a Labour government that deflated in 1929–31 (and then split), while the Swedish SDP was creating wealth by reflating. In 1945, whatever the welfare achievements of the Labour government, it dismantled most of the war-time planning arrangements and handed the power of wealth creation back to the City. In the 1960s the failure of planning and the abolition of the Department of Economic Affairs happened under the Wilson Labour government. In the 1970s the Labour government of Callaghan contributed to the failure of the Social Contract. That covers *all* the majority governments of Labour. And in the 1983 election campaign Labour leader Michael Foot constantly contrasted 'people' and 'profits', handing wealth creation over to capital and the Conservatives, reserving only its civilized use for Labour. The Party still refuses to utter the obscenity 'income policy'!

In all these ways the power of the British working class, and of its unions and main party, has been essentially reactive. It has depended on capitalists creating wealth, and then labour hits them. True, the act of hitting may damage. Unions may resist productivity deals, better manning practices, the introduction of new products, the closure of obsolete firms and industries. But none of that is fundamental. In any case, as Pollard concludes, their intransigence is more an effect of decline than a cause: 'An environment of cuts and stagnation has turned them into reactionary and destructive bodies' (1982, p. 118). Once there is a profits squeeze then class struggle can hurt. It can hurt even more if, as in Britain, capital does not now know how to create wealth, and labour does not try to create it. It is the cause not of decline, but of a steepening of the downward spiral.

Consequences and alternatives

British industrial decline continues. Unemployment has risen to about 15 per cent, the highest among the advanced industrial countries. Manufacturing employment is now well below 30 per cent of total employment, having been above 40 per cent in 1950. Even full-time service employment is now static, and will begin falling if there is a lagged effect of manufacturing output on the demand for services. North Sea oil is papering over the balance of payments but will run down in the 1990s. Most economic prognostications are gloomy, casting doubt on whether Britain will be able to continue to afford its twentieth century welfare state achievements.

The sociologist can add gloom too. Massive unemployment and the contraction of the manufacturing base are bad enough in themselves, but they also have divisive effects. They are unevenly spread, so that some regions, and especially the inner cities and ethnic minorities, take the brunt of it. At the moment the South of England minus inner London, and small towns throughout most of the country, are somewhat cloistered from the worst effects of recession. Given the emergence of 'Two Britains' – though they are not simply North and South – it is difficult to find political consensus for any alternative strategy. An open economy favours commercial capital and rentier investment abroad. It also favours the successful multinationals operating from Britain (though Williams' analysis of GEC may indicate that they are concentrating their investment and job expansion programmes abroad). Most of the South-East of England now lives off this international economic sector, in the split social world of the service sector — split because financial and commercial services and headquarters staff of multinationals provide well-paid non-manual employment, yet they also generate the lowest paid service employment in shops, restaurants, transport etc. Yet the price of their recent growth, through an open economy and the dominance of commercial capitalism, has been the stagnation of those regions and classes dependent on most manufacturing industries. Public planning is especially difficult because, as Massey and Meegan (1982) have shown, an open economy exposes every town and region to the uncertainties of the world economy. Britain's economy looks less like a single unit and more difficult to plan.

Political reactions are also divided. A willingness to use violence to express discontent seems mostly confined to the black communities. The white working class seems somewhat demoralized. The predominantly white working class organized in national unionism and the Labour Party is largely in inner cities and regions hit by the most declining industries. They, naturally but unfortunately, espouse the politics of economic defence. They seek to protect existing jobs and industries, when that may be economically indefensible; and they are not attracted by an alternative strategy of political economy which might reflate, but still at the cost of their present jobs.

None of the political parties offers a clear, coherent solution. The Conservatives give priority to profit and so are realistic about obsolete industries and encouraging to new entrepreneurs. But they are controlled fundamentally by commercial, not industrial, capital and so are least likely to introduce a massive programme of industrial investment or a judicious measure of industrial protection and planning. The Labour Party has a clear, if crude, notion of the problem and the main part of the remedy: aid industrial investment and attack the hegemony of the City. But Labour seems unable to attract the support of industry in a corporatist strategy. This is partly because industry is the old enemy in the defensive class struggle, partly because Labour cannot promise effective wage restraint. The Liberal/SDP Alliance offers a combination of both sets of policies, some good, some bad, but no apparent overall strategy and little prospect of power.

So what will happen and what might alternatively happen? We should not expect any government to bring about a dramatic reversal of fortunes. The record of government intervention in the economy in any capitalist country shows that it has almost never made a massive difference, for better or for worse. Nevertheless, it might be possible to halt the absolute decline, perhaps even to turn the corner. Over a period of 50–100 years Britain might recover gradually to being one of the leading, most dynamic medium-sized capitalist economies. This is possible – such a degree of recovery has been achieved more than once in modern history by France. The last recovery occurred in the immediate post-war years thanks in large measure to concerted national planning – to which the British record can be very unfavourably compared (Hall, 1986). However, as I have stressed, this would involve tackling some of the central institutions of our ruling class: its dominance by commercial capitalism, its internationalism and its militarism. It is no small task.

The most probable scenario is continued decline, both because of the power of the major institutions I have described and because of the lack of political will and unity to change them. At some point soon, perhaps in the 1990s when the oil revenues will largely cease, we will arrive at a vital crunch point. Will the continued collapse of manufacturing also induce a collapse of services, as most economists believe? Or will Britain's divisions exacerbate, with commercial capital and the multinationals able to go it alone, generating enough employment (along with smaller, low-paid industries supplying local markets at low cost) to keep unemployment down to perhaps 20 per cent? These seem to me to be the two alternative scenarios of decline. In either case, by the year 2000 it will be as difficult to remember the Greatness of Britain as it is now to remember the Empire of Spain.

References

Bairoch P. 1976: *Commerce exterieur et development economique de l'Europe au XIXe siecle.* Paris: Mouton.

—— 1982: 'International industrialization levels from 1750 to 1980'. *Journal of European Economic History*, vol. 11.

Crafts N. F. R. 1985: *British Economic Growth during the industrial revolution.* Oxford: Clarendon Press.
Eversley D. E. C. 1967: 'The home market and economic growth in England, 1750–80', in E. L. Jones and G. E. Mingay (eds), *Land, Labour and Population in the Industrial Revolution.* London: Arnold.
Freeman C. 1978: 'Technical innovation and British trade performance', in F. Blackaby (ed), *De-industrialisation.* London: Heinemann.
Gamble A. 1981: *Britain in Decline.* London: Macmillan.
Glyn A. and Harrison J. 1980: *The British Economic Disaster.* London: Pluto Press.
Hall P. A. 1986: *Governing the Economy: the Politics of State Intervention in Britain and France.* Cambridge: Polity Press.
Hu Y. 1975: 'National attitudes and the financing of industry', *Political and Economic Planning,* broadsheet no. 559.
Ingham G. K. 1984: *Capitalism Divided? The City and Industry in British Social Development.* London: Macmillan.
Lee C. H. 1986: *The British Economy since 1700: A Macroeconomic Perspective.* Cambridge: Cambridge University Press.
Longstreth F. 1979: 'The city, industry and the state', in C. Crouch (ed.), *State and Economy in Contemporary Capitalism.* London: Croom Helm.
—— 1983: 'State economic planning in a capitalist society: the political sociology of economic policy in Britain, 1940–1979', unpublished PhD thesis, London School of Economics.
Mann M. 1975: 'The ideology of intellectuals and other people in the development of capitalism', in L. N. Lindberg, R. Alford, C. Crouch and C. Offe (eds), *Stress and Contradiction in Modern Capitalism.* Lexington, Mass: D. C. Heath.
Massey D. and Meegan R. 1982: *The Anatomy of Job Loss: the How, Why and Where of Employment Decline.* London: Methuen.
McCloskey D. 1985: 'The industrial revolution 1789–1860: a survey', in J. Mokyr (ed.), *The Economics of the Industrial Revolution.* London: Allen and Unwin.
Pahl R. E. and Winkler J. 1974: 'The economic elite: theory and practice', in P. Stanworth and A. Giddens (eds), *Elites and Power in British Society.* Cambridge: Cambridge University Press.
Pawson E. 1979: *The Early Industrial Revolution.* New York: Harper and Row.
Pollard S. 1965: *The Genesis of Modern Management.* London: Arnold.
—— 1982: *The Wasting of the British Economy.* London: Croom Helm.
Rubinstein W. D. 1974: 'British millionaires, 1809–1949', *Bulletin of the Institute of Historical Research,* vol. 48.
—— 1977: 'Wealth, elites and the class structure of modern Britain', *Past and Present,* no. 76.

Scott J. 1982: *The Upper Classes: Property and Privilege in Britain.* London: Macmillan.

Wiener M. 1981: *English Culture and the Decline of the Industrial Spirit 1850–1980.* Cambridge: Cambridge University Press.

Williams K., Willams J. and Thomas D. 1983: *Why are the British Bad at Manufacturing?* London: Routledge and Kegan Paul.

Wilson H. 1971: *The Labour Government 1964–70: A Personal Record.* London: Weidenfeld and Nicolson.

Index

absolutism 5, 15, 27, 113–18
Austria, Austria–Hungary 148, 158, 200, 201, 232
authoritarian monarchy xii, 190, 191, 196–203, 205–6
authoritarian socialism xii, 190, 203–5

capitalism vii, viii, x, xi, xii, 27, 36–7, 39, 46, 69, 73, 86, 115–20, ch. 4, 163–4, 188, 192–4, 196, 216–35
  defined 136
China, Chinese Empire x, 5, 12, 34, 42–5, 47–50, 52, 55–7, 61–4, 65
citizenship xii, 151, 156, 158–9, 162, 184, 188–9, 191–8, 204
citizen warfare xii, 135, 151, 166, 171
the City of London 212, 218, 222, 229
class conflict, struggle x, xii, 1, 19, 24, 33, 41, 52, 56, 69, 119, 148–9, 158, 161, 163, 164, 188, 190, 194, 230
classes viii, x–xi, 3–4, 15, 17, 24, 27, 29, 30, 39, 40–2, 47, 50, 52, 54, 55, 73, 115, 149, 154
  international viii, 149, 152, 163
  national viii, 148, 150, 152, 159, 163

ruling or dominant xii, 3, 13, 14, 22, 29, 35, 49, 59, 138, 188, 190, 217, 221, 228
transnational viii, 149, 152–3, 163
compulsory cooperation 21–3, 58
conquest 21, 60, 63–5, 68–9, 137
constitutional regimes 114, 116–18, 191

despotic power 1, 5, 7–11, 21–30, 48, 57, 99

economic power vii, ix, xii–xiii, 10, 16, 120

Fascism, Nazism xii, 2, 8, 57, 70, 190, 203–6
feudalism 7, 12, 26–7, 38–40, 73–4, 85, 87, 112, 115, 141, 153
France 138, 155, 169, 171

geopolitical power, geopolitics vii, viii, ix, x, xi, xii, 27, 124, 128, 132, 151–65, 171, 177, 191
Germany, Prussia 20, 57–9, 70, 130, 142, 147–8, 154, 155, 167, 171, 196–9, 202–4, 213, 214, 219, 232
Great Britain, Britain xi, xii, 3, 8, 18, 27–8, 40, ch. 3, 138, 142,

148, 155, 168, 174, 185, 189, 191–4, 202–3, ch. 8
Greece 24, 34, 131, 148
Gumplowicz 2, 126, 148

ideological power, ideology vii, ix, 4, 10, 16–17, 29
industrialization, Industrial Revolution 24, 34, 70, 119, 137, 142, 154, 190, 212–13, 217
infrastructural power 1, 6, 8, 9, 11, 19, 20, 23, 25–30, 190
  defined 5, 7

Japan 20, 28, 70, 199, 202, 215

liberalism, liberal theory i, 126, 146–9, 151, 164, 172–3, 190, 192–5, 196, 205–7, 213

Marx, Marxism vii, x, xi, 1, 2, 15, 33, 35–42, 63–4, 69, 75, 86, 111, 126–7, 140, 148, 172, 198, 230
militarism viii, ix, xi, xii, 21, ch. 4, 158–9, 170, 175–7, 186–7, 217, 227
militarist theory 2, 20, 150
militarized socialism 166, 177, 180, 181–3, 186
military power vii, ix, xii–xiii, 4, 10, 16–18, 57–68, 75, 110, 116–18, 120, ch. 6, 205–8
military strategy 13, 63, 87–8, 90–1, 96–9, 132–3, ch. 6
deterrence science militarism 178, 180, 185
mode of production 136–7, 139, 144, 186

nation-state, national state x, 135–6, 139, 144, 186

nuclear deterrence xii, 132, 159, 161, 171, 178, 185
nuclear war xi, 134, 167, 184
nuclear weapons viii, xii, 70, 133, 144, 159, 177–8, 179, 185, 207–8

Oppenheimer 2, 20, 39, 75

political power vii, xiii, 70

reform, reformism xii, 190, 195–6, 198, 231–2
Rome, Roman Empire x, 5, 8–9, 12, 20–3, 34, 37–40, 42–5, 47, 49–50, 52–8, 62, 65–7, 85, 131, 134–5, 137
Russia, Soviet Union xii, 2, 5, 8, 11, 20, 24–5, 35, 47–8, 57, 59, 132, 143, 147, 160–1, 162–4, 176, 180–3, 199–200, 203

Scandinavia 195, 232
socialism vii, 231
Spain 138, 211–12
spectator-sport militarism xii, 159–60, 166, 177, 184–6
Spencer x, 20, 21, 33, 35, 39, 57–9, 61–4, 68
state viii, xi, ch. 1
  defined 3, 4, 26, 74
  elite 3, 6–8, 15, 18–19, 22, 29, 30, 55, 151
  expenditures xi, 75–8, 91–113, 130, 134–5
  revenues 75–84, 87–90, 94–113
Sweden 211, 232

unions 46, 193, 198, 204, 230–1, 233
United States vii, xii, 28, 40, 70, 132, 147–8, 160, 174, 176,

180, 183, 191–4, 202, 213, 215, 227

war viii, ix, xi, xii, 8, 13, 53, 62–3, 70, 90–118, 126, 129–35, 140, 142–4, 146, 148, 153, 157–9, 163, 167–9, 171–4

Weber, Weberian theory 3, 4, 15, 23, 29, 33, 38, 40, 65, 74–5

working class xii, 15, 24, 50, 163, 175, 193, 198, 202, 233–4